# Quadrennial Catalogue of the Hartford Public High School, 1904

## Hartford Public High School (Hartford, Conn)

HIGH SCHOOL BUILDING, ENLARGED, 1897

FOR FLOOR PLANS, SEE PAGES 165-168

HIGH SCHOOL BUILDING, ENLARGED, 1897

FOR FLOOR PLANS, SEE PAGES 165-168

HIGH SCHOOL BUILDING, ENLARGED, 1897

FOR FLOOR PLANS, SEE PAGES 165-168

# QUADRENNIAL CATALOGUE

## OF THE

# HARTFORD

# PUBLIC HIGH SCHOOL

*"Docc, Disce, aut Discede"*

# 1904

Hartford Press

THE CASE, LOCKWOOD & BRAINARD COMPANY

1905

# Teachers
## 1904

**EDWARD H. SMILEY, A.M.**
**Principal**
244 Collins Street

**R. ESTON PHYFE, A.B.**
**Vice-Principal**
**History**
233 Sargeant Street

**FRANK P. MOULTON, A.M.**
*Hartford Grammar School Teacher*
**Latin**
245 Collins Street

**DAVID G. SMYTH, A.B.**
**Mathematics and Physics**
46 Willard Street

**HOMER W. BRAINARD, A.B.**
**Mathematics**
88 Kenyon Street

**CLEMENT C. HYDE, A.B.**
**Science**
80 Church Street

**FRANKLIN H. TAYLOR, A.M.**
**Latin**
136 Allen Place

**ALFRED M. HITCHCOCK, A.M.**
**English**
158 Sargeant Street

**FRANK J. PRESTON**
**Woodworking**
16 Cone Street

**LEWIS W. ALLEN**
**Physical Training**
155 Beacon Street

**ARTHUR B. BABBITT**
**Constructive Drawing**
611 Albany Avenue

**SAMUEL M. ALVORD, A.B.**
**Latin and Greek**
254 Ashley Street

**FREDERICK S. MORRISON, A.B.**
**Greek**
63 Deerfield Avenue

**GEORGE B. KINGSBURY, A.M.**
**Bookkeeping**
229 Sargeant Street

**WILLIAM C. HOLDEN, M.E.**
**Metal Work**
237 Sigourney Street

**WALTER F. KENRICK, A.M.**
**English and Latin**
21 Marshall Street

**RALPH L. BALDWIN**
**Vocal Music**
81 Tremont Street

**KATHERINE BURBANK**
**Librarian**
714 Asylum Avenue

**CLARA A. PEASE**
**Science**
1492 Broad Street

**LUCY O. MATHER**
**Mathematics**
747 Asylum Avenue

**ANNA H. ANDREWS, Ph.B.**
**Mathematics**
167 Beacon Street

**MARY L. HASTINGS**
**English**
69 Elm Street

**JENNIE A. PRATT**
**Algebra and History**
South Glastonbury

**MAY B. BALD, A.B.**
**English and History**
235 Sisson Avenue

**ELISABETH W. STONE, B.L.**
**Science**
40 Allen Place

**MARGARET T. HEDDEN**
**Domestic Science**
26 Whitney Street

**ALICE L. COLE, A.B.**
**Latin**
31 Farmington Avenue

**ELISABETH M. BRANDT**
**French and German**
235 Sisson Avenue

**LOUISE G. STUTZ**
**French and German**
47 Farmington Avenue

**KATHERINE L. HILLS**
**Physical Training**
202 Windsor Avenue

**ELIZABETH C. WRIGHT, A.B.**
**Algebra and English**
115 Allen Place

**HELEN L. WOLCOTT, A.B.**
**Mathematics**
Wethersfield

**CLARA A. BENTLEY, A.B.**
**English**
193 Sisson Avenue

**MARY A. SAWTELLE, Ph.B.**
**French**
'23 Marshall Street

**JANE MacMARTIN**
**German**
21 Marshall Street

**CATHERINE A. GARDNER, A.B**
**Latin and Mathematics**
19 Sargeant Street

## MARY E. ALEXANDER
**Stenography**
31 Russ Street

## CORA GREENWOOD
**Free-Hand Drawing and Design**
17 Haynes Street

## HARRIET ROBBINS, A.B.
**History and Mathematics**
Wethersfield

## EDITH L. RISLEY, B.S.
**English and Mathematics**
290 Sigourney Street

## EVA M. GOWING, A.B.
**French and German**
31 Russ Street

## ELDORA J. BIRCH, B.S.
**Laboratory Assistant**
East Hartford

## ELIZABETH F. FRAZER
**Bookkeeping and Typewriting**
751 Asylum Avenue

## F. ELIZABETH MACK
**English and Elocution**
Windsor

## MARY C. WELLES, Ph.D.
**English and German**
Newington

## ANNIE L. HOLCOMB
**Secretary**
154 Capitol Avenue

## GRACE E. HYDE
**Principal's Assistant**
80 Church Street

HARTFORD HIGH SCHOOL TELESCOPE.

Object Glass 9½ inches Aperture

BY ALVAN CLARK & SONS, Cambridge, Mass.
Equatorial by WARNER & SWASEY, Cleveland, Ohio.

# HISTORY OF THE SCHOOL

THE colonial records of Connecticut show that a classical school was in existence in Hartford as early as the year 1638. In 1642 the town voted to settle £30 a year upon the school. For the next twenty, years it was supported partly by appropriations made from time to time for that purpose by the town and partly by the tuition fees of its pupils. During this time two sons of Governor John Winthrop were here as pupils, and before 1662 ten graduates of Harvard College, from Hartford, had received their preparation for college in this school.

The first bequest in its favor was from William Gibbons, in 1655, who gave to the town of Hartford 30 acres of land in the town of Wethersfield for the support of a Latin school. In the year 1659 it received a small donation from John Talcott.

In 1660 the town voted that " Mr. Wyllys and Mr. Stone be a committee to consider what way may be best for the endowing a free school, and return their judgment at some town meeting."

In 1664 the trustees under the will of Governor Edward Hopkins gave to the town of Hartford the sum of £400 for the support of the school; it was further endowed in 1673 by a grant from the Connecticut colony of 600 acres of land lying in what is now the town of Stafford; in 1680 it received a donation of £50 from James Richards.

Governor Edward Hopkins was born in Shrewsbury, England, in 1600; in 1637 he emigrated to Boston, but soon after came to Hartford.

He was the first secretary of state of the colony of Connecticut, and deputy governor under the constitution of 1638. He was governor in 1640, 1646, 1648, 1650, 1652, and 1654, while in the alternate years after 1646 he was deputy governor. In 1653 he returned to England, although according to the colonial records he was governor of Connecticut in 1654. After his return to England he inherited from his brother the office of Warden of the Fleet ("otherwise called the King's Gate of the Fleete"), and Keeper of the Palace of Westminster, and was elected a member of Parliament. He died in 1657.

His will, dated London, March 7, 1657, contained the following provisions: "The residue of my estate there [in New England] I do hereby give and bequeath to my father, Theophilus Eaton, Esq., Mr. John Davenport, Mr. John Cullick, and Mr. William Goodwin, in full assurance of their trust and faithfulness in disposing of it according to the true intent and purpose of me the said Edward Hopkins, which is, to give some encouragement in those foreign plantations for the breeding up of hopeful youths, both at the grammar school and college, for the public service of the country in future times. . . . My farther mind and will is, that, within six months after the decease of my wife, £500 be made over into New England, according to the advice of my loving friends Major Robert Thomson and Mr. Francis Willoughby, and conveyed into the hands of the trustees before mentioned, in farther prosecution of the aforesaid public ends, which, in the simplicity of my heart, are for the upholding and promoting the kingdom of the Lord Jesus Christ in those parts of the earth."

As Governor Hopkins in his will did not designate the places or schools to be benefited by his bequest, on the 13th of June, 1664, two of the trustees having died, the survivors, the Rev. John Davenport of New Haven and Mr. William Goodwin of Hadley, signed an instrument from which the following is a literal transcript:

"Wee therefore ye said John Davenport and Wm. Goodwin the only survivors of ye said Trustees that we may answer the sd trust Reposed in us, Doe order and dispose of ye sd Estate, as ffolloweth, viz.: To ye towne of Hartford we do give ye sum of ffower hundred pounds of wch Hills ffarme shall be a part att ye same price att wch it was sold by us and the pay Ready to be delivered, if there had been noe Interruption, the Rest of the 400lb in such debts, and goods as we or or Agents shall see mett, provided that this part be Improved according to ye ends of the Donor, viz., for the erecting and maintaining of a schoole at Hartford. . . . We doe further order and appoint the Rest of ye estate of the said Edward Hopkins Esq., (the debts being paid) to be all of it equally divided betweene the townes of Newhaven and Hadley to be in both those townes managed and Improved for the erecting and maintaining of a schoole, in each of the sd townes. . . . Only provided yt one hundred pounds out of yt halfe of ye estate wch Hadley hath, shall be given and paid to Harvard College soe soone, as we the said John Davenport and Wm. Goodwin soe meet, and to be ordered as we or or assignes shall judge most conducing to the end of ye Donor."

Harvard College received £100 from the proceeds of the estate in New England, and after the death of Mrs. Hopkins,* which occurred

---

* Mrs. Hopkins outlived all the original trustees of the New England estate, as well as the executor and residuary legatee of the estate in England. Governor

in 1699, forty-two years after the death of her husband, a suit in Chancery was begun against the executor in England, and in 1712 this Court decreed that the legacy and interest, amounting then to £800, should be paid to Governor Dudley of Massachusetts, and twenty other trustees, for the benefit of Harvard College and the Cambridge Grammar School; so that, as a result of Governor Hopkins's bequest, the Hartford Grammar School Fund, derived from this and previously mentioned sources, was largely increased, and there is a Hopkins fund in New Haven, and also in Hadley and Cambridge, Massachusetts.

The town of Hartford, through committees chosen for the purpose, continued for more than a century to manage the school and the funds accruing from the above-mentioned sources, until, upon a petition of the town, the State Legislature, in May, 1798, incorporated the school under the name of " The Hartford Grammar School," and appointed a board of trustees, with power to fill all vacancies occasioned by death or otherwise; so that the obligations of the town to maintain a " Latin school," as stipulated in the will of William Gibbons, to provide " for the breeding up of hopeful youths at the grammar school," as stipulated by Governor Hopkins, and to maintain a free school " for the schooling of all who should come, in the Latin and English languages," according to the conditions of the colonial grant, were performed from 1798 to 1847 by the Grammar School.

At an adjourned meeting of the First School Society of Hartford, held November 5, 1839, to hear the report of the committee appointed at the annual meeting to take into consideration the expediency of establishing a high school, it was

---

Winthrop, senior, in his Journal of Occurrences in New England, under date of 1644, makes mention of her in the following language:

" Mr. Hopkins, the governor of Hartford upon Connecticut, came to Boston, and brought his wife with him (a godly young woman, and of special parts), who was fallen into a sad infirmity upon her divers years, by occasion of her giving herself wholly to reading and writing, and had written many books. Her husband, being very loving and tender of her, was loath to grieve her, but he saw his error, when it was too late. For if she had attended her household affairs, and such things as belong to women, and not gone out of her way and calling to meddle in such things as are proper for men, whose minds are stronger, &c., she had kept her wits, and might have improved them usefully and honorably in the place God had set her. He brought her to Boston, and left her with her brother, one Mr. Yale, a merchant, to try what means might be had here for her. But no help could be had." — Savage Ed. of Winthrop's History of New England, vol. ii, p. 216.

voted, " That it is expedient that a public high school be established at the earliest period at which suitable arrangements can be made." After eight years this was done.

The year 1847 witnessed a notable revolution in educational matters in Hartford ; up to that time the privileges of the higher school had been confined to boys, but during that year the PUBLIC HIGH SCHOOL, as at present organized, was established by the town of Hartford for the " free instruction in the higher branches of an English, and the elementary branches of a classical education for all the male and female children of suitable age and acquirements who may wish to avail themselves of its advantages." This was accomplished by the energetic and untiring efforts of such men as James M. Bunce, Amos M. Collins, D. F. Robinson, Rev. Dr. Burgess, Dr. Henry Barnard, and the Rev. Dr. Bushnell.

At a public meeting held on the 5th of January, 1847, at the Center schoolhouse, it was again resolved " to be expedient to establish a high school in the First School Society of Hartford, and that the Society's committee be asked to call a special meeting for the consideration of the subject."

At this meeting, which was held on the 11th of January, it was

*Voted,* That Amos M. Collins, Rev. Dr. Burgess, D. F. Robinson, Walter Pease, Edward Button, Roderick Terry, and Timothy M. Allyn be a committee on behalf of this Society, to inquire as to the expediency of establishing a public high school wherein shall be taught such branches of general education as are usually taught in schools of like character, and cannot now be thoroughly acquired in the district schools, such high school to be under the regulations now provided by law, or hereafter to be provided by this Society; also to inquire as to the number of scholars of each sex of the proper age and attainment to attend such high school; also to inquire as to a suitable location, plan of building, expenses thereof, and the current expenses of supporting such a school, and what per cent. tax will be required for that purpose; also whether and upon what terms the funds of the Hartford Grammar School can be made available for its support, and to report the same, together with such other information as they may think advisable, to a future meeting of this Society.

After seven weeks of inquiry and consideration, the majority of this committee, through the Rev. George Burgess, submitted to a special meeting of the Society, held at the City Hall on the 1st of March, 1847, a report in which the several subjects referred to the committee were considered, and closed by submitting the following resolutions for the action of the Society:

1. *Voted,* That this Society proceed to establish a free high school for instruction in the higher branches of an English, and the elementary branches of a classical education, for all the male and female children of suitable age and acquirements in this Society who may wish to avail themselves of its advantages.

2. *Voted,* That D. F. Robinson, Thomas Belknap, James M. Bunce, Walter Pease, Jr., Edward Button, E. D. Tiffany, and A. M. Collins be and they are hereby appointed a building committee, who are empowered and directed in behalf of and for the account of this Society to purchase such site or lot of land, with or without buildings thereon, as in their judgment shall most economically and best accommodate the Society for a public English and classical high school, and forthwith proceed to remodel, fit up, or erect, as they may find it necessary, a suitable building and outhouses for said school, with accommodations for not less than two hundred and fifty scholars of both sexes; also to prepare the grounds, erect necessary fences, provide suitable chemical, philosophical, and astronomical apparatus for said school; also to place in said building the necessary stoves and furnaces, seats, desks, and fixtures, the whole not to exceed in expenditure twelve thousand dollars.

3. *Voted,* That the Society's committee be and they are hereby directed to borrow on the credit of this Society such sums of money, not exceeding in all twelve thousand dollars, as the building committee, appointed by a previous vote of this Society, shall need in the performance of their duties as specified in said vote, and pay over the same to said committee from time to time as required, taking proper vouchers therefor.

4. *Voted,* That a committee of nine, consisting of the Rev. Dr. Burgess, William J. Hamersley, D. F. Robinson, James M. Bunce, Rev. Dr. Bushnell, Rev. Dr. Turnbull, Francis Parsons, Gurdon Robins, and N. H. Morgan, be appointed to make, if practicable, such agreement with the trustees of the Hartford Grammar School as in their opinion shall be just and reasonable for making the funds of said Grammar School available for the support of the high school or some department thereof; also that the action of the committee in these premises be binding upon the Society.

It should be mentioned here that the original appropriation by the town was found insufficient, and that the sum of $2,250

2

was raised by the members of the building committee, Mr. Bunce contributing $1,000, and Mr. Robinson and Mr. Collins $500 each.

No further action on the part of the Society was called for until August 6, 1847, when the committee charged with the erection of the building, having reported that the same would be ready for occupancy before the close of the year, was authorized to employ teachers, and make such other arrangements as were necessary for the opening of the school.

At the annual meeting held on the 29th of October, the committee reported that the building was completed, that Joshua D. Giddings of Providence, Rhode Island, had been appointed principal, and that arrangements had been effected with the trustees of the Grammar School by which they would supply and sustain a teacher for the Classical Department. At this meeting it was

*Voted,* That D. F. Robinson, Thomas Belknap, James M. Bunce, Walter Pease, Jr., Edward Button, E. D. Tiffany, and A. M. Collins be a committee to organize the said school at the earliest practicable time; to make all necessary rules and by-laws for its regulation; to determine the qualifications of the scholars desirous of being admitted thereto, either by themselves or through such persons as they may appoint for the purpose; to decide all questions relating to the admission of children and youth, provided that no [Hartford] scholars shall be admitted for pay; to provide for the expulsion of refractory and unmanageable pupils; and to discharge all the functions relating to said school which will not interfere with the school laws of the State.

The High School was formally opened December 1, 1847. The first principal, Mr. Joshua D. Giddings, remained only one term; he was succeeded by Mr. Thomas K. Beecher, who held the place for two years; Mr. McLauren F. Cook then became principal, and remained for one term, succeeded by Mr. Cephas A. Leach, who also left at the close of one term, so that during the first three years the school had four principals.

In 1851 Mr. T. W. T. Curtis became principal of the school and remained for ten years; he was succeeded in 1861 by Mr. Hiram A. Pratt, who remained for three years and five months.

There was then an interregnum of four months, during which the school was temporarily in charge of the vice-principal.   In May, 1865, Mr. Samuel M. Capron took charge of the school and retained it until his death, on January 4, 1874, a period of eight years and eight months.

He was succeeded by Mr. Joseph Hall, who retained the position for twenty years.

At a meeting of the High School committee held on the 8th of November, 1893, the resignation of Mr. Hall as principal of the school was accepted, he being made Principal Emeritus, and Mr. Charles Henry Douglas was chosen in his stead.   The following resolutions in relation to Mr. Hall's resignation were passed:

WHEREAS, Mr. Joseph Hall, principal of the Hartford Public High
    School since 1874, has signified his desire to retire from the posi-
    tion so long and creditably held by him, it is
Voted, That his resignation as principal of the school be, and is
hereby, accepted, the same to take effect upon the assumption of the
duties of the office by his successor.   And
WHEREAS, In the opinion of this committee, the school cannot afford
    to entirely dispense with the experience, knowledge, and services
    of Mr. Hall, therefore, it is
Voted, That he be continued in the High School at one-half his
present salary during the pleasure of the committee, to perform such
duties as may be required of him by the committee and principal.   And
it is further
Voted, That in accepting the resignation of Mr. Hall the committee
express and place on record their appreciation of his faithful, judicious,
and successful services, extending over a period of more than thirty
years.   For twenty years he has been at the head of the school.   Its
record during all this period, and the rank which it holds among the
educational institutions of New England, are the strongest and most
eloquent testimonials to his excellence as a teacher, his wisdom as an
administrator, and to the purity of his character.   In partial recognition
thereof, and as a slight tribute to his long, faithful, and efficient service
to the school, he is hereby appointed its Principal Emeritus.

Mr. Hall retained the position of Principal Emeritus until his death, which occurred June 10, 1896.

In April, 1895, the resignation of Mr. Douglas was accepted, and Mr. Edward H. Smiley, the present principal, who has been connected with the school since 1890, was elected to the principalship.

THE FIRST HIGH SCHOOL BUILDING, which was erected in 1847 at the corner of Asylum and Ann Streets, was a plain, three-story, brick structure, about 70 feet long by 40 feet wide. The entire cost of the building, completely furnished, including the land, was less than $15,000. The school occupied this building until 1870, when the lot, 135 by 150 feet, was sold for $61,500.

In 1869 a building was erected upon the present High School lot on Asylum Hill, in Hopkins Street. The lot was 305 feet front and 295 feet deep. The building was 100 feet long by 85 feet wide, and cost, including the lot, $160,000.

This building was enlarged in 1877, at a cost of $24,000, by the erection of an additional building communicating with it.

The enlarged building, with all its contents, was destroyed by fire on January 24, 1882. Within less than one week the school was again opened in temporary quarters in Batterson's Block, corner of Asylum and High Streets.

A town meeting was held on February 6, at which the High School committee for that year, Mr. James G. Batterson, Mr. James L. Howard, Rev. Edwin P. Parker, Rev. George Leon Walker, and Mr. Edward S. White, were appointed a building committee, and an appropriation of $200,000 was made for erecting a new building. Additional appropriations, amounting in all to $85,000, were afterwards made by the town for the purpose of finishing the building and supplying it with furniture, library, and apparatus.

Mr. George Keller of Hartford was appointed architect. The first stone of the foundation was laid on May 12, 1882, and the building was occupied by the school on January 3, 1884.

This building faces the east; it is in the secular gothic style, and is fireproof; the basement walls are of rock-faced brown stone; the outer walls above the basement are of Philadelphia pressed brick, with dressings of brown stone for the doors and windows. All the floors are laid upon brick arches supported by iron beams; the stairs are of stone supported by brick arches, and the plastering of the walls and ceilings is laid directly upon the brick without lath; the outer walls of the building are 20 inches thick, and enclose an air space of 4 inches, thus securing perfect dryness of the inner surface; the partition walls, all of which are of brick and extend from the floor of the basement to the roof of the building, are 20 inches thick up to the level of the first floor, and from the first floor to the roof are 16 inches in thickness. The building is 236 feet long, and averages 100 feet in width.

In the south end of the basement, communicating with each other by means of archways, are four rooms, each 31 by 43 feet, which are used as lunch rooms and play rooms for the boys; in the north basement there are corresponding rooms for the girls. In the front of the basement is a room, 30 by 44 feet, intended originally for a laboratory for the classes in chemistry, but used now for a bicycle room.

The first story had originally four entrances, with doors opening outward, two on the front, one on the north, and one on the west side. A reception-room, 15 by 30 feet, and the principal's office, 15 by 20 feet, are at the left of the main entrance. Next is a room, 30 by 44 feet, which is used both for a teachers' library and the main office; this room is connected by electric bells and speaking tubes with all parts of the building, and here is located an electric clock which controls all signals and the individual clocks in the various rooms; adjoining this room is a recitation-room, 15 by 30 feet. On this floor are four school-rooms, each 41 by 33 feet, for the Fourth Class, and three for the Third Class; also five dressing-rooms for the Third and Fourth Classes, and one for the use of teachers.

The second story, which is reached by three broad stairways, one in the north end of the building and one each on the east and west sides, contained originally an assembly hall, 64 by 100 feet, capable of seating twelve hundred persons. During the summer of 1896 this assembly hall was divided into four school-rooms, each 41 by 33 feet, which are used for the Senior and Junior Classes. This story contains also a Senior Class room, 30 by 60 feet; two Junior Class rooms, each 30 by 40 feet; a lecture-room, 30 by 40 feet, three recitation-rooms, and a book-room. There are also on this floor four dressing-rooms for the use of the Senior and Junior Classes.

In the third story the only rooms originally finished were for the use of the classes in drawing and for the boys' debating club, but during the summer of 1890 eight additional rooms were made, and five years later an unfinished room in the observatory tower was finished, making an excellent recitation-room for about thirty pupils. Still another change was made during the summer of 1903, when the space at the south end of the building was converted into six excellent rooms, three of which have been fitted up for the use of the Business Department.

There are two towers in this building, one, 126 feet high, which originally contained a clock, and another, 98 feet high, containing the astronomical observatory, which is surmounted by a hemispherical revolving dome, 17 feet in diameter. This is furnished with a telescope having an object glass of 9½ inches aperture, made by Alvan Clark & Sons of Cambridge, Massachusetts. Its focal length is 11 feet and 4 inches; its declination circle is graduated on silver to 15', and by vernier reads to 1'. The hour circle is graduated to single minutes, and reads by vernier to five seconds. The equatorial mounting and driving clock and the revolving dome were made by Warner & Swasey of Cleveland, Ohio.

Recognizing the necessity of enlarging the school building at an early date, the town purchased, in October, 1893, for $50,000 all the land adjoining the High School grounds on the north, with a frontage of 300 feet on Asylum Street.

In November, 1896, the town of Hartford appropriated $160,000 for an extension to the High School building.

This extension was designed by the architect, Mr. Keller, and the plans were made so as to include a manual training building, for which, also, an appropriation had been voted.

The original building has an area of 23,500 square feet, while the extension has an area of 26,000, and the manual training building 8,500 more, so that the entire addition to the High School is nearly 1½ times its original area.

So extensive an addition to a building already complete in itself is not easily made, yet the new building is joined to the old one so skillfully that the façade on Hopkins Street presents one harmonious whole, not suggesting in the least the idea of an addition. The extension is executed in substantially the same kind of materials, and the new roof is fireproof as well as the rest of the building. The addition extends northerly toward Asylum Street 190 feet, leaving a court in the rear, over 40 feet wide, for light and air between the new building and the old. This court is enclosed on three sides only, being open toward the west. On the front of the building a staircase tower, containing a clock with four dials, is placed 40 feet north of the old clock tower, and is of similar design. The space between these towers on the first floor is devoted to the main entrance to the building, giving ample vestibule and lobby room. This entrance is very properly made a prominent feature of the design, coming, as it does, practically in the center of a façade nearly 450 feet long. Three wide, arched doorways, flanked by the two staircase towers, each 24 feet square and 126 feet high, give a commanding effect to the front.

The main corridor is continued in a straight line toward the north, and leads to a porch at the north end of the building. At the right of this porch, inside the building, is a wide stairway leading down to the basement and up to the third floor. The front of the building is occupied on the first floor by two school-rooms and a reading-room, each 30 by 40 feet, and a dressing-room, 14 by 30 feet. The light in these school-rooms comes from the longer side of the rooms, so that the inner wall is but 30 feet from the windows. On the second floor, above these rooms, are three science laboratories, each 30 by 40 feet, with a store-room, 14 by 30 feet, adjoining. Over the vestibule, between the two central towers, are two recitation-rooms, each 20 by 20 feet. On this floor, on the other side of the main corridor, is an assembly hall, 70 feet wide, 106 feet long, and about 46 feet high. It has windows on three sides, and a gallery at the south end. At the north end is a teachers' platform. The principal entrance to the hall is at the south end, but there are also side entrances from the main corridor. The floor and gallery give accommodations for about fourteen hundred persons. South of the assembly hall is a lobby, 20 feet wide and 70 feet long, leading directly from the hall to the two central staircases contained in the towers. A teachers' dressing-room, 15 by 24 feet, opens off from this lobby. The gymnasium occupies the entire space under the assembly hall, and is 24 feet high. An instructors' room, examination rooms, lockers for boys and girls, and other necessary accommodations are suitably arranged in the basement, which is well lighted.  On the third floor are two science laboratories, with apparatus room and teachers' laboratory adjoining, one recitation-room, one store-room, and a large school-room which occupies the space between the towers.

At a town meeting held in October, 1895, a committee was appointed to consider all matters pertaining to the establishment of a manual training·school in Hartford, and to investigate the advisability of such a school and the cost of the establishment and maintenance of the same.  This committee consisted of six citizens of Hartford, namely: Messrs. Jacob L. Greene, George H. Day, Joseph A. Graves, John J. McCook, Andrew F. Gates, and J. A. Mulcahy.  The results of the investigation of this committee were submitted to a town meeting held some two months later, and, so far as they pertain to the High School, are embodied in the following votes:

*Voted,* That the High School committee be, and they hereby are, directed to build an addition to the present High School, to be devoted to purposes of manual instruction, as follows:

For girls: In cooking, sewing, drawing, wood-carving, and clay
          modeling.
· For boys: In woodwork, ironwork, drawing, and wood-carving.
To supply the same with proper furniture and apparatus, and to secure the requisite number of teachers for instruction in the same.

*Voted,* That said committee be, and they hereby are, authorized to expend for the erection of said addition to the High School the sum of $12,000, and for the furniture and equipment of the same the further sum of $10,000; and that the treasurer be directed to honor such drafts as may be made from time to time by the said committee for the above-mentioned purposes, not exceeding in the aggregate the amounts hereby designated and appropriated.

*Voted,* That said High School committee be, and they hereby are, appointed a building committee for the purposes mentioned in the two preceding votes, and that they be authorized to add to their number at such times and in such manner as may to them seem best.

                              J. L. GREENE,
                              G. H. DAY,
                              J. A. GRAVES,
                              J. J. McCOOK,
                              A. F. GATES,
                              J. A. MULCAHY,
                                   *Committee.*

The report of this committee was adopted in town meeting, together with the votes recommended by the committee. Inasmuch as the appropriation called for exceeded the sum of $10,000, the charter of the city of Hartford required that the action of this town meeting be approved by a vote of the town by check-list. At the spring election in April, 1896, the town, by a very large sustaining vote, appropriated the sum called for in this report, and at the next meeting of the Board of School Visitors definite action was taken towards establishing manual training in our public schools.

The High School committee for this year, Messrs. Charles E. Thompson, Joseph Schwab, Edward J. Mulcahy, Flavel S. Luther, and Francis R. Cooley, after careful investigation, found that the sum recommended by the citizens' committee, $12,000, would not be sufficient for erecting the manual training building with such additional rooms and conveniences as they deemed necessary for its highest efficiency. Upon their recommendation the town voted, at the election held November 5, 1896, to appropriate the further sum of $16,500 for this purpose, and the sum of $160,000, as before stated, for the High School extension.

The manual training building is placed in the rear of the extension, and 43 feet away from it, and is of mill construction. It is a two-story and basement building, 132 feet long by 64 feet wide. The basement and the first and second floors are even with the corresponding floors in the extension, and are connected with them by corridors 8 feet wide. The basement contains the forging shop and an experimental laboratory, with an engine-room and engine for furnishing power for the manual training shops. The first story contains the woodworking and machine shops, molding and metal-working rooms, an office for the superintendent, stock-room, locker, and store-rooms. The second floor is arranged for the drawing-room, modeling-room, carving, sewing, cooking, locker, store, and toilet-rooms.

The system of heating and ventilation, which was under the supervision of Prof. Charles B. Richards of the Sheffield Scientific School, Yale, includes both the old and the new part of the main building and the manual training building. A large fan supplies air to both buildings in all the class-rooms and recitation-rooms, assembly hall and gymnasium.

This air, before entering the fan, passes over tempering coils, by means of which it is heated to a temperature of about 65 degrees. Directly in front of the fan (which is a double discharge), on either side, is placed a group of supplementary heaters, that on the east side for the entire main building, and that on the west side for the manual training building.

. At each of these supplementary heaters provision is made for causing the air either to pass over this heating surface or to pass by without touching it, and two lines of piping convey the air from each heater to the several vertical flues in each building. The air which passes over the heating surface is carried in the lower pipe, which is called the " hot-air " pipe, and the air which passes by is carried in the upper, which is called the " tempered-air " pipe, thus forming what is commonly called the " double-pipe system."

At the base of each vertical flue a connection is made with each pipe, so arranged with mixing dampers, which are automatically controlled by the temperature of the rooms, that a constant temperature is maintained. Supplementary heating surface is also placed in each room under the windows. The corridors and all rooms other than those before mentioned are heated by direct radiation. Steam is supplied to all the heating surface in the main building, the old as well as the new part, by a battery of four boilers 54 inches in diameter. These four boilers are run at a pressure of from 2 to 10 pounds, and all returns to them from the direct radiation are by gravity. A fifth boiler, 66 inches in diameter, is run at a pressure of about 60 pounds, and is used chiefly for furnishing power to run the supply-fan engine, an engine for generating electricity, and a special engine for the manual training building.

The indirect heating of the manual training building is accomplished by using the exhaust steam from these engines, supplemented by live steam from the fifth boiler, through a reducing valve, at a back pressure not exceeding 6 pounds per square inch. This exhaust steam is also utilized in the tempering coils, for tempering the air before it enters the large supply-fan, and is also used in mild weather in the indirect heaters for the main building, by means of a by-pass. The exhaust steam first passes through a feed-water heater.

The returns from all the indirect surface are trapped into a receiver and automatically conveyed to the boilers by a pump.

The removal of the foul air from the main building is accomplished by a large exhaust-fan in the attic, operated by an electric motor, all of the vent flues being connected with a foul air chamber in the attic, from which the fan delivers the air into one of the towers and thence out of doors.

The ventilation of the manual training building is through heated flues in the walls, all of which extend out of and above the roof, and are fitted with dampers just under the ceiling of the top floor.

Ample ventilating flues are also provided in each of the wardrobe rooms, and in these rooms a line of steam-pipes runs along the partitions close to the floor, in order to dry the clothing in wet weather.

The water-closets, which are entered from the wardrobe rooms on each floor, are entirely outside the building, and each has its own system of warming, ventilation, and drainage, which is also entirely outside the building.

The electricity which is generated supplies power to the large ventilating fan in the attic of the main building, and to a few lights in the engine-room and air chamber.

# REQUIREMENTS FOR ADMISSION, ETC.

ALL candidates for admission to the High School must be twelve years of age. If from the Brown, South, Second North, West Middle, Arsenal, Washington Street, Northeast, or Northwest schools, they must have been members of the first class of the first department of such schools for one year, and must also be recommended by the principal of the school which they last attended as qualified by attainments and character to become members of the High School. They must also, at the time of their application, present a certificate of the requirements herein named, signed by the principal of the school which they last attended. If not so certified for promotion to the High School, they will be obliged to pass the regular examination in reading, writing, spelling, arithmetic, geography, grammar, and history of the United States.

The regular examination occurs at the close of the summer term, in June, but those prevented by sickness or other sufficient cause from attending it are allowed a special examination at certain times during the year.

Candidates residing out of Hartford, if qualified in the above-mentioned or equivalent studies, may be admitted at any time when school is in session on a special examination which shall be satisfactory to the Principal and to the Superintendent of Public Schools. It should be understood, however, that this examination is not designed to be in any essential respect on a lower standard than the other.

In examinations each candidate receives printed questions upon the principal studies which are to be answered only in writing.

The charge for tuition to pupils whose parents or guardians reside elsewhere than in Hartford is $3.25 per week.

## IRREGULAR PUPILS

It is expected that those who enter the school will join some one of the regular classes in any department, take the studies prescribed for that class, and attend all the school sessions. But in special cases, when delicacy of health requires it, pupils are allowed to become irregular both in attendance and recitations.

## DISCIPLINE

Copies of the " Regulations of the High School " may be had upon application to any of the teachers.

Parents are kept informed of the standing of their children in scholarship, attendance, and deportment by reports issued at regular intervals. These reports must be returned with the signature of the parent or guardian.

## EXAMINATIONS

Written examinations occur in January and June, and no pupil is allowed to advance to the next class who has failed to pass them satisfactorily.

## GRADUATION

Diplomas are presented at the close of the school year, in June, to those who have completed the regular course of study. Original essays and orations are prepared by the graduating class, and a limited number of these are read or recited on the day of graduation.

Pupils who wish to extend their course of study after graduation are received into any department, and allowed to pursue any studies which they may have omitted in the regular course, or which they may wish to review. It should be understood, however, that they are subject to the same rules and regulations as the other pupils, regarding scholarship, attendance, and deportment.

There are two prize funds, established respectively by the Classes of 1878 and 1888, from the income of which $5.00 is given each year to those members of the graduating class who write and deliver an oration and essay in the best manner. There is also a fund established by the Class of 1889, which yields $5.00 to the pupil who passes the best Latin examinations in the four years' course, a like fund established by the Class of 1896, which yields $5.00 to the pupil who passes the best examinations in Mathematics for the four years, and one given by the Class of 1900, yielding the same amount to the pupil who passes the best examinations in English.

# Questions used in Recent Examinations of Candidates

## ARITHMETIC

I. Copy and add: 30460; 5207; 78.003; 83000; 486.000575; 8278; 23.961; 203040; 306.0708; 9070; 243.81; 62873.979.

If the product of two numbers is 346712, and one of the factors is 76, what is the other factor?

What is cancellation? Divide, using cancellation:

$$15 \times 80 \times 27 \times 28 \text{ by } 7 \times 20 \times 8.$$

Find the least common multiple of 4, 14, 28, and 98. Find the greatest common divisor of 1313 and 4108.

II. The product of three numbers is $\frac{4}{5}$; two of the numbers are $2\frac{1}{4}$ and $\frac{7}{8}$ ; what is the third?

Reduce $\dfrac{\frac{5}{8} \text{ of } 16.125}{4\frac{3}{8}}$ to a decimal fraction.

$\frac{1}{4}$ of $\frac{4}{5}$ is what part of $\frac{7}{11}$?

Divide $\dfrac{3\frac{3}{8} + \frac{4}{5} + \frac{1}{11}}{\frac{3}{4} \text{ of } 5\frac{5}{7}} \times \dfrac{6}{7}$ by $\dfrac{133}{141}$.

III. A wall of 700 yards in length was to be built in 29 days; 12 men were employed on it for 11 days, and only completed 220 yards: how many men must be added, to complete the wall in the required time?

IV. If a barn is 50 feet wide and the ridge-pole is 12 feet above the eaves, what will be the length of the rafters?

What is the area of a circle 5 feet in diameter?

V. What is the simple interest on $3,750.87 for 2 years and 9 months at 8 per cent.?

The interest of $3,675 for 3 years is $771.75; what is the rate?

VI. By selling 12 pounds of tea for $7.56 a dealer gains 5 per cent.; what does he gain or lose per cent. by selling 50 pounds of the same tea for $31?

VII. A traveler, on reaching a certain place, found that his watch, which kept correct time for the place he left, was 2 hr. 22 m. slower than the local time. Had he traveled eastward or westward, and how far, in circular measure, had he come?

VIII. On a railroad 149 mi. 243 rd. 4 yd. 2 ft. long, there are 18 stations, including one at each end of the road. What is the average distance between the stations?

IX. How many bricks, 8 inches long and 4 inches wide, will pave a yard that is 100 feet by 50 feet?

How many acres are there in 250 city lots, each of which is 25 feet by 100 feet?

X. A, B, and C rent a farm for $270. A puts 200 sheep on it; B, 150; and C, 100. After 6 months A sells ⅘ of his flock to C, and 3 months later B sells ⅔ of his to A. How much of the rent should each pay at the end of the year?

## GRAMMAR

I. Define monosyllable, dissyllable, vowel, diphthong, adverb, personal pronoun.

Write down all the relative pronouns that you know.

Write four short sentences containing:

(a) a predicate adjective.
(b) a verb in the passive voice.
(c) a verb in the active voice, progressive form.
(d) a relative clause.

II. Decline the personal pronoun of the third person, masculine gender.

Form the plural of *pencil, half, goose, monkey.*

Form the possessive singular and plural of *cat, city, child, fox.*

Compare *heavy, little, beautiful, rapidly.*

III. Give the principal parts of *steal, catch, go, hurry.*

Write the present and the perfect infinitive, active and passive, of the verb *praise.*

Conjugate the verb *go* in the past tense, indicative mood; first in the simple form, then in the progressive form.

Conjugate the verb *help* in the present perfect tense, indicative mood, passive voice.

Conjugate the verb *drive* in the present subjunctive active.

IV. Parse the italicized words in the following sentence: *Before* daybreak, *aroused* by a slight noise, the soldiers *rushed* from the camp *to see* who *were coming;* but the *enemy's* scouts, *hearing* the footsteps, *had fled before* they *could be captured.*

V. Tell whether the sentence preceding is compound or complex, and why. Point out the subordinate clauses, and tell what each modifies. What two verbs does *but* connect?

VI. Write a single paragraph, not over a page in length, on one
of the following topics:
    Directions for making something.
    One of my friends.
    Reasons why I wish to write correctly.

VII-VIII. Write a letter to a friend, giving the history of one day in
your life. Make the letter about two pages long, with
heading, introduction, superscription, etc.

IX-X. Write a composition at least two pages long on one of the
following topics:
    How John Allen won Priscilla.
    One of the best times I have ever had.
    Paul Revere's ride.
    How I spent the Fourth last year, and how I plan to
    spend it this year.
    Some things I expect to enjoy while attending high
    school.

## GEOGRAPHY

I. What distinction is there between a bay, a fiord, and a harbor?
Locate one of each. How are deltas formed? Locate two
delta plains.
What is the heat equator? What countries does it cross in
June?

II. Give the ocean boundaries of North America. What is the ex-
tent of the central plain of the continent? What rivers drain
it and into what waters? In which part are there large lakes?
Name two. Locate and give the characteristics of the part
called the wooded plain; the prairies; the northern plain.
Locate the Gulf of California, Yucatan, Sitka, Lake Nicaragua,
Nova Scotia, Martinique.

III. Which parts of Europe are mountainous? What countries lie
wholly or in part in the lowland? What waters are on the
west of Russia? south of Russia?
In what direction from the Arctic Circle is Iceland? Nova
Zembla? Archangel? Hammerfest?

IV. Through what countries does the Rhine flow? Locate and tell
something about Lucerne, Berlin, Dresden, Havre, Venice,
Mt. Vesuvius, Vienna. What waters are connected by Strait
of Otranto? Strait of Dover?
Describe the position of Denmark and name its capital.
Compare the coast of Norway with that of Spain. What ex-
ports might these countries exchange, and from what ports?

V. What is the largest country of Asia? What physical barriers have served to separate its inhabitants from those of other countries?

What and where are the two greatest seaports of India? Which has better opportunities for European commerce? Why?

VI. Draw a map of Africa. Place upon it four large rivers and name them. Name the bodies of water surrounding the continent; locate Cape Colony, Sahara Desert, Egypt, Kongo state, and Madagascar.

VII. Compare South America with Africa as to

    (a) Position and size.

    (b) Native races.

    (c) Occupation and development by whites.

    (d) Physical and political relation to other continents.

VIII. In what region of the United States does each of the following occur? Anthracite coal, bituminous coal, iron ore, wheat, natural gas, cotton, corn, rice, silver, petroleum.

IX. Through what states does the Missouri River pass, and what ones does it separate? Name a city situated upon it in each state. Describe the flood plain of the Mississippi; its value and danger to its inhabitants.

Locate and describe Niagara Falls, Minneapolis, Yellowstone Park, Grand Rapids, Savannah.

X. Compare New England with any equal area between the Rocky and Appalachian Mountains in regard to

    (a) Surface.

    (b) Large cities.

    (c) Industries.

    (d) Population.

## HISTORY

I. Write on the discoveries of —

    (a) John Cabot.

    (b) Cartier.

    (c) De Soto.

    (d) Cortez.

    (e) Magellan.

II. Describe the most important events of the administration of Thomas Jefferson.

3

III. Give an account of —
    (a) John Paul Jones and the Bon Homme Richard.
    (b) Perry on Lake Erie.
    (c) Farragut at New Orleans and Mobile Bay.
    (d) Dewey at Manilla.

IV. Give the main facts regarding —
    (a) The Missouri Compromise. .
    (b) The Wilmot Proviso.
    (c) The Dred Scott Decision.
    (d) The Kansas-Nebraska Act.

V. Show with a map or by words —
    (a) The extent of the United States in 1783.
    (b) The addition that was acquired in 1803.
    (c) The part that was secured in 1819.
    (d) What we got by the Mexican War.
    (e) What we got by the Spanish-American War.

VI. Tell what you know of John Brown, John C. Fremont, Miles Standish, William Lloyd Garrison, Robert Morris.

VII. During whose administration did the Civil War begin? Contrast the way in which the president of that time acted towards the seceding states with the way in which President Jackson acted towards South Carolina when that state threatened to secede in 1832. To what was the Republican party pledged when it elected Lincoln in 1860? How long did the Civil War last? How were the slaves set free? How were the seceded states restored to their former position in the Union?

VIII. Under what forms of government has Connecticut been governed since the coming of Thomas Hooker? Who are the national senators of Connecticut? How many representatives does Connecticut have in the lower house of Congress? How many electoral votes will Connecticut have in the next presidential election?

IX. What do you understand by —
    (a) A protective tariff.
    (c) The president's cabinet.
    (c) The veto power.
    (d) The spoils system.
    (e) Civil service reform.

X. Write on the principal features of the life of Theodore Roosevelt.

# EVENING HIGH SCHOOL

IN October, 1903, the High School Committee, after conference with the Board of School Visitors, and with their hearty approval, voted to establish an evening department of the school under the name of the Evening High School.

During the first year, from October 12, 1903 to March 11, 1904, fifty-nine sessions of the school were held on Monday, Wednesday, and Friday evenings, with a total registration of five hundred and seventy-five, and an average attendance of two hundred and fifty-four.

The number of sessions for the present year, 1904-5, will be about the same as for 1903-4. The total registration has been five hundred and seventy-seven, with an average attendance of two hundred and ninety-one.

By vote of the High School Committee Mr. David G. Smyth was appointed Principal in charge, and Mr. Edward H. Smiley Principal *ex-officio*.

## REQUIREMENTS FOR ADMISSION

Those who have been admitted at any time to the High School, or have completed the ninth grade in any grammar school of this city, and are not attending any day school, and those who are recommended by the Principal of the Evening Grammar School, may be admitted to the various classes without an examination. Others are required to present satisfactory evidence that they are prepared to pursue successfully the studies which they may select.

## SUBJECTS TAUGHT

English, French, German, Algebra, Geometry, Trigonometry, Physics, Chemistry, Bookkeeping, Typewriting, Stenography, Wood-working, Metal-working, Free-hand Drawing, and Constructive Drawing.

# COURSES OF STUDY

*The English Course* includes the usual literary, scientific, and mathematical studies of a high school.

*The Classical Course* includes a General Classical and a College Preparatory Course.

*The Scientific Course* furnishes a preparation for admission to any of the scientific schools.

*The Manual Training Course* prepares for admission to any of the scientific schools, or for manufacturing or industrial pursuits.

*The Commercial Course* is designed for pupils who desire special preparation for business.

## ELECTIVES

In addition to the regular studies, the following *Electives* are open to the students in each course:

Free-hand and Constructive Drawing, Vocal Music, Physical Training.

## ENGLISH COURSE

### First Year — Fourth Class

studies indicate the number of recitations per week

History (½ year) . . . 5
. . . . . . 5
. . . . . . 5

### 1 Year — Third Class

. . . . . . 2
. . . . . . 5
r) . . . . . 5
ear) }
f year) } . . . . 5

### Year — Junior Class

two years of this course, except English, are op-
t is 15 recitations a week, — 18 if three-period Eng-

. . . . 3 or 5
iced Algebra . . . 5
ir) . . . . . 5
. . . . . 5
. . . . . 5
alf year) . . . . 5
f year) . . . . 5

### 1 Year — Senior Class

. . . . 3 or 5
ir) . . . . . 5
Chemistry . . . . 5
Geology (1st half year) . . . . 5
Astronomy or Physiology (2d half year) . . . 5
Modern History . . . . . . 5

## GENERAL CLASSICAL COURSE

### First Year — Fourth Class

| | |
|---|---|
| English (½ year), Grecian History (½ year) . . . | 5 |
| Algebra . . . . . . . . . | 5 |
| Latin . . . . . . . . . | 5 |

### Second Year — Third Class

| | |
|---|---|
| English . . . . . . . . | 2 |
| Geometry . . . . . . . . | 5 |
| Latin (Cæsar) . . . . . . . | 5 |
| English History (1st half year) ⎱ . . . . | 5 |
| Botany or Physics (2d half year) ⎰ | |

### Third Year — Junior Class

All the studies of the last two years of this course, except English and Latin, are optional. The *minimum requirement* is 18 recitations a week.

| | |
|---|---|
| English . . . . . . . . | 3 |
| Latin (Cicero) . . . . . . . | 5 |
| French or German (1st year) . . . . . | 5 |
| Physics (continued) . . . . . . | 5 |
| Zoölogy . . . . . . . . | 5 |
| Physical Geography (1st half year) ⎱ . . . | 5 |
| Ancient or Mediæval History (2d half year) ⎰ | |

### Fourth Year — Senior Class

| | |
|---|---|
| English . . . . . . . . | 3 |
| Latin (Virgil) . . . . . . . | 5 |
| French or German (2d year) . . . . . | 5 |
| Chemistry . . . . . . . | 5 |
| Geology (1st half year) . . . . . | 5 |
| Astronomy or Physiology (2d half year) . . . | 5 |
| Modern History . . . . . . | 5 |

## COLLEGE PREPARATORY COURSE

### First Year — Fourth Class

| | |
|---|---|
| English (½ year), Grecian History (½ year) . . . | 5 |
| Algebra .. . . . . . . . | 5 |
| Latin . . . . . . . . . | 5 |

### Second Year — Third Class

| | |
|---|---|
| English . . . . . . . . . | 2 |
| Geometry . . . . . . . . . | 5 |
| Latin (Cæsar) . . . . . . . . | 5 |
| Greek or a Modern Language . . . . . | 5 |
| *Physics (2d half year) . . . . . . | 5 |

### Third Year — Junior Class

| | |
|---|---|
| English . . . . . . . . . | 3 |
| Advanced Algebra (1st half year) . . . . | 5 |
| Geometry (2d half year, for boys) . . . . | 5 |
| Roman History (2d half year) . . . . . | 5 |
| Latin (Cicero) . . . . . . . | 5 |
| Greek or 2d year of a Modern Language . . . | 5 |
| *Physics (continued) . . . . . . | 5 |

### Fourth Year — Senior Class

| | |
|---|---|
| English . . . . . . . . | 3 |
| Latin { Virgil . . . . . . | 5 |
| { Ovid, for boys . . . . . . | 2 |
| Greek or 3d year of a Modern Language . . . | 5 |
| Modern Language (1st year) or } . . . . | 5 |
| Chemistry or Zoölogy } | |

* Elective

## SCIENTIFIC COURSE

### First Year — Fourth Class

| | |
|---|---|
| English (½ year), Grecian History (½ year) . . . | 5 |
| Algebra . . . . . . . . . | 5 |
| Latin . . . . . . . . . | 5 |

### Second Year — Third Class

| | |
|---|---|
| English . . . . . . . . | 2 |
| Geometry . . . . . . . . | 5 |
| Latin (Cæsar) . . . . . . . | 5 |
| English History (1st half year) }<br>Botany or Physics (2d half year) } . . . . | 5 |

### Third Year — Junior Class

| | |
|---|---|
| English . . . . . . . . | 3 |
| Solid Geometry and Advanced Algebra . . . . | 5 |
| *Latin — Cicero (1st half year) }<br>History Reviews (2d half year) } . . . . | 5 |
| French or German (1st year) . . . . . . | 5 |
| *Physics (continued) . . . . . . . | 5 |

### Fourth Year — Senior Class

| | |
|---|---|
| English . . . . . . . . | 3 |
| Advanced Algebra and Trigonometry . . . . | 5 |
| French or German (2d year) . . . . . | 5 |
| Chemistry . . . . . . . . | 5 |

* Elective

# MANUAL TRAINING COURSE

## First Year — Fourth Class

### REQUIRED SUBJECTS

English . . . . . . . . 2
Algebra . . . . . . . . 5
Constructive Drawing 2 }
Woodwork 5 } Boys . . . . 7
Free-hand or Constructive Drawing 2 )
Sewing 2 } Girls . . . 8
Cooking 4 )

### ELECT ONE

Latin, French, or German . . . . . . 5

## Second Year — Third Class

### REQUIRED SUBJECTS

English . . . . . . . . 2
Geometry . . . . . . . . 5
Constructive Drawing 4 }
Woodwork (½ year), Forging (½ year) 4 } Boys . . 8
Free-hand or Constructive Drawing 2 }
Sewing (2), Cooking (4) 6 } Girls . . . 8

### ELECT ONE

Latin (Cæsar), French (2d year), or German (2d year) . . 5
English History (1st half year) }
Botany or Physics (2d half year) } . . . . . 5

## MANUAL TRAINING COURSE

### Third Year — Junior Class

REQUIRED SUBJECTS

English . . . . . . . . . 3
Constructive Drawing 4 }
Metal Work           5 } Boys . . . . . 9
Free-hand or Constructive Drawing 2 }
Sewing (2), Cooking(4)            6 } Girls . . . 8

ELECT TWO

Solid Geometry and Advanced Algebra . . . . 5
Latin (Cicero) . . . . . . . . 5
French or German (1st year) . . . . . . 5
Physics (continued) . . . . . . . 5
Zoölogy . . . . . . . . . 5
Physical Geography (1st half year) }
Mediæval History (2d half year) } . . . . 5
Commercial Work . . . . . . . . 5

### Fourth Year — Senior Class

REQUIRED SUBJECTS

English . . . . . . . . . 3
Constructive Drawing          4 }
Metal Work and Applied Science 4 } Boys . . . . 8
Free-hand or Constructive Drawing 4 }
Modeling (2), Carving (2)         4 } Girls . . . 8

ELECT TWO

Latin (Virgil) . . . . . . . . 5
Advanced Algebra and Trigonometry . . . . . 5
French or German (2d year) . . . . . . 5
Chemistry . . . . . . . . . 5
Geology (1st half year) . . . . . . . 5
Astronomy or Physiology (2d half year) . . . 5
Modern History . . . . . . . . 5
Commercial Work . . . . . . . . 5

## COMMERCIAL COURSE

### First Year — Fourth Class

REQUIRED SUBJECTS

| | |
|---|---|
| English | 2 |
| Algebra | 5 |
| Bookkeeping, Business Arithmetic, and Penmanship | 5 |

ELECT ONE

| | |
|---|---|
| French, German, or Grecian History | 5 |

### Second Year — Third Class

REQUIRED SUBJECTS

| | |
|---|---|
| English | 2 |
| Geometry | 5 |
| Bookkeeping, Business Correspondence, and Penmanship | 5 |
| Commercial Geography | 2 |

*ELECT ONE

| | |
|---|---|
| †Stenography and Typewriting | 7 |
| French or German (2d year) | 5 |
| English History (1st half year) } | |
| Botany or Physics (2d half year) } | 5 |

---

* The pupil may substitute for a five-period elective a year's work in manual training as shown on pages 37 and 38.

† The course in Stenography covers two years. It may be begun in the second or the third year.

## COMMERCIAL COURSE

### Third Year — Junior Class

#### REQUIRED SUBJECTS

| | |
|---|---|
| English | 3 |
| Advanced Bookkeeping, Banking, Business Arithmetic, and Penmanship | 5 |

#### *ELECT TWO

| | |
|---|---|
| Stenography and Typewriting | 7 |
| French or German (1st year) | 5 |
| Physics (continued) | 5 |
| Zoölogy | 5 |
| Physical Geography (1st half year) }<br>Mediæval History (2d half year) } | 5 |

### Fourth Year — Senior Class

#### REQUIRED SUBJECTS

| | |
|---|---|
| English | 3 |
| Advanced Office Work | 3 |
| Commercial Law | 2 |
| United States History and Civics | 5 |

#### *ELECT ONE

| | |
|---|---|
| Stenography and Typewriting | 7 |
| French or German (2d year) | 5 |
| Chemistry | 5 |
| Geology (1st half year) | 5 |
| Astronomy or Physiology (2d half year) | 5 |
| Modern History (1st half year) | 5 |

* The pupil may substitute for a five-period elective a year's work in manual training as shown on pages 37 and 38.

# TEXT-BOOKS

MATHEMATICS. — Hall and Knight's Elementary Algebra, Schultze and Sevenoak's Plane Geometry, Wentworth's Geometry, Estill's Numerical Problems in Plane Geometry, Phillips and Fisher's Geometry of Space, Wentworth's Plane Trigonometry and Tables, Four-Place Logarithmic Tables.

ENGLISH. — Lewis's First Manual of Composition, Pancoast's Introduction to English Literature. Webster's, Worcester's, the Century, and the Standard dictionaries. Appropriate editions of the English classics studied are recommended from time to time.

HISTORY. — Myers's Rome: Its Rise and Fall, Myers's History of Greece, Myers's Mediæval and Modern History, Montgomery's Leading Facts of English History, McLaughlin's History of the American Nation.

SCIENCE. — Stevens's Introduction to Botany, Bergen's Foundations of Botany, Dryer's Lessons in Physical Geography, Young's Elements of Astronomy, Avery's School Physics, Gilley's Principles of Physics, Jackson and Price's Elementary Book on Electricity and Magnetism, Snyder and Palmer's 1,000 Problems in Physics, Bradbury's Elementary Chemistry, Bradbury's Laboratory Manual of Chemistry, Dana's Geological Story, Martin's The Human Body, Jordan, Kellogg and Heath's Animals, A Text-Book of Zoölogy.

FRENCH. — Fraser and Squair's French Grammar, Chardenal's Complete French Course, Super's Preparatory French Reader, Bowman's Scientific French Reader, Selections from classical and contemporary French authors, Grandgent's French Composition, Gasc's French-English Dictionary.

GERMAN. — Harris's German Composition, Hatfield's German Composition, Horning's German Composition, Joynes-Meissner's German Grammar, Otis's Elementary German, Dippold's Scientific German Reader, Perrin's Pamphlets for

German Declension, Guerber's Märchen und Erzählungen, Von Jagemann's German Prose Composition, Poll's German Prose Composition, Selections from classical and contemporary German authors, Whitney's German-English Dictionary.

LATIN. — Allen and Greenough's New Latin Grammar, Collar and Daniell's First Year Latin, Allen and Greenough's Cæsar, Allen and Greenough's Cicero, Allen and Greenough's Ovid, Greenough and Kittredge's Virgil, Moulton and Collar's Preparatory Latin Composition, Bullion's or White's Latin Lexicon, Smith's Classical Dictionary, Lindsay's Nepos.

GREEK. — Goodell's School Grammar of Attic Greek, Hadley's Greek Grammar, White and Morgan's Illustrated Dictionary to Xenophon's Anabasis, Goodwin's Greek Reader, Bonner's Greek Composition, Seymour's Homer's Iliad, Perrin and Seymour's Homer's Odyssey, Seymour's Introduction to the Language and Verse of Homer, Jones's and Collar and Daniell's Greek Prose Composition, Liddell and Scott's Greek Lexicon, Autenrieth's Homeric Dictionary (Keep's edition), Morrison and Goodell's Greek Lessons for Beginners, Woodruff's and Pearson's Greek Prose Composition.

MUSIC. — Emerson's School and College Hymnal, Tomlins's The Laurel Song Book.

BOOKKEEPING. — Adams's Commercial Geography, Bowen-Merrill's Modern Business Bookkeeping, Lyons's Commercial Law, Palmer's Method of Business Writing, Williams and Rogers's Seventy Lessons in Spelling, Williams and Rogers's Business and Social Correspondence, Williams and Rogers's Commercial Arithmetic, Packard's New Commercial Arithmetic, Williams and Rogers's Introductive Bookkeeping, Williams and Rogers's Theoretical and Practical Complete Bookkeeping, Eaton's Business Forms, Customs, and Accounts, Chandler's Practical Shorthand.

DRAWING. — Anthony's Machine Drawing, Anthony's Mechanical Drawing, Meyer's Machine Design.

# PRIZES

THE prizes for the past four years have been awarded as follows:

For the year ending June, 1901

For the best scholarship, as shown by the monthly standing and the annual examinations: —

| | | |
|---|---|---|
| Senior Class — | $15 | EMMA P. HIRTH |
| "      " | 10 | W. ARTHUR COUNTRYMAN, JR. |
| Junior Class — | $15 | CLARA E. LANG |
| "      " | 10 | LEON E. DIX |
| Third Class — | $15 | WILLIAM H. GOODWIN |
| "      " | 10 | CHARLES F. TAYLOR |
| Fourth Class — | $15 | FAITH F. BOLLES |
| "      " | 10 | FREDERIC J. CORBETT |

In Elocution

| | | |
|---|---|---|
| Reading — | $10 | HELEN C. WAY |
| " | 5 | CHARLOTTE W. BURTON |
| Declamation — | $10 | EDWARD L. DONAGHUE |
| " | 5 | VINCENT C. BREWER |

The '78 prize for the best oration —

$5    JOHN H. THOMPSON

The '88 prize for the best essay —

$5    ANNA E. O'BRIEN

The '89 prize for the best Latin examination for four years —

$5    W. ARTHUR COUNTRYMAN, JR.

The '96 prize for the best Mathematical examination for four years —

$5    EMMA P. HIRTH

The 1900 prize for the best English examination for four years —

$5    W. ARTHUR COUNTRYMAN, JR.

The Daniel Goodwin Scholarship in Trinity College was awarded to — W. ARTHUR COUNTRYMAN, JR.

For the year ending June, 1902

SCHOLARSHIP

| | | |
|---|---|---|
| Senior Class — | $15 | CLARA E. LANG |
| "      " | 10 | LEON E. DIX |
| Junior Class — | $15 | WILLIAM H. GOODWIN |
| "      " | 10 | MINNIE K. HASTINGS |

Third Class — $15   FAITH F. BOLLES
"         "      10   FREDERIC J. CORBETT
Fourth Class — $15   HELEN F. DWYER
"         "      10   MARION M. WELCH

In Elocution

Reading —      $10   KATHERINE E. GOLDBERG
"              5   IDA M. DRESSER
Declamation —  $10   LEON R. JILLSON
"              5   SOLOMON PORISS

The '78 prize for the best oration —
$5   MORRIS TUCH

The '88 prize for the best essay —
$5   ALICE S. GRISWOLD

The '89 prize for the best Latin examination for four years —
$5   CLARA E. LANG

The '96 prize for the best Mathematical examination for four years —
$5   EDWIN W. TILLOTSON

The 1900 prize for the best English examination for four years —
$5   MARTHA GARDNER

The Daniel Goodwin Scholarship in Trinity College was awarded to —
LEON E. DIX

### For the year ending June, 1903

#### SCHOLARSHIP

Senior Class — $12.50   *RAYMOND N. DICKINSON
"         "   12.50   *GRACE C. STRONG
Junior Class — $15   FAITH F. BOLLES
"         "      10   FREDERIC J. CORBETT
Third Class — $15   HELEN F. DWYER
"         "      10   MARION M. WELCH
Fourth Class — $15   SAMUEL M. COHEN
"         "      10   ANNA E. FRANZEN

The '78 prize for the best oration —
$5   GOODWIN B. BEACH

The '88 prize for the best essay —
$5   KATHERINE E. GOLDBERG

The '89 prize for the best Latin examination for four years —
$5   WILLIAM H. GOODWIN

The '96 prize for the best Mathematical examination for four years —
$5   . CHARLES F. TAYLOR

The 1900 prize for the best English examination for four years —
$5   MINNIE K. HASTINGS

The Daniel Goodwin Scholarship in Trinity College was awarded to —
WILLIAM H. GOODWIN

---

* First and second prizes equally divided.

## PRIZES

For the year ending June, 1904

SCHOLARSHIP

| | | |
|---|---|---|
| Senior Class — | $15 | FAITH F. BOLLES |
| " " | 10 | CARL G. F. FRANZEN |
| Junior Class — | $15 | HELEN F. DWYER |
| " " | 10 | MARION M. WELCH |
| Third Class — | $15 | NINA W. MORGAN |
| " " | 10 | SAMUEL M. COHEN |
| Fourth Class — | $15 | LOUIS KOFSKY |
| " " | 10 | CARLTON S. WAY |

Batterson Prize Debate —
Athena *vs.* Hopkins Debating Club
       Won by Hopkins Debating Club
    First prize was awarded to —
                   SAUL BERMAN
    Second prize was awarded to —
                   HELEN B. KEYES
The '78 prize for the best oration —
            $5    B. HALSEY SPENCER
The '88 prize for the best essay —
            $5    HELEN E. GRAVES
The '89 prize for the best Latin examination for four years —
            $5    FAITH F. BOLLES
The '96 prize for the best Mathematical examination for four years —
            $2.50   *FAITH F. BOLLES
            2.50   *HORACE V. S. TAYLOR
The 1900 prize for the best English examination for four years —
            $5    FREDERIC J. CORBETT

The Daniel Goodwin Scholarship in Trinity College was awarded to —
       FREDERIC J. CORBETT

---

\* Prize equally divided.

#### NUMBER OF PUPILS FOR YEAR ENDING JUNE, 1901

|  | Girls | Boys | Total |
|---|---|---|---|
| Graduate Class   .   .   . | 23 | 5 | 28 |
| Senior Class   .   .   . | 67 | 46 | 113 |
| Junior Class   .   .   . | 89 | 67 | 156 |
| Third Class   .   .   . | 111 | 124 | 235 |
| Fourth Class   .   .   . | 187 | 196 | 383 |
| Total   .   .   .   . | 477 | 438 | 915 |

#### NUMBER OF PUPILS FOR YEAR ENDING JUNE, 1902

|  | Girls | Boys | Total |
|---|---|---|---|
| Graduate Class   .   .   . | 15 | 7 | 22 |
| Senior Class   .   .   . | 80 | 59 | 139 |
| Junior Class   .   .   . | 68 | 97 | 165 |
| Third Class   .   .   . | 155 | 131 | 286 |
| Fourth Class   .   .   . | 192 | 213 | 405 |
| Total   .   .   .   . | 510 | 507 | 1,017 |

#### NUMBER OF PUPILS FOR YEAR ENDING JUNE, 1903

|  | Girls | Boys | Total |
|---|---|---|---|
| Graduate Class   .   . | 10 | 4 | 14 |
| Senior Class   .   .   . | 65 | 79 | 144 |
| Junior Class   .   .   . | 98 | 93 | 191 |
| Third Class   .   .   . | 135 | 124 | 259 |
| Fourth Class   .   .   . | 189 | 205 | 394 |
| Total   .   .   .   . | 497 | 505 | 1,002 |

#### NUMBER OF PUPILS FOR YEAR ENDING JUNE, 1904

|  | Girls | Boys | Total |
|---|---|---|---|
| Graduate Class   .   . | 17 | 6 | 23 |
| Senior Class   .   .   . | 92 | 71 | 163 |
| Junior Class   .   .   . | 96 | 81 | 177 |
| Third Class   .   .   . | 143 | 130 | 273 |
| Fourth Class   .   .   . | 199 | 228 | 427 |
| Total   .   .   .   . | 547 | 516 | 1,063 |

# CALENDAR FOR 1904-1905

FALL TERM ends December 23, 1904
WINTER TERM begins January 3, 1905
WINTER EXAMINATIONS, January 25, 26, and 27, 1905
WINTER TERM ends April 14, 1905
SUMMER TERM begins May 1, 1905
SUMMER EXAMINATIONS, June 14, 15, and 16, 1905
GRADUATION DAY, June 23, 1905
ALUMNI MEETING, evening of June 23, 1905
SUMMER TERM ends June 23, 1905
EXAMINATION OF CANDIDATES, June 26 and 27, 1905
FALL TERM begins September 13, 1905

# SCHOOL HOURS

| | | |
|---|---|---|
| 8.45 to 8.55 | Opening exercises |
| 8.55 to 9.44 | First recitation period |
| 9.49 to 10.36 | Second recitation period |
| 10.41 to 11.28 | Third recitation period |
| 11.31 to 11.51 | Recess |
| 11.54 to 12.41 | Fourth recitation period |
| 12.46 to 1.33 | Fifth recitation period |

# VACATIONS AND HOLIDAYS

The vacations are as follows: One of two weeks, called the Easter vacation; one beginning with the close of the usual school exercises on the last Friday in June, and ending on Tuesday preceding the second Wednesday in September following; and one beginning with the day before Christmas, and closing with the day after New Year's.

The regular holidays are Fast Day, Thanksgiving Day, with the day following, Lincoln Day, Washington's Birthday, Memorial Day, Commencement Day at Trinity College, and every Saturday.

# THE ALUMNI ASSOCIATION
### OF THE
# HARTFORD PUBLIC HIGH SCHOOL
## INCORPORATED 1889

| | |
|---|---|
| EDWARD H. SMILEY | . . . . . . PRESIDENT |
| ARCHIBALD A. WELCH, 1878 | . . . VICE-PRESIDENT |
| LUCY O. MATHER, 1884 . | . . . VICE-PRESIDENT |
| FREDERICK S. MORRISON | . . RECORDING SECRETARY |
| ATWOOD COLLINS, 1869 . | . . . . TREASURER |

## CORRESPONDING SECRETARIES

| | | | |
|---|---|---|---|
| Charles H. Owen | Class of 1855 | Harry D. Olmsted | Class of 1881 |
| Jane L. Sheldon | " 1856 | Mrs. Charles R. Hansel | " 1882 |
| Mrs. George H. Warner | " 1858 | Arthur Perkins | " 1883 |
| Morton W. Easton | " 1859 | Annie L. Holcomb | " 1884 |
| Roswell F. Blodgett | " 1860 | David G. Smyth | " 1885 |
| Mrs. Oscar B. Purinton | " 1861 | Marian H. Jones | " 1886 |
| John H. Brocklesby | " 1862 | Edward H. Abbot | " 1887 |
| Joseph L. Barbour | " 1863 | Elizabeth Fay | " 1888 |
| Charles E. Gross | " 1864 | Jane W. Stone | " 1889 |
| Bernadotte Perrin | " 1865 | Mrs. Charles L. Taylor | " 1890 |
| Eliza F. Mix | " 1866 | Wilfred W. Savage | " 1891 |
| Frederick B. Edwards | " 1867 | Walter H. Clark | " 1892 |
| George H. Seyms | " 1868 | Ernest A. Wells | " 1893 |
| James S. Tryon | " 1869 | Horace B. Clark | " 1894 |
| Mrs. Goodwin Brown | " 1870 | Frances A. McCook | " 1895 |
| Mrs. Charles E. Gross | " 1871 | Frank E. Hale | " 1896 |
| Lucy S. Williams | " 1872 | F. Raymond Sturtevant | " 1897 |
| Mrs. Charles T. Russ | " 1873 | Mary F. Whiton | " 1898 |
| Lillian A. Andrews | " 1874 | Eliot R. Clark | " 1899 |
| Charles A. Pease | " 1875 | Helen C. Lincoln | " 1900 |
| Charles E. Chase | " 1876 | W. Arthur Countryman, Jr. | " 1901 |
| Emily V. Barnard | " 1877 | Carolyn B. Taylor | " 1902 |
| Archibald A. Welch | " 1878 | Lucy E. McCook | " 1903 |
| Clarence H. Wickham | " 1879 | Alice K. O'Connor | " 1904 |
| Charles G. Case | " 1880 | | |

A reunion of the Alumni is usually held on the evening of graduation day, to which all members of graduated classes (whether graduates or not) are invited.

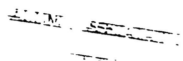

THE ASSOCIATION will always keep
women deeply interested...

As stated in its articles, the
purpose or promotion of ...
receiving gifts in, various ...
objects specified ...
among the ...

The committee will ...
which may be ...
which is to be ...
connected with ...
donors.

It is intended ...
reach some of through ...
aid in some way ...
way through them

# THE ALUMNI ASSOCIATION
### OF THE
## HARTFORD PUBLIC HIGH SCHOOL

As implied in the statement above quoted, it is true that every year there are graduates from the School, girls and boys, earnestly desirous of going to college, but prevented from doing so because of lack of funds.

The number of living graduates of the School is now about *three thousand*. Of this number less than *one hundred and twenty* belong to the Alumni Association.

The funds in the hands of the Treasurer, Mr. Atwood Collins, as shown by his last annual report, March 21, 1904, are as follows:

## OBJECT DESIGNATED BY DONORS
### (INCOME ONLY AVAILABLE)

| | | |
|---|---|---|
| Class of 1878, | $203.21 | Prize for best Graduation Oration |
| Class of 1888, | 144.42 | "    "    "    "    Essay |
| Class of 1889, | 133.67 | "    "    " Latin Examinations |
| Class of 1896, | 131.36 | "    "    " Mathematical Examinations |
| Class of 1900, | 196.64 | "    "    " English Examinations |
| Batterson Fund, | 505.00 | "    "    " Debate |
| | $1,903.30 | |

## GENERAL FUND
### (PRINCIPAL AND INCOME AVAILABLE)

| | |
|---|---|
| Amount received from membership fees, . . . | $733.06 |
| Loaned to member of Class of 1903 to assist in defraying College expenses, . . . . . . . . . | 145.00 |
| Balance available for rendering further assistance, | $588.06 |

From this statement it will readily be seen that it is very desirable to increase the membership of the Association in order to carry out more fully one of the chief purposes for which the organization was formed, namely, to assist worthy students to secure a college education.

Any graduate of this school, or any person who has been regularly employed as a teacher in this school, may become a member of this Association on application to the Secretary, and payment of the fee of five dollars for a life membership.

The officers of the Association shall be one President, two Vice-Presidents, one Recording Secretary, and one Treasurer.

The regular annual meeting of the Association is held on the _____ at half-past seven in the evening, at the High School

At the last annual meeting it was voted to instruct the Executive Committee to bring the matter in printed form to the attention of the Alumni with the hope and expectation that if the purpose of the Association were more fully understood by the Alumni in general its membership would be greatly increased.

The payment of *five dollars* by any graduate constitutes a life membership.

It is hoped that this year we can add *five hundred* names to the membership list and a like number every succeeding year, and thus so increase the general fund that the income will be sufficient to enable us, by gift or loan, to broaden the educational opportunities of a considerable number of our earnest and deserving graduates.

The Secretary of the Association, Mr. F. S. Morrison, will be in the reception room on the first floor, at the close of the exercises in the hall, for the purpose of giving membership certificates to such as may wish to join the Association.

For the convenience of those who are not prepared to pay the membership fee at this time, the inclosed card has been prepared.

This card may be left with the Secretary, who will send it to the given address as a reminder.

Those whom this communication reaches through the mail are requested to send their membership fee to Mr. Atwood Collins, Treasurer of the Association, Hartford, Conn.

EDWARD H. SMILEY, *President*
ARCHIBALD A. WELCH, *Vice-President*
LUCY O. MATHER, *Vice-President*
ATWOOD COLLINS, *Treasurer*
FREDERICK S. MORRISON, *Secretary*

THE EXECUTIVE COMMITTEE

Any graduate of this school, or any person who has been regularly employed as a teacher in this school, may become a member of this Association on application to the Secretary, and payment of the fee of five dollars for a life membership.

The officers of the Association shall be one President, two Vice-Presidents, one Recording Secretary, and one Treasurer.

The regular annual meeting of the Association is held on the third Monday in March, at half-past seven in the evening, at the High School building.

Copies of the constitution may be obtained from the Secretary, or any one of the officers.

In June, 1903, the Alumni Association received a gift of five hundred dollars from Mrs. Charles C. Beach in memory of her father, the late James G. Batterson, the income from which will be used as prizes for debate

# H. P. H. S. DEBATING CLUB

### ORGANIZED 1882

Meetings on alternate Fridays at 12.50 P.M.

### Officers since 1900

*Presidents*

HOWARD GOODWIN
LEWIS B. WHITTEMORE
CLIFFORD B. MORCOM
JAMES W. WILLIAMS
WILLIAM H. GOODWIN
RAYMOND T. PAUSCH

JAMES J. PAGE
FREDERIC J. CORBETT
HORACE V. S. TAYLOR
ROBERT M. KEENEY
JOSEPH K. HOOKER

*Secretaries*

DAVID B. HENNEY
CLEVELAND PERRY
HORACE O. KILBOURN
THOMAS G. WRIGHT, JR.
CLARENCE W. SEYMOUR

FREDERIC J. CORBETT
ROBERT B. ENGLISH
HAROLD B. KEYES
JOSEPH K. HOOKER
LEWIS G. HARRIMAN

---

# THE ATHENA

### ORGANIZED 1889

Meetings on alternate Fridays at 12.50 P.M.

### Officers since 1900

*Presidents*

NELLIE ROBBINS
M. LOUISE GLAZIER
DOROTHY W. DAVIS

JULIET L. CLAGHORN
ALICE K. O'CONNOR
LOIS ANGELL

*Secretaries*

CLARA E. LANG
ANNA L. HASTINGS
MINNIE K. HASTINGS

GRACE C. STRONG
HELEN E. GRAVES
HELEN B. KEYES

# THE HOPKINS DEBATING CLUB

ORGANIZED 1900

Meetings on alternate Thursdays at 12.50 P.M.

## Officers since 1900

### Presidents

JOSEPH H. TWICHELL
WILLIAM W. WALKER
CHESTER R. BROWN
WARREN S. CHAPIN

CHARLES N. ST. JOHN
LOUIS S. BUTHS
ARTHUR R. ST. JOHN

### Secretaries

HAROLD W. ROGERS
HENRY G. BARBOUR
CHARLES M. SMITH
CHARLES N. ST. JOHN

LOUIS S. BUTHS
EDWARD F. AHEARN
THOMAS J. MOLLOY

---

# INTER-CLUB DEBATES

## March 20, 1903

### Athena vs. Hopkins Debating Club

Subject — *Resolved:* That the abolishment of the canteen was justifiable.

ATHENA

*Affirmative*

DOROTHY W. DAVIS
JULIET L. CLAGHORN
HELEN L. MERRIAM

HOPKINS D. C.

*Negative*

WARREN S. CHAPIN
HERBERT J. STEANE
DONALD B. WELLS

Won by the Athena

## April 2, 1903

### Athena vs. H. P. H. S. Debating Club

Subject — *Resolved:* That fear exerts a greater influence over the human race than ambition.

| ATHENA | H. P. H. S. D. C. |
|---|---|
| *Affirmative* | *Negative* |
| GRACE C. STRONG | THOMAS G. WRIGHT, JR. |
| LUCY E. McCOOK | GOODWIN B. BEACH |
| MINNIE K. HASTINGS | WILLIAM H. GOODWIN |

Won by the Athena

## May 8, 1903

### H. P. H. S. Debating Club vs. Hopkins Debating Club

Subject — *Resolved:* That the disfranchisement of the negroes in the south is unjust.

| HOPKINS D. C. | H. P. H. S. D. C. |
|---|---|
| *Affirmative* | *Negative* |
| SAUL BERMAN | CLARENCE W. SEYMOUR |
| CLEVELAND C. SOPER | HORACE V. S. TAYLOR |
| SAMUEL J. GOLDBERG | HORACE O. KILBOURN |

Won by the Hopkins Debating Club

# LIST OF TEACHERS

## OF THE LATIN SCHOOL, THE FREE SCHOOL, AND THE HARTFORD GRAMMAR SCHOOL
### 1638-1847

JOHN HIGGINSON . . . . . . 1637 and 1638
  Educated in the Grammar School in Leicester, Eng-
    land; afterwards Chaplain of the fort in Say-
    brook.

WILLIAM COLLINS . . . . . . 1640
  "A young scholar and preacher from Barbadoes."

WILLIAM ANDREWS . . . . . . { 1643-1647
{ 1654-1656

  One of the original emigrants from Newtown; "an
    educated man, and held in high consideration by
    his townsmen."

JOHN RUSSELL, A.B., Harvard, 1645 . . . 1648
SAMUEL FITCH . . . . . . 1650-1653
JOHN DAVIS, A.B., Harvard, 1651 . . . . 1656
WILLIAM PITKIN . . . . . . 1660-1663
  Educated for the law in Norwich, England. The
    first Attorney for the Colony.

CALEB WATSON, A.B., Harvard, 1661 . . . 1674-1705
  After Mr. Watson's retirement in 1705, the town an-
    nually voted him £10 until his death in 1725. In
    1725, on petition for "aid to the Rev. Mr. Caleb
    Watson, now advanced to an exceeding old age,
    spent in the office of schoolmaster, a great and
    constant benefactor to the colony," the Upper
    House of the General Court also ordered £10 to
    be paid him out of the public treasury.

The record of the names of teachers from 1705 to 1740 is lost;
  but from votes relating to the school which were passed by
  the town from time to time, the school is known to have
  been in continuous operation during that period.

NOAH WELLES, A.B., Yale, 1741 . . . . 1741-1744
  Tutor in Yale, and clergyman at Stamford, Conn.
    A prominent candidate for the presidency of
    Yale in 1766.

ELEAZAR WALES, A.B., Yale, 1753 . . . . 1753-1755

NEHEMIAH STRONG, A.B., Yale, 1755 . . .     **1755**
     Tutor in Yale, 1757-60, and first Professor of Mathe-
       matics and Natural Philosophy, 1770-81; author
       of "Astronomy Improved."

JOSEPH HOWE, A.B., Yale, 1765 . . .     **1765**
     Tutor in Yale, 1769-72, and pastor of the New
       South Church in Boston, 1773-75.

SOLOMON PORTER, A.B., Yale, 1775 . . .     **1789–1792**
     Private Secretary of Gen. Lafayette, at South Wind-
       sor, in 1778. City Surveyor and Collector of the
       port of Hartford. Made first survey and map of
       the city in 1790.

GEORGE JAFFREY PATTEN, A.B., Brown, 1792 . .     **1792-1799**

ELISHA CHAPMAN, A.B., Yale, 1797 . . .     **1798-1799**
     Physician in New London, Conn.

ALANSON HAMLIN, A.B., Yale, 1799 . . .     **1799**
     Attorney at Law in Danbury and Bridgeport, Conn.

THOMAS ADAMS, A.B., Yale, 1800 . . . .     **1800-1804**

STEDMAN ADAMS, A.B., Yale, 1801 . . . .     **1805**

JOHN McCURDY STRONG, A.B., Yale, 1806 . . .     **1806**

SHELDON CANDEE, A.B., Yale, 1805 . . . .     **1806**
     Attorney at Law in Hartford.

AMASA LOOMIS, A.B., Yale, 1807 . . . .     **1808**

JOHN LANGDON, A.B., Yale, 1809 . . . .     **1810**
     Tutor in Yale, 1811-15.

ISAAC PARSONS, Rev., A.B., Yale, 1811 . . .     **1811**

JOHN WITTER, A.B., Yale, 1812 . . . .     **1812-1815**
     Tutor in Yale, 1815-17.

HORACE HOOKER, A.B., Yale, 1815 . . . .     **1816**
     Tutor in Yale, 1817-22; author of twelve volumes of
       " Bible History."

LYMAN COLEMAN, A.B., Yale, 1817 . . .     **1817-1819**
     Tutor in Yale, 1820-25, and Professor of Latin and
       Greek in the College of New Jersey, 1823-29, and
       Professor of Greek in Lafayette College, Easton,
       Pa., 1840-72.

SOLOMON STODDARD, A.B., Yale, 1820 . . .     **1820-1822**
     With Prof. E. A. Andrews, author of "Andrews and
       Stoddard's Latin Grammar." Tutor in Yale,
       1822-26, and Professor of Greek and Latin in
       Middlebury College, Middlebury, Vt.

EDWARD BEECHER, A.B., Yale, 1822 . . .     **1822-1824**
     Tutor in Yale College, President of Illinois College,
       clergyman in Boston, 1846-56, and author of
       " The Conflict of Ages."

WILLIAM MOSELEY HOLLAND, A.B., Yale, 1824 . . 1824-1826
Tutor in Yale, and Professor of Greek and Latin in
Washington (now Trinity) College, 1831-37.

ASHBEL SMITH, A.B., Yale, 1824 . . . . 1826
Texan Minister to the United States, Great Britain,
France, and Spain, 1838-44.

ELIJAH P. BARROWS, JR.,* A.B., Yale, 1826 . . 1826-1830
Professor of Sacred Literature in Western Reserve
College, 1837-52, of Hebrew in Andover Theo-
logical Seminary, 1853-66, and same in Oberlin
College.

WILLIAM CARTER, A.B., Yale, 1828 . . . 1828-1830
Tutor in Yale, 1830-33.

FREDERICK A. P. BARNARD, A.B., Yale, 1828 . . 1828-1830
Professor in the University of Alabama, 1837-54,
President of the University of Mississippi, and
President of Columbia College, 1864-88.

JOHN E. EDWARDS, A.B., Yale, 1828 . . . 1829
SELDEN W. SKINNER . . . . . 1829-1830
ISAAC W. STUART,* A.B., Yale, 1828 . . . 1831-1832
Professor of Latin and Greek in the College of South
Carolina, 1833-45; author of "Hartford in the
Olden Time" and "Life of Jonathan Trumbull."

ANTHONY D. STANLEY, A.B., Yale, 1830 . . . 1832
Professor of Mathematics in Yale, 1836-53; author
of Treatise on Logarithms.

FRANCIS FELLOWES,* A.B., Amherst, 1826 . . 1832
THATCHER THAYER, A.B., Amherst, 1831 . . . 1833
Tutor in Amherst, 1833-35.

EVANGELINUS APOSTOLIDES SOPHOCLES,* A.B., Amherst,
1833 . . . . . . . 1833-1836
Tutor and Professor of Greek in Harvard, 1840-83,
and author of "Sophocles' Greek Grammar."

WILLIAM N. MATSON, A.B., Yale, 1833 . . . 1833
Judge of Probate and Reporter of the Supreme Court.

NATHAN PERKINS SEYMOUR, A.B., Yale, 1834 . . 1834-1836
Tutor in Yale, 1836-40. Professor of Greek and
Latin in Western Reserve College.

THEODORE L. WRIGHT,* A.M., Yale, 1833 . . . 1836-1841

JOHN D. POST, A.B. . . . . . . { 1837-1840
1845

C. P. BORDENAVE, Teacher of French and Spanish . 1837-1843
JOHN W. NORTHAM . . . . . . 1837-1838
HENRY F. BRIGGS . . . . . . 1837-1839

* After 1826 the Principal is marked thus (*).

| | |
|---|---|
| I. Winter . . . . . . . | 1838 |
| Saul Alvord . . . . . . . | 1839-1840 |
| Benjamin H. Coe, Teacher of Drawing . . . | 1839-1841 |
| H. T. Wells . . . . . . . | 1840 |
| C. F. Peake . . . . . . . | 1840 |
| W. A. Grover . . . . . . . | 1840 |
| Levi N. Tracy,* Rev., A.B., Dartmouth, 1834 . . | 1841-1845 |
| Henry Elijah Parker, A.B., Dartmouth, 1841 . . | 1841-1843 |

Tutor in Dartmouth, clergyman, 1847-66, and Professor of Latin in Dartmouth, 1866-92.

| | |
|---|---|
| David Burnett Scott . . . . . | 1841-1843 |

Educated in Edinburgh for St. Andrew's University, Scotland. Teacher in the public schools of New York City, 1846-69. Professor of English Literature, Rhetoric, and Belles-Lettres in the College of the City of New York, 1870-94. Author of three school histories of the United States. Died June 10, 1894.

| | |
|---|---|
| G. W. Winchester . . . . . . | 1841 |
| John B. Talcott, A.B., Yale, 1846 . . . | { 1841-1842 <br> { 1846-1847 |

Tutor in Middlebury College, Middlebury, Vt., 1848; tutor in Yale, 1848-51; Mayor of New Britain, Conn., 1880-81. Died Feb. 21, 1905.

| | |
|---|---|
| Otto F. Jacobson, Teacher of French and German . | 1844 |
| Oliver D. Cooke, 2d . . . . . . | 1845 |
| Joseph Monds, Teacher of Modern Languages . . | 1845 |
| Lewis R. Hurlbutt,* A.B., Yale, 1843 . . . | 1846-1847 |

Tutor in Yale, 1848-51; M.D., in 1850. Physician at Stamford, Conn.

---

* After 1826 the Principal is marked thus (*).

# LIST OF TEACHERS SINCE 1847

☞ The names of Principals are in capitals; the names of those who taught for only one term or as substitutes are omitted from this list.

| NAME | CAME | WENT | REMARKS |
|---|---|---|---|
| JOSHUA D. GIDDINGS | Dec., 1847 | April, 1848 | Died Jan., 1891 |
| WILLIAM B. CAPRON | Dec., 1847 | July, 1853 | Principal of the H. G. S., Missionary at Madura, India. Died Oct. 6, 1876 |
| HELEN M. WHEATON | Dec., 1847 | Dec., 1851 | Mrs. Bethuel C. Farrand, Port Huron, Mich. Died June 4, 1901 |
| MARIETTA M. BARTLETT | Jan., 1848 | July, 1848 | Mrs. Henry L. Ellsworth. Died April 17, 1856 |
| THOMAS K. BEECHER | June, 1848 | July, 1850 | Rev., Elmira, N. Y. Died 1900 |
| MARY B. BROGNARD | June, 1848 | Dec., 1850 | Philadelphia, Pa. Deceased |
| OLIVIA DAY | Jan., 1849 | Jan., 1850 | Mrs. Thomas K. Beecher. Died 1856 |
| SOPHIA C. STEVENS | Jan., 1849 | July, 1851 | Mrs. Wm. Page, New York, N. Y. Died 1892 |
| MARION M. GOODRICH | Jan., 1850 | Dec., 1850 | Died 1858, Burlington, Vt. |
| MARY C. TORREY | Jan., 1850 | July, 1850 | Burlington, Vt. |
| McLAUREN F. COOK | Sept., 1850 | Dec., 1850 | Died 1875, Chelsea, Mass. |
| CEPHAS A. LEACH | Dec., 1650 | May, 1651 | Rev., Editor *Times*, Sedalia, Mo. Died Jan. 16, 1887 |
| THEODOSIA L. OSBORNE | Jan., 1851 | June, 1854 | Died in San Francisco, Cal., Jan. 2, 1855 |
| THOMAS W. T. CURTIS | July, 1851 | April, 1861 | Principal Hillhouse High School, New Haven, Conn. Died 1888 |
| ERSKINE J. HAWES | Sept., 1851 | July, 1852 | Rev., Plymouth, Conn. Died July 7, 186, |
| SARAH B. HOOKER | Jan., 1852 | April, 1854 | Mrs. Wm. B Capron, Boston, Mass., late Missionary of the A. B. C. F. M. |
| F. JULIUS BUSCH | May, 1852 | July, 1858 | Teacher of Drawing. Lost in the *Austria*, Sept. 13, 1858 |
| SARAH A. FLANDERS | Dec., 1852 | May, 1853 | Mrs. C. D. Herbert, Monroe, Conn. |
| SAMUEL M. CAPRON | Sept., 1853 | | Principal of the H G S. until May, 1865; after that time of both schools until his death, Jan. 4, 1874 |
| ELLEN A. HUNT | May, 1855 / Jan., 1858 | Sept., 1856 / July, 1862 | Mrs. Henry F. Clark, Brooklyn, N. Y. Died 1900 |
| MARY A. DODGE | Sept., 1855 | July, 1858 | "Gail Hamilton," Hamilton, Mass. Died Aug. 17, 1896 |

| NAME | CAME | WENT | REMARKS |
|---|---|---|---|
| B. Ludolph | Sept., 1855 | | Teacher of German. Died April, 1856 |
| Thomas H. Tucker | Sept., 1855 | July, 1856 | Melrose, Mass. |
| F. M. Serenbetz | May, 1856 | April, 1857 | Teacher of German, Kansas |
| Charles W. Huntington } | Sept., 1856<br>Sept., 1866 | July, 1858<br>Dec., 1868 | Hartford, Conn. |
| Timothy K. Wilcox | Sept., 1856 | July, 1858 | Died 1863, Chicago, Ill. |
| Caroline L. Tallant | Nov., 1856 | April, 1861 | Died Nov. 6, 1877 |
| Samuel Hermann | May, 1857 | April, 1858 | Teacher of German, Kansas Died 1890 |
| Bertha Olmsted | May, 1858 | April, 1861 | Mrs. Wm. W. Niles, Concord, N. H. |
| John W. Stancliff | May, 1858 | Dec., 1858 | Died 1891 |
| William W. Niles | Sept., 1858 | July, 1860 | Rt. Rev Bishop of the Diocese of New Hampshire, Concord, N. H. |
| Frances L. Bushnell | Sept., 1858 | April, 1860 | Died July 26, 1899, Hartford, Conn. |
| Mary H. Parsons | Sept., 1858 | April, 1860 | Mrs. Watson Webb, Hartford, Conn. |
| Catharine C. Wilcox | Sept., 1859 | July, 1860 | St. Louis, Mo. |
| Francis E. Manley | Jan., 1860 | April, 1861 | Died Jan. 11, 1898, Melrose, Mass. |
| Elisabeth H. Gillette | May, 1860 | April, 1861 | Mrs. George H. Warner, Hartford, Conn. |
| Charlotte J. Braddock | May, 1860 | April, 1867 | Mrs. Charlotte J. Merriman, Hartford, Conn. |
| Virginia H. Hubbard | May, 1860 | July, 1861 | Mrs. Thomas W. T. Curtis, New Haven, Conn. |
| Jane L. Sheldon | Sept., 1860 | April, 1861 | Hartford, Conn. |
| William E. Bullock | Sept., 1860 | July, 1861 | Barrister, New York, N. Y. |
| Louis Bail | Sept., 1860 | July, 1871 | Died 1894, Newark, N. J. |
| Wesley C. Ginn | May, 1861 | Dec., 1863 | Delaware, Ohio |
| Jane Goldthwaite | May, 1861 | July, 1862 | Hartford, Conn. |
| Victor Alvergnat | May, 1861 | | Teacher of French. Died May, 1877 |
| HIRAM A. PRATT | Sept., 1861 | Feb., 1865 | Died Nov. 22, 1901, Faribault, Minn. |
| Leopold Simonson | Sept., 1861 | | Teacher of German. Died Jan., 1892 |
| Arthur N. Hollister | May, 1862 | April, 1869 | Died Jan., 1897, Hartford, Conn. |
| Roswell Parish | May, 1862 | July, 1863 | Master in Mechanic Arts High School, Boston, Mass. |
| JOSEPH HALL | Sept., 1863 | | Vice-Principal until the death of Mr. Capron, Jan. 4, 1874; Principal until Nov 8, 1893; Principal Emeritus until his death, June 10, 1896 |
| Marietta S. Fletcher | Sept., 1863 | July, 1865 | Mrs. John E. Sinclair, Worcester, Mass. |
| Chester Holcombe | Jan., 1864 | July, 1864 | Newark, N. Y. |
| Charles E. Willard | Sept., 1864 | May, 1866 | Died Jan. 24, 1898, New York, N. Y. |

| NAME | CAME | WENT | REMARKS |
|---|---|---|---|
| RALPH G. HIBBARD | April, 1865 | June, 1901 | New Britain, Conn. Died Jan. 26, 1904 |
| JOHN A. MARTIN | May, 1865 | April, 1866 | Teacher of Writing, Hartford, Conn. Died Sept. 19, 1901 |
| KATHERINE BURBANK | Sept., 1865 | | |
| REESE B. GWILLIM | May, 1866 | July, 1868 | Attorney at Law, New York, N. Y. |
| MARTHA F. HENRY | May, 1867 / May, 1869 | July, 1867 / July, 1869 | Mrs. Nathan F. Peck, Hartford, Conn. |
| MARGARET BLYTHE | Sept., 1867 | July, 1872 | Hartford, Conn. Died 1900 |
| JOHN LEWIS | Sept., 1868 | July, 1869 | Attorney at Law, Oak Park, Ill. |
| MARY A. COOKE | Sept., 1868 | April, 1873 | Mrs. Franklin F. Knous, New Haven, Conn. |
| MARSHALL R. GAINES | May, 1869 | July, 1872 | Rev., President of Tillotson College, Austin, Tex. |
| BERNADOTTE PERRIN | Sept., 1869 / Sept., 1874 / Sept., 1879 | July, 1870 / April, 1876 / July, 1881 | Professor in Yale University, New Haven, Conn. |
| EMMA G. HOLLISTER | May, 1870 | July, 1870 | Mrs. Lucien M. Royce, Hartford, Conn. |
| FRANK R. CHILDS | Sept., 1870 | Oct., 1890 | Hartford, Conn. |
| ANGE A. PATTOU | Oct., 1870 | July, 1872 | Teacher of Vocal Music, New York, N. Y. |
| ELIZABETH P. KEEP | May, 1871 | July, 1872 | Mrs. George W. Avery, Hartford, Conn. |
| AVIS C. KNIBLOE | Sept., 1871 | April, 1885 | Died 1894 |
| CHARLES MEUTH | Sept., 1872 | April, 1873 | Teacher of Drawing |
| WILLIAM L. CUSHING | Sept., 1872 | July, 1873 | Headmaster of Westminster School, Simsbury, Conn. |
| ALEXANDER R. MERRIAM | Sept., 1872 | July, 1874 | Rev., Professor in Theological Seminary, Hartford, Conn. |
| EMMA L. WARNER | Sept., 1872 | July, 1884 | Teacher in High School, Westfield, Mass. |
| SARA J. SMITH | May, 1873 | June, 1889 | Principal of Private School, Woodside, Hartford, Conn. |
| ALICE L. SEAVEY | May, 1873 / May, 1875 | July, 1873 / Dec., 1876 | Mrs. F. H. Chapin, Hartford, Conn. Died 1838 |
| EDWARD S. HUME | Sept., 1873 | July, 1874 | Rev., Missionary of A. B. C. F. M., Bombay, India |
| JANE A. BIDWELL | Sept., 1873 | April, 1878 | Mrs. Edwin H. Wilson, Cambridge, Mass. |
| IRVING EMERSON | Sept., 1873 | June, 1901 | Died May 28, 1903, Hartford, Conn. |
| ABBY M. WILLIAMS | May, 1874 | Sept., 1887 | Died Nov 22, 1895, Hartford, Conn. |
| HENRY B. B. STAPLER | Sept., 1874 | July, 1875 | Attorney at Law, New York, N. Y. |
| HENRY S. GULLIVER | Sept., 1875 | July, 1877 | High School, Waterbury, Conn. |
| EDWIN H. WILSON | Sept., 1876 | July, 1879 | Died Nov. 29, 1901, Cambridge, Mass. |
| ELLEN E. UPSON | Sept., 1876 | April, 1881 | Mrs. Frank G. Woodworth, Tougaloo, Miss. |
| MME. J. DE B. DRAPER | Sept., 1877 | Dec., 1882 | Hartford, Conn. |

5

| NAME | CAME | WENT | REMARKS |
|---|---|---|---|
| THOMAS D. GOODELL | Sept., 1877 | Dec., 1888 | Professor in Yale University, New Haven, Conn. |
| ELIZA H. LORD | April, 1878 | July, 1878 | Buffalo, N. Y. |
| MARY C. KIPP | Sept., 1878 | July, 1879 | Mrs. E. W. Seeger, Springfield, Mass. |
| KATHARINE L. HASKELL | May, 1879 | July, 1879 | Mrs. Charles S. Osborn, Atchison, Kans. |
| MALVINA A. HOWE | Sept., 1879 | June, 1895 | Miss Porter's School, Farmington, Conn. |
| MARY B. MATHER | Sept., 1879 / May, 1883 | July, 1882 / June, 1898 | Died in Hartford, Conn. May 23, 1902 |
| MARY W. WOLCOTT | Jan., 1881 | July, 1885 | Mrs. John Barstow, Manchester, Vt. |
| WINFRED R. MARTIN | Sept., 1881 | Sept., 1887 | Professor in Trinity College. Hartford, Conn. |
| WILLIAM E. JUDD | Sept., 1882 | July, 1885 | Principal of Hamilton Grammar School, Holyoke, Mass. |
| CLARA VAN VLECK | Sept., 1884 | July, 1888 | Middletown, Conn. |
| CLARA A. PEASE | May, 1885 | | |
| JULIA W. COLE | May, 1885 | April, 1887 | Mrs. Edward A. Cole, Kensington, Conn. Died 1887 |
| FREDERICK S. MORRISON | Sept., 1885 | | |
| FANNY H. WELLS | Sept., 1885 | June, 1893 | Mrs. Edmund C. Noyes, Evanston, Ill. Died Oct. 21, 1895 |
| HIRAM B. LOOMIS | Sept., 1886 | July, 1887 | Principal of Bernhard Moos School, Chicago, Ill. |
| GRACE UPSON | May, 1887 | June, 1889 | Mrs. Robert A. Mahan, Marianna, Ark. |
| CHARLES S. CHAPIN | Sept., 1887 | June, 1890 | Principal of Rhode Island Normal School, Providence, R. I. |
| LUCY O. MATHER | Sept., 1887 | | |
| JENNY VAN VLECK | Jan., 1888 | June, 1893 | Teacher in Girls' Central High School, Brooklyn, N. Y. |
| WINFIELD C. GRAHAM | Sept., 1888 | June, 1897 | Hartford, Conn. |
| EDWIN M. PICKOP | Jan., 1889 | Dec., 1890 | Rev., Nichols, Conn. |
| KATE MITCHELL | May, 1889 | Mar., 1895 | Mrs. John E. Jenkins, Kingston, Pa. |
| ELIZA L. McCOOK | May, 1889 | Dec., 1894 | Mrs. Logan H. Roots, Hankow, China |
| HARRIET A. HOLBROOK | Sept., 1889 | | Died March 20, 1890 |
| HENRY C. WHITE | Sept., 1889 | Dec., 1897 | Hartford, Conn. |
| ANNA H. ANDREWS | Sept., 1889 | | |
| EDWARD H. SMILEY | Sept., 1890 | | Vice-Principal until May, 1895; since then Principal |
| R. ESTON PHYFE | Sept., 1890 | | Vice-Principal since July 15, 1902 |
| ANNETTE E. BISHOP | Sept., 1890 | June, 1892 | Mrs. Harvey M. Ives, Fairfield, Maine |
| FRANK P. MOULTON | Oct., 1890 | | |
| WARREN F. GREGORY | Jan., 1891 | June, 1896 | With Lee & Shepard, Boston, Mass. |
| DAVID G. SMYTH | Sept., 1891 | | |
| HOMER W. BRAINARD | Sept., 1891 | | |
| MARY L. HASTINGS | Sept., 1891 | | |

| NAME | CAME | WENT | REMARKS |
|---|---|---|---|
| OTTO B. SCHLUTTER | Jan., 1892 | June, 1899 | Hartford, Conn. |
| CAROLYN L. EMERSON | Sept., 1892 | June, 1894 | Mrs. George Mooney, Mendham, N. J. |
| CAROLINE R. LEVERETT | May, 1893 | June, 1897 | Plymouth, N. H. |
| HOWARD H. C. BINGHAM | Sept., 1893 | Feb., 1897 | Principal of Lawrence Academy, Groton, Mass. |
| BERTHA H. SMITH | Oct., 1893 | Mar., 1898 | Mrs. Charles L. Taylor, Hartford, Conn. |
| JENNIE A. PRATT | Oct., 1893 | | |
| CHARLES H. DOUGLAS | Nov., 1893 | April, 1895 | With D. C. Heath & Co., Boston, Mass. |
| ALICE A. STEVENS | June, 1894 | June, 1897 | Teacher in Girls' High School, Brooklyn, N. Y. |
| CLEMENT C. HYDE | Sept., 1894 | | |
| AGNES W. GARVAN | Jan., 1895 | June, 1898 | Hartford, Conn. |
| MARY R. BEACH | April, 1895 | June, 1898 | Teacher in Wadleigh High School, New York, N. Y. |
| MARIE DE LA NIÈPCE | May, 1895 | Dec., 1901 | Mrs. William G. Craig, Hartford, Conn. |
| MAY B. BALD | Sept., 1895 | | |
| FRANKLIN H. TAYLOR | Sept., 1895 | | |
| ANNA C. WALTER | Sept., 1895 | June, 1901 | Middletown, Conn. |
| BURLEIGH S. ANNIS | Sept., 1896 | June, 1904 | Chattanooga, Tenn. |
| ALFRED M. HITCHCOCK | April, 1897 | | |
| ELISABETH W. STONE | Sept., 1897 | | |
| CHARLES B. HOWE | Sept., 1897 | June, 1902 | Teacher in Mechanic Arts, High School, Boston, Mass. |
| FRANK J. PRESTON | Sept., 1897 | | |
| IDELLE B. WATSON | Sept., 1897 | June, 1898 | Dresden, Germany |
| CAROLINE A. JACOBS | Sept., 1897 | June, 1898 | Mrs. Albert M. Gray, New York, N. Y. |
| MARGARET T. HEDDEN | Sept., 1897 | | |
| ELMA A. NICHOLS | Sept., 1897 | June, 1902 | Mrs. Frederick A. Ladd, West Somerville, Mass. |
| C. LOUISE WILLIAMS | Jan., 1898 | June, 1900 | Hartford, Conn. |
| SOPHIA D. TRACY | Jan., 1898 | June, 1900 | Hartford, Conn. |
| ALICE L. COLE | Feb., 1898 | | |
| LEWIS W. ALLEN | Sept., 1898 | | |
| ELISABETH M. BRANDT | Sept., 1898 | | |
| BERTHA E. LOVEWELL | Sept., 1898 | June, 1903 | Mrs. George L. Dickinson, Hartford, Conn. |
| CORA H. COOLIDGE | Sept., 1898 | June, 1900 | Fitchburg, Mass. |
| ELIZABETH B. FOWLER | Sept., 1898 | June, 1900 | Mrs. John L. Haines, Glenshaw, Pa. |
| LOUISE G. STUTZ | Sept., 1898 | | |
| KATHERINE L. HILLS | Sept., 1898 | | |
| HARRIETT W. FOOTE | Oct., 1898 | June, 1902 | Mrs. Herbert A. Taylor, Upper Montclair, N. J. |
| ARTHUR B. BABBITT | Jan., 1899 | | |
| ELIZABETH C. WRIGHT | Sept., 1900 | | |
| SAMUEL M. ALVORD | Sept., 1900 | | |
| HERMANN N. MATZEN | Sept., 1900 | Sept., 1902 | Berlin, Germany |

| NAME | CAME | WENT | REMARKS |
|------|------|------|---------|
| HELEN L. WOLCOTT | Sept., 1900 | | |
| CLARA A. BENTLEY | Sept., 1900 | | |
| MEDORA E. LOOMIS | Sept., 1900 | June, 1901 | Teacher in High School, Woodside, N. Y. |
| EDITH F. MONTAGUE | Sept., 1900 | June, 1902 | Mrs. Henry W. White Hartford, Conn. |
| JOSEPH D. FLYNN | Sept., 1901 | June, 1903 | Instructor in Trinity College, Hartford, Conn. |
| RICHMOND P. PAINE | Sept., 1901 | Sept., 1902 | Hartford, Conn. |
| MARY A. SAWTELLE | Sept., 1901 | | |
| JANE MacMARTIN | Sept., 1901 | | |
| LOUISE H. BAKER | Jan., 1902 | . | Died in Hartford, Conn., Jan. 4, 1904 |
| GEORGE B. KINGSBURY | Sept., 1902 | | |
| WILLIAM C. HOLDEN | Sept., 1902 | | |
| CATHERINE A. GARDNER | Sept., 1902 | | |
| MARY E. ALEXANDER | Sept., 1902 | | |
| CORA GREENWOOD | Jan., 1903 | | |
| WALTER F. KENRICK | Sept., 1903 | | |
| HARRIET ROBBINS | Sept., 1903 | | |
| EDITH L. RISLEY | Sept., 1903 | | |
| EVA M. GOWING | Feb., 1904 | | |
| RALPH L. BALDWIN | Mar., 1904 | | |
| ELDORA J. BIRCH | Sept., 1904 | | |
| ELIZABETH F. FRAZER | Sept., 1904 | | |
| F. ELIZABETH MACK | Sept., 1904 | | |
| MARY C. WELLES | Nov., 1904 | | |

# LIST OF GRADUATES

There were no diplomas or special forms of graduation until 1854, and the school records up to that date do not show accurately who completed the course of study. The lists for years previous to 1854 probably contain the names of all who would have been entitled to a diploma, with those of a very few who apparently lacked less than six months of completing the course.

In order that our Quadrennial Catalogue may give as complete and accurate information as possible concerning the Alumni, every graduate is earnestly requested to notify his class secretary of any change in name, address, or title of any member of the class, or of any other facts which may be of general interest.

## 1848

| NAMES | RESIDENCES |
|---|---|
| CHARLES M. BLISS, A.M., Yale..................... | Bennington, Vt. |
| JONATHAN B. BUNCE, President Phœnix Mutual Life Insurance Company ........................... | Hartford, Conn. |
| DOMINICK MAGUIRE, A.B., Holy Cross...Died, 1865 | |
| JOHN MULLIGAN, REV., D.D., Holy Cross.Died, 1861 | |
| JOHN G. PARSONS, REV., A.B., Wesleyan..Died, 1853 | |
| J. WARD SMYTH, A.M., Trinity..........Died, 1875 | |

## 1849

| | |
|---|---|
| MARTHA A. SEARS.........Mrs. Benjamin Haskell, | Atchison, Kans. |
| HENRY I. BLISS, A.B., Yale..............Died, 1896 | |
| JULIUS CATLIN, A.M., Yale..............Died, 1893 | |
| CHARLES E. FOX........................Died, 1858 | |
| WILLIAM M. HUDSON, A.B., Yale, M.D., Jefferson Med. Coll......................Died, 1901 | |
| JOHN C. PARSONS, A.M., Yale..........Died, 1898 | |
| CHARLES E. PERKINS, A.M., Williams.............. | Hartford, Conn. |
| HENRY C. ROBINSON, A.M., LL.D., Yale, Mayor of Hartford, 1872-4 ...................Died, 1900 | |
| ROBERT O. TYLER, West Point, 1853, Maj. Gen. U. S. A.............................Died, 1874 | |

## 1850

| | |
|---|---|
| LAURA C. SHEPARD...........Mrs. Samuel Breese, | Oneida, N. Y. |
| ALICE E. TERRY..Mrs. Howard S. Collins, Died, 1877 | |
| AUSTIN C. DUNHAM, A.M., Yale................... | Hartford, Conn. |
| FRANCIS FELLOWES, A.B., Yale...........Died, 1870 | |
| ROLAND E. GRISWOLD......................... | Hartford, Conn. |
| WILLIAM H. GROSS....................Died, 1891 | |
| THOMAS P. MULLIGAN...................Deceased | |
| JOSEPH MORGAN SMITH, REV., A.B., Yale..Died, 1883 | |
| ALBERT E. STILLMAN.......................Died, 1889 | |
| WILLIAM VERY ................................ | Hartford, Conn. |
| LEWIS L. WELD, COL., A.M., Yale Died in the army, 1865 | |
| SAMUEL WHITING, A.B., Williams................. | Clearwater, Minn. |
| MATTHEW N. WHITMORE, A.B., LL.B., Yale Died, 1893 | |

## 1851

| NAMES | RESIDENCES |
|---|---|
| CAROLINE A. BOLLES........................... | Hartford, Conn. |
| ALICE C. GALLAUDET, Mrs. H. Clay Trumbull | |
| Died, 1891 | |
| JANE GOLDTHWAITE .............................. | Hartford, Conn. |
| ELLEN M. HOTCHKISS, Mrs. John M. Parker | |
| Died, 1900 | |
| ESTHER C. POST............Mrs. E. Henry Barnes, | New Haven, Conn. |

EDWARD M. GALLAUDET, B.S., A.M., LL.D., Trinity, ⎫
    Ph.D., Columbian, LL.D., Yale, President and ⎬   Washington, D. C.
    Professor of Moral and Political Science, Gal- ⎪
    laudet College, Washington, D. C............ ⎭

| JAMES J. GOODWIN............................... | New York, N. Y. |
| THEODORE LYMAN, A.B., Yale.................... | Hartford, Conn. |

## 1852

| | |
|---|---|
| MARTHA E. CARRIER.......Mrs. Lyman A. Spencer, | Hartford, Conn. |
| LAVINIA M. HOLMAN............................. | New York, N. Y. |
| JULIETTE HOUSE...........Mrs. Joseph N. Spencer, | Hartford, Conn. |
| MARY E. JENISON..........Mrs. Richard W. Bliss, | Jamestown, N. Dak. |
| BERTHA OLMSTED.........Mrs. William W. Niles, | Concord, N. H. |
| EMILY G. ROBERTS............Mrs. Linus T. Fenn, | West Hartford, Conn. |

FRANCIS BEACH, West Point, 1857, Col. U. S. A.
                            Died, 1872
EDWIN C. BOLLES, REV., A.M., Trinity, Ph.D., St. ⎫
    Laurence, S.T.D., Tufts, Professor of English ⎬   Tufts College, Mass.
    and American History in Tufts College...... ⎭
CHARLES E. BULKELEY, A.M., Yale, Capt. 1st C. V. A.
    Died at Battery Garesche, Va., 1864

| STEPHEN CONDIT, A.B., Yale ..........Died, 1897 |
| CHARLES E. FELLOWES, A.B., Yale........Died, 1904 |
| DANIEL E. HOLCOMB, A.B., Trinity......Died, 1869 |
| ALFRED S. ROBINSON....................Died, 1878 |
| EDWARD W. SEYMOUR, A.M., Yale, M.D., |
|     Jefferson Med. Coll.................Died, 1880 |
| CHARLES G. SOUTHMAYD, A.B., Yale.....Died, 1885 |

## 1853

| MARY GOLDTHWAITE......................Died, 1858 | |
| HARRIET ROWELL .............................. | Hartford, Conn. |
| MARY J. SPENCER........................Deceased | |
| | |
| JAMES S. BROOKS............................... | Hartford, Conn. |

## 1854

SHELDON GOODWIN, A.B., Yale..........Died, 1881
ARTHUR N. HOLLISTER, A.M., Yale.......Died, 1897
NORMAND SMITH, A.B., Yale, M.D., Columbia
                          Died, 1896

## 1855

CHARLES H. OWEN, Corresponding Secretary

HENRY W. CAMP, MAJ., A.B., Yale
    . Killed near Richmond, Va., 1864
BENJAMIN S. CATLIN, A.M., M.D., Yale..Died, 1871
EDWARD GOODRIDGE, REV., A.M., D.D., Trinity....... Exeter, N. H.
FERGUS L. KENYON, REV., A.M., Princeton.Died, 1902
CHARLES H. OWEN, A.M., Yale, LL.B., Harvard,
    Brev. Maj. 1st C. V. A........................ Hartford, Conn.
EDWARD H. PERKINS....................Died, 1876
JAMES A. SMITH.......................Died, 1897
GEORGE P. WELLES, A.M., Yale..................... Chicago, Ill.

## 1856

JANE L. SHELDON, Corresponding Secretary

SOPHIA W. BIGELOW..........Mrs. Abel Sampson, Unknown
ANNA E. BLODGETT........Mrs. Frederic A. Francis, Hartford, Conn.
JULIA B. BURBANK............................. Hartford, Conn.
ELMA J. HOOKER........................Deceased
EMMA M. HUNT.............Mrs. George Tucker, Northampton, Mass.
MARY ROWELL.............Mrs. Zalmon A. Storrs, Hartford, Conn.
JANE L. SHELDON................................. Hartford, Conn.
CORNELIA TRASK.......................Died, 1883
ANNA B. VERY..........,...Mrs. Francis S. Drake, Hartford, Conn.
CORNELIA A. WATROUS........................... Hartford, Conn.

CHARLES H. BUNCE, Ph.B., Yale................... Wethersfield, Conn.
THEODORE C. GLAZIER, A.B., Trinity......Died, 1874
GEORGE C. PERKINS, A.M., Yale.........Died, 1875
JOHN D. TUCKER, A.B., Yale...........Died, 1904

## 1857

In 1857 the Board of School Visitors voted to extend the course of study from four to five years; consequently there were no graduates this year.

## 1858

MRS. GEORGE H. WARNER, Corresponding Secretary

JANE F. BLODGETT..............Mrs. Milton Santee, Hartford, Conn.
KATHERINE BURBANK, Librarian of Public High
    School ...................................... Hartford, Conn.
ELISABETH H. GILLETTE....Mrs. George H. Warner, Hartford, Conn.
KATE L. HAYDEN................................. Hartford, Conn.
SARAH C. PACKARD, Mrs. George F. Hills, Died, 1863
ELIZABETH W. PARSONS, Mrs. Frederick E. Goodrich, Boston, Mass.
CAROLINE E. ROBINSON, Mrs. James A. Smith
                             Died, 1881
HENRIETTA SHELDON.........Mrs. Albert L. Hunt, Hartford, Conn.
MARY A. STARKWEATHER.....Mrs. Mary A. Crosby, Chicago, Ill.
FRANCES E. TRASK.........Mrs. Horace J. Morse, Brooklyn, N. Y.

| NAMES | RESIDENCES |
|---|---|
| HEBER H. BEADLE, REV., A.B., Yale................ | Bridgeton, N. J. |
| JOSEPH L. BLANCHARD............................ | Hartford, Conn. |
| REESE B. GWILLIM, A.M., Wesleyan................ | Brooklyn, N. Y. |
| WILLIAM W. HOUSE, A. B., Yale. Died in the army, 1863 | |
| ALBERT L. HUNT........................Died, 1900 | |
| WILLIAM L. MATSON, A.M., Yale, LL.B., Columbia, | Hartford, Conn. |
| AUGUSTUS MORSE, A.M., Trinity........Died, 1871 | |
| HENRY L. PASCO, Maj. 16th C. V. I......Died, 1882 | |
| WILLIAM D. PENFIELD, A.M., Trinity............. | Cobalt, Conn. |
| DWIGHT D. WILLARD, A.M., Princeton...Died, 1877 | |
| ALANSON WORK........................Died, 1881 | |

### 1859

#### MORTON W. EASTON, Corresponding Secretary

| | |
|---|---|
| MORTON W. EASTON, A.B., Ph.D., Yale, M.D., Columbia, Professor of English and Comparative Philology in University of Pennsylvania....... | Philadelphia, Pa. |
| ROSWELL PARISH, A.M., Yale..................... | Brookline, Mass. |
| CHARLES H. WESSON, A.B., Yale, LL.B., Columbia .........................Died, 1873 | |

### 1860

#### ROSWELL F. BLODGETT, Corresponding Secretary

| | | |
|---|---|---|
| ANN E. HORTON.........Mrs. William J. Roberts, | Hartford, Conn. |
| ELLEN A. PETTIBONE, Mrs. Charles S. Field | Died, 1870 |
| MARY C. PHILLIPS...............Mrs. George Lee, | Hartford, Conn. |
| SARAH W. STARKWEATHER..Mrs. William Streeter, | Rochester, N. Y. |
| | |
| WILLIAM A. AYRES, A.B., Yale................... | Hartford, Conn. |
| ROSWELL F. BLODGETT........................... | North San Diego, Cal |
| JAMES W. CLARK, REV., A.M., Trinity............. | Washington, D. C. |
| SAMUEL W. DOBIE......................Died, 1863 | |
| FREDERICK E. GOODRICH, A.B., Yale............... | Boston, Mass. |
| HENRY S. GOODWIN....................Died, 1864 | |
| GEORGE H. HEBARD....................Died, 1902 | |
| CHARLES D. HILLS, REV., A.M., Wesleyan, S.T.D., Claflin ..................................... | Laconia, N. H. |
| THOMAS HOOKER, A.B., Yale..................... | New York, N. Y. |
| SAMUEL HUNTINGTON, A.B., Yale, LL.B., Columbia, | Plainfield, N. J. |
| CHARLES T. MARSTON..................Died, 1889 | |
| EDWARD T. MATHER, A.B., Yale.........Died, 1870 | |
| HENRY E. OWEN, A.B., Yale, M.D., Columbia...... | New York, N. Y. |
| STEPHEN C. PIERSON, A.B., Yale.................. | Meriden, Conn. |
| WILLIAM H. B. PRATT, A.B., Yale, M.D., Columbia, | Brooklyn, N. Y. |
| WILLIAM G. SUMNER, A.B., Yale, LL.D., Univ. of East Tennessee, Professor of Political and Social Science in Yale University................... | New Haven, Conn. |
| EDGAR T. WELLES, A.M., Yale.................... | New York, N. Y. |
| RICHARD K. WOODRUFF, Capt. 30th C. V. I. Wounded at Petersburg, Va. Died in hospital, 1864 | |

## 1861

MRS. OSCAR B. PURINTON, Corresponding Secretary

HARRIET E. CALLENDER....Mrs. Edward N. Havens, Bridgeport, Conn.
EMMA C. DICKINSON, Mrs. Frank E. Flint, Died, 1871
MARIA HOWARD......Mrs. Ethan Curtis, Died, 1879
ALICE E. RAMSEY......................Died, 1896
ELIZA W. SCHULZE, Mrs. George H. Burdick
                                        Died, 1901
AMELIA E. SMITH............Mrs. J. Austin Pease, Hartford, Conn.
MALENA G. TURNER.......Mrs. Oscar B. Purinton, Hartford, Conn.

DANIEL P. DEWEY, 2d Lieut. Company A, 25th C. V.
    A. Killed at Irish Bend, La., 1863
ROBERT P. KEEP, A.B., Ph.D., Yale.......Died, 1904
BENAJAH H. PLATO...................Died, 1904
WILLIAM H. ROBERTS............................. Hartford, Conn.
CHARLES H. B. TREMAINE, REV., A.B., Trinity
                                        Died, 1882

## 1862

JOHN H. BROCKLESBY, Corresponding Secretary

This year the five years' course was abandoned, and consequently two classes were graduated.

GEORGIANA L. FRENCH, Mrs. Edward W. Watson
                                        Died, 1896
ALICE M. HAVENS..........Mrs. Thomas R. Berry, Hartford, Conn.
HANNAH P. LATIMER, Mrs. Stephen C. Pierson
                                        Died, 1883
CAROLINE H. LOOMIS........................... Denver, Colo.
HARRIET E. MORGAN...................Died, 1863
SARAH A. MORGAN, Mrs. George S. A. Young
                                        Died, 1900
ANNA C. NEWTON...........Mrs. Anna C. Hawley, Hartford, Conn.
JANE A. OWEN........Mrs. deB. Randolph Keim, Washington, D. C.
ADELAIDE A. TRASK, Mrs. Cardella E. Brown
                                        Died, 1883
ELIZABETH UTLEY.........Mrs. Charles L. Tuttle, Hartford, Conn.
LOUISA VERY..........Mrs. Hervert B. Langdon, Hartford, Conn.
JANE E. WILLIAMS....................Died, 1863

ALEXANDER D. ANDERSON, A.B., Yale, LL.B., Univ.
    of Mich.............................Died, 1901
JOHN H. BROCKLESBY, A.M., Trinity............... Hartford, Conn.
EDWARD B. BRONSON, A.B., Yale, M.D., Columbia... New York, N. Y.
G. PIERREPONT DAVIS, A.B., Yale, M.D., Columbia... Hartford, Conn.
WILLIAM D. GALLAGHER................Died, 1885
ROBERT HARBISON, A.M., Princeton.....Died, 1903
GEORGE F. HAWLEY, M.D., Columbia............... Chicago, Ill.
CHARLES C. HAYDEN, A.B., Trinity............... New York, N. Y.
HENRY K. HUNTINGTON, A.B., Trinity, M.D., N. Y.
    Univ. .............................Died, 1897
WILLIAM A. MATHER...................Died, 1865
WALTER MITCHELL ....................Died, 1868

| NAMES | RESIDENCES |
|---|---|
| ISAAC PIERSON, REV., A.B., Yale.................. | West Medford, Mass. |
| JOHN F. TRACY................................... | Vernon Center, Conn. |
| | |
| ELLEN M. BUCK..........Mrs. John W. Overand, | St. Louis, Mo. |
| FRANCES A. CALDWELL.....Mrs. George Wadsworth, | Hutchinson, Kans. |
| ELIZABETH M. CRANE......Mrs. Charles C. Fengar, | Sitka, Alaska |
| CAROLINE B. DODD.......Mrs. Emerson W. Belden, | Hartford, Conn. |
| MINDWELL L. HASTINGS....Mrs. Stephen C. Pierson, | Meriden, Conn. |
| | |
| OLIVER D. COOKE......................Died, 1866 | |
| WAYLAND TRASK ......................Died, 1905 | |
| FRANCIS W. WATERMAN.......................... | Rockford, Ill. |

## 1863

### JOSEPH L. BARBOUR, Corresponding Secretary

| | |
|---|---|
| MARY A. BRIGHAM......................Died, 1882 | |
| SARAH M. GLAZIER, A.M., Vassar, Mrs. John M. Bates ....................................... | Lincoln, Nebr. |
| ELLA S. HUTCHINSON..................Died, 1874 | |
| ELLA M. HYDE................................. | Windsor Locks, Conn. |
| ANGELINA KELLOGG.......Mrs. Chester G. Munyan, | Hartford, Conn. |
| IRENE H. PACKARD...........Mrs. George F. Hills, | Hartford, Conn. |
| HARRIET E. SEYMOUR......Mrs. Frank M. Seymour, | Wauwatosa, Wis. |
| ELLEN TUTTLE...........Mrs. D. Waldo Johnson, | Hartford, Conn. |
| | |
| WILLIAM T. BACON, A.M., Yale, M.D., N. Y. Univ., | Hartford, Conn. |
| JOSEPH L. BARBOUR.............................. | Hartford, Conn. |
| CHARLES T. COLLINS, REV., A.B., Yale...Died, 1883 | |
| WILLIAM A. KEEP......................Died, 1867 | |
| JAMES S. McCLAY......................Died, 1884 | |
| ERNEST G. STEDMAN, A.B., Yale, LL.B., Columbia... | New York, N. Y. |
| DEFOREST WILLARD, M.D., Ph.D., Univ. of Pa., A.M., Lafayette, Professor of Orthopedic Surgery in University of Pennsylvania, President of American Surgical Association............... | Philadelphia, Pa. |

## 1864

### CHARLES E. GROSS, Corresponding Secretary

| | |
|---|---|
| JULIA M. ADAMS................................ | Hartford, Conn. |
| JENNY H. APGAR............. .Mrs. Louis L. Davis, | Philadelphia, Pa. |
| ELLEN F. GILLETTE......Mrs. Sanford A. Gabrielle, | Hartford, Conn. |
| ISABEL L. GRISWOLD............................. | Hartford, Conn. |
| FRANCES B. HAVENS.....Mrs. Roderick W. Farmer, | Hartford, Conn. |
| ELLA G. MORSE........................Died, 1894 | |
| FANNY T. PEASE........Mrs. William Porter, Jr., | Hartford, Conn. |
| ELLEN M. PHILLIPS............................. | Hartford, Conn. |
| ELIZABETH G. SMITH.... .................... | Hartford, Conn. |
| ELIZABETH J. STEELE............................ | Springfield, Mass. |
| M. ADELINE TIFFANY............................ | Hartford, Conn. |
| LOUISE G. TRASK.........Mrs. Cardella E. Brown, | Hartford, Conn. |
| ALICE VERY.................Mrs. Thomas J. Gill, | Hartford, Conn. |

| NAMES | RESIDENCES |
|---|---|
| Lucius A. Barbour.............................. | Hartford, Conn. |
| Henry A. Beers, A.M., Yale, Professor of English Literature in Yale University.................. | New Haven, Conn. |
| John S. Greenfield, A.B., Wesleyan....Died, 1870 | |
| Charles E. Gross, A.M., Yale.................. | Hartford, Conn. |
| James W. Holcombe, A.M., Yale.................. | London, Eng. |
| James S. Loomis......................Died, 1866 | |
| Terrence Scollon.....................Died, 1868 | |
| Lucius Tuttle.................................. | Boston, Mass. |

## 1865

### VINCIT QUI ENITITUR

### Bernadotte Perrin, Corresponding Secretary

| | |
|---|---|
| Mary C. Beach..............Mrs. Steven Rogers, | Chicago, Ill. |
| Emily C. Bowers......................Died, 1865 | |
| Ella J. Brace................Mrs. Ella J. Stamp, | Edgewood, R. I. |
| Mary J. Chapin...........Mrs. George F. Capen, | Bloomfield, Conn. |
| Elizabeth K. Holmes.....Mrs. Henry P. Johnston, | New York, N. Y. |
| Isadore King..............Mrs. James H. Willard, | Philadelphia, Pa. |
| Julia G. Litchfield...........Mrs. Julia G. Hills, | Hartford, Conn. |
| Georgiana C. Rogers..........Mrs. Isaac H. Coe, | Hartford, Conn. |
| Frances E. Watrous...................Died, 1894 | |

| | |
|---|---|
| Arthur K. Brocklesby, A.M., Trinity............. | Hartford, Conn. |
| William C. Brocklesby, A.M., Trinity............ | West Hartford, Conn. |
| Ezra Brooks.................................... | New York, N. Y. |
| Frank R. Childs, A.M., Yale..................... | Hartford, Conn. |
| Luther C. Glazier.............................. | Hartford, Conn. |
| John M. Holcombe, A.M., Yale.................. | Hartford, Conn. |
| Bernadotte Perrin, Ph.D., Yale, LL.D., Western Reserve Univ., Professor of Greek Literature and History in Yale University................ | New Haven, Conn. |
| Elisha Stanley........................Died, 1875 | |
| Cornelius Sullivan, A.B., Yale, LL.B., N. Y. Died, 1878 | |
| Henry T. Terry, A.B., Yale, Professor in University of Tokio........................................ | Tokio, Japan |
| Charles H. Thacher............................ | Springfield, Ill. |
| Charles T. Weitzel, Rev., A.M., Yale...Died, 1896 | |
| Francke S. Williams, A.M., Yale, LL.B., Columbia...........................Died, 1882 | |

## 1866

### FINIS NONDUM EST

### Eliza F. Mix, Corresponding Secretary

| | |
|---|---|
| Sarah A. Backus............................... | Hartford, Conn. |
| Julia R. Brewster.....Mrs. Nathaniel H. Loomis, | Amherst, Mass. |
| Ella L. Eldredge, Mrs. Benjamin Macy..Died, 1895 | |
| Hattie M. Ellis.......Mrs. Francis C. Sturtevant, | Hartford, Conn. |
| Hannah M. Fish................................ | Hartford, Conn. |
| Martha F. Henry..........Mrs. Nathan F. Peck, | Hartford, Conn. |

| NAMES | RESIDENCES |
|---|---|
| EMMA M. IVES | Brooklyn, N. Y. |
| MARTHA E. LOOMIS | Hartford, Conn. |
| ELIZA F. MIX | Hartford, Conn. |
| JENNIE M. POST...........Mrs. Ira D. Van Duzee, | Boston, Mass. |
| LUCY W. STOCKBRIDGE, Mrs. Charles L. Burdett | |
| Died, 1896 | |
| SUSIE E. TERRY.........Mrs. James R. Matthews, | West Hartford, Conn. |
| MARY S. WATERMAN | Hartford, Conn. |
| | |
| PERCY S. BRYANT, A.M., Trinity | East Hartford, Conn. |
| ARTHUR H. DAY | Glencoe, Ill. |
| SAMUEL A. GALPIN, LL.B., Columbian, A.M., Yale | |
| Died, 1902 | |
| GEORGE F. GOODMAN.....................Died, 1868 | |
| CHARLES H. HAMLIN, REV., A.B., Yale | Easthampton, Mass. |
| JAMES D. JOHNSON, M.D., Columbia.....Died, 1884 | |
| CHARLES H. ROOT.....................Died, 1867 | |
| WILLIAM TUCKER | Hartford, Conn. |
| SIMEON A. WATROUS | Waterbury, Conn. |

## 1867

### PER ASPERA AD ASTRA

### FREDERICK B. EDWARDS, Corresponding Secretary

| | |
|---|---|
| MARY P. ANDRUSS.....................Died, 1902 | |
| GEORGIANA BIGELOW.......Mrs. Frank S. Kellogg, | Hartford, Conn. |
| MARY FAIRCHILD...........Mrs. Charles W. Cook, | West Medway, Mass. |
| JANE E. FISHER.........Mrs. William J. Roberts, | Hartford, Conn. |
| MARY E. KLINE.....Mrs. Thomas J. Gill, Died, 1873 | |
| JULIA L. SMITH.........Mrs. Frederick A. Adkins, | Hartford, Conn. |
| IVA J. TOWNSEND.....................Died, 1903 | |
| | |
| HENRY BALDWIN, A.M., Yale | New York, N. Y. |
| CHARLES HOPKINS CLARK, A.M., Yale, Editor of the Hartford *Courant* | Hartford, Conn. |
| FREDERICK B. EDWARDS | Hartford, Conn. |
| FREDERICK W. HARRIMAN, REV., A.M., D.D., Trinity, | Windsor, Conn. |
| CHARLES S. HASTINGS, Ph.D., Yale, Professor of Physics in Yale University | New Haven, Conn |
| EDWARD T. OWEN, A.B., Ph.D., Yale, Professor of French Language and Literature in University of Wisconsin | Madison, Wis. |
| WILBERT W. PERRY, A.B., Yale, LL.B., Columbia | |
| Died, 1895 | |

## 1868

### ALTA PETENS

### GEORGE H. SEYMS, Corresponding Secretary

| | |
|---|---|
| MARY S. BASSETT........Mrs. George E. C. Augur, | Hartford, Conn. |
| FLORA J. CHANDLER, Mrs. William D. Yorke | |
| Died, 1878 | |
| LOUISE A. CHURCH.......Mrs. William J. Tolhurst, | Hartford, Conn. |

| NAMES | RESIDENCES |
|---|---|
| MARY A. COOKE.........Mrs. Franklin F. Knous, | New Haven, Conn. |
| KATE F. ELLIS................................... | Hartford, Conn. |
| MARY C. FRANCIS..........Mrs. Frank H. Pierce, | Mount Carmel, Conn. |
| MARTHA S. GOODRICH......Mrs. Chauncey H. Eno, | Simsbury, Conn. |
| ELLA T. GRISWOLD..........Mrs. Isaac J. Lansing, | Scranton, Pa. |
| IDA V. HAMMOND............................... | Whitinsville, Mass. |
| HARRIET T. HOLMES....Mrs. Charlemagne Holmes, | Hadlyme, Conn. |
| ANNIE D. LOOMIS, Mrs. Edward R. Parmelee | |
| Died, 1889 | |
| EFFIE F. MILLER....Mrs. George Foster, Died, 1877 | |
| MARY H. MORGAN.......Mrs. Samuel B. St. John, | Hartford, Conn. |
| ALICE M. RILEY................................ | Burnside, Conn. |
| HARRIET L. ROBINSON..................Died, 1880 | |
| FANNY M. SMITH............................... | New Hartford, Conn. |
| LIZZIE SMITH...........Mrs. Charles S. Hastings, | New Haven, Conn. |
| JOANNA H. VAN RENSSELAER..................... | Cambridge, Mass. |
| MARY N. WELLES...............Mrs. John Isham, | Minneapolis, Minn. |
| | |
| FREDERICK H. AYRES........................... | Sandusky, Ohio |
| HENRY D. BARNARD.....................Died, 1884 | |
| CHARLES G. BARTLETT, A.M., Yale, Principal of the | |
| Black Hall School........................... | Black Hall, Conn. |
| JOSHUA BELDEN ............................... | Newington, Conn. |
| ALBERT M. CURRY, A.B., Yale, M.D., Univ. of Pa... | Brooklyn, N. Y. |
| CHARLES C. DEMING, A.B.. Yale, LL.B., Columbia.. | New York, N. Y. |
| HENRY C. DEMING, A.B., Yale.................... | New York, N. Y. |
| GEORGE A. OVIATT, A.B., Yale, M.D., Columbia...... | South Sudbury, Mass. |
| WILLIAM B. PARSONS............................ | Ella, Oregon |
| HENRY T. SCUDDER, A.M., Wesleyan................ | Marinette, Wis. |
| GEORGE H. SEYMS, A.M., Trinity.................. | Hartford, Conn. |
| CHARLES C. STEARNS, REV., A.M., Yale............. | Hartford, Conn. |
| WILLIAM H. STRONG............................. | Detroit, Mich. |
| EDWARD C. TERRY, Ph.B., Yale.................... | Hartford, Conn. |

## 1869

### VIRES ACQUIRIMUS EUNDO

### JAMES S. TRYON, Corresponding Secretary

| | |
|---|---|
| HARRIET F. BARROWS............................ | Hartford, Conn. |
| KATE M. BIDWELL......................Died, 1870 | |
| JOSEPHINE M. CHAPIN.......Mrs. Edgar A. Smith, | West Somerville, Mass. |
| SUSAN T. CLARK................................ | Hartford, Conn. |
| EMMA E. COOLEY...........Mrs. D. P. Williams, | Unknown |
| LILLIE E. DANIELS..........Mrs. James M. Burns, | Pittsfield, Mass. |
| IDA V. DAWSON.............Mrs. Wilbur F. Prior, | Hartford, Conn. |
| ELLA A. FULLER.............Mrs. Henry M. Mayer, | Hartford, Conn. |
| FLORINE GRISWOLD........Mrs. James T. Patterson, | Milford, Conn. |
| FANNIE H. HAZEN..........Mrs. John B. Talcott, | New Britain, Conn. |
| HELEN L. LYMAN.......Mrs. Marcus M. Johnson, | Hartford, Conn. |
| NELLIE A. PARRISH.............Mrs. Henry Avery, | Portland, Oregon |
| ELLA L. PEMBER........Mrs. Charles F. Harwood, | Stafford Springs, Conn. |
| | |
| HENRY A. BLAKE, REV., A.B., Brown.............. | Rochester, N. H. |
| WILLIAM H. BURKETT..................Died, 1886 | |
| NORMAN H. BURNHAM, REV., A.B., Yale........... | Thompsonville, Conn. |

| NAMES | RESIDENCES |
|---|---|
| JOHN F. BURT.................................... | Waltham, Mass. |
| CHARLES H. CAMP........................Died, 1872 | |
| GEORGE N. CLARK............................... | Hartford, Conn. |
| ATWOOD COLLINS, A.B., Yale...................... | Hartford, Conn. |
| DANIEL FARRELL........................Died, 1890 | |
| CHARLES P. HOWARD, B.S., Mass. Inst. of Technology, | Hartford, Conn. |
| WILLIAM D. HUBBARD............................. | West Hartford, Conn. |
| JOHN B. KNAPP, M.D., Columbia.................. | New York, N. Y. |
| NATHAN F. MILLER.............................. | Bloomfield, Conn. |
| ADDISON PERRIN........................Died, 1871 | |
| OWEN D. RIST.................................. | East Hartford, Conn. |
| JAMES H. ROBERTS, REV., A.B., B.D., Yale, Missionary A. B. C: F. M........................... | Kalgan, China |
| FREDERICK J. SHEPARD, A.B., Yale.................. | Buffalo, N. Y. |
| CHARLES W. SKINNER............................ | Hartford, Conn. |
| JAMES S. TRYON................................ | Rumford, R. I. |

## 1870

### A POSSE AD ESSE

### Mrs. Goodwin Brown, Corresponding Secretary

| | | |
|---|---|---|
| ROSABEL S. ATTLETON.......Mrs. Rosabel S. Mayer, | Hartford, Conn. |
| MARY E. BOOTH................................. | Chicago, Ill. |
| EMMA A. BRIGGS.........Mrs. Willard M. Lovell, | Windsor, Conn. |
| EMMA S. COMINGS......................Died, 1876 | |
| NELLIE L. FAIRCHILD........Mrs. George R. Hewitt, | West Medway, Mass. |
| ALICE M. FLOWER...........Mrs. James F. Lummis, | Bridgeton, N. J. |
| IDA E. HODGE................Mrs. Austin L. Cutler, | Warehouse Point, Ct. |
| EMMA G. HOLLISTER.........Mrs. Lucien M. Royce, | Hartford, Conn. |
| ELIZABETH NORTON............................... | Kensington, Conn. |
| ALICE L. SEAVEY, Mrs. Frederick H. Chapin Died, 1888 | |
| SOPHIE D. SEYMOUR.......Mrs. Charles C. Stearns, | Hartford, Conn. |
| M. ALICE SHERMAN............................. | West Hartford, Conn. |
| CARLOTTA N. SMITH.............................. | New York, N. Y. |
| SARAH J. THOMPSON......Mrs. Clarence B. Lummis, | Cedarville, N. J. |
| ADA M. VINTON...............Mrs. Henry C. Dean, | New York, N. Y. |
| LILIAN S. WOODHOUSE........Mrs. Goodwin Brown, | Yonkers, N. Y. |

| | |
|---|---|
| CHARLES W. CLARK, A.M., Yale, J.U.D., Göttingen, Ph.D., Columbia, Licencié en droit, Paris...... | Hartford, Conn. |
| JOHN F. CLARK...........................Died, 1901 | |
| WILLIAM F. HENNEY, A.M., Princeton, Mayor of Hartford, 1904-6 ........................... | Hartford, Conn. |
| DANIEL R. HOWE, A.B., Yale...................... | Hartford, Conn. |
| FREDERICK S. LYMAN............................. | Augusta, Maine |
| CHARLES S. MILLS.............................. | Westfield, Mass. |
| GILBERT G. MOSELEY, A.B., Yale.................. | Hartford, Conn. |
| FRANK H. OLMSTED, A.B., Yale, LL.B., Columbia Died, 1886 | |
| WILLIAM K. PHILLIPS....................Died, 1874 | |
| EDWARD D. ROBBINS, A.B., LL.B., Yale............. | Wethersfield, Conn. |
| ARTHUR F. SKEELE, REV., A.M., Amherst.......... | Painesville, Ohio |
| HENRY B. SKEELE............................... | Savannah, Ga. |
| JAMES W. SMITH........................Died, 1876 | |
| GEORGE M. STEARNS, A.B., Yale.................. | Unknown |
| EDMUND ZACHER, A.B., LL.B., Yale............... | Branford, Conn. |

## 1871

NE TENTES AUT PERFICE

MRS. CHARLES E. GROSS, Corresponding Secretary

LYDIA W. BALLOU............................... Hartford, Conn.
MARY G. BARKER.............Mrs. Mary G. Foster, Hartford, Conn.
ANNA R. BEEBE.......Mrs. Louis Kraft, Died, 1899
JANE A. BIDWELL...........Mrs. Edwin H. Wilson, Cambridge, Mass.
IDA J. FENN..................................... Schenectady, N. Y.
LUCILLE H. FOSTER.......Mrs. William A. Erving, West Hartford, Conn.
HELEN R. HAZEN...........Mrs. David G. Gordon, Bostonia, Cal.
ADELAIDE H. KING......Mrs. Frederick S. Bidwell, Windsor Locks, Conn.
EMMA M. KING................................. Hartford, Conn.
SARAH H. LOOMIS...........Mrs. Albert H. Pitkin, Hartford, Conn.
ROSABELLE R. MARSHALL....Mrs. Thomas T. Welles, New Haven, Conn.
FRANCES A. PARKER, Mrs. James S. Birden
                                          Died, 1897
MARTHA A. PATTERSON........................... Hartford, Conn.
HARRIET PLAISTED..........:..Mrs. David Shirrell, Montreal, Canada
HARRIET J. SPENCER.......Mrs. Joseph O. Goodwin, East Hartford, Conn.
NELLIE C. SPENCER.........Mrs. Charles E. Gross, Hartford, Conn.
ANNA M. STAMM.........Mrs. William A. Smith, New York, N. Y.
GRACE G. STANLEY.......Mrs. Thomas W. Wilbor, New Britain, Conn.
ALICE M. STEARNS.............................. Hartford, Conn.
ANNA J. WOODHOUSE.......Mrs. Joseph L. Barbour, Hartford, Conn.

CHARLES L. BARTLETT, A.B., Yale.................. Chicago, Ill.
T. BELKNAP BEACH.............................. Hartford, Conn.
HENRY BLODGET, A.B., Yale, M.D., Bellevue Hosp.
    Med. Coll. .................................. Bridgeport, Conn.
GEORGE W. ELY.........................Died, 1896
HENRY S. HOUSE............................... Hartford, Conn.
SAMUEL F. JONES............................... Winchester, Mass.


## 1872

ESSE QUAM VIDERI

LUCY S. WILLIAMS, Corresponding Secretary

ELIZA A. BECKWITH...........Mrs. George Ogden, Everett, Mass.
HATTIE BISSELL...........Mrs. Edward S. Jackson, Rockville, Conn.
ALICE M. CHAPMAN............................. Hartford, Conn.
ELLA B. CONE.............Mrs. Charles W. Pratt, Hartford, Conn.
CORA W. GUION........Mrs. William C. Russell, Hartford, Conn.
MARY J. HARRIS................................ Wethersfield, Conn.
BELLE L. HART...............Mrs. George L. Bell, Hartford, Conn.
ELLA M. HOUSTON........Mrs. Eugene E. Clements, New Haven, Conn.
ANNA P. HYDE..............Mrs. Charles H. Coye, Windsor Locks, Conn.
SARAH E. LOOMIS.........Mrs. Charles A. Vallette, St. Louis, Mo.
BELLE S. MOSELEY.............................. Hartford, Conn.
ROSA A. POST..............Mrs. Charles D. Hoxie, Brooklyn, N. Y.
MARIA E. PRICE........................Died, 1872
M. LOUISE ROWLES.......Mrs. George W. Fowler, Hartford, Conn.
ALIDA A. SEARS........................Died, 1877
CHARLOTTE L. SHEPARD, Mrs. Charlotte L. McMurray, Hartford, Conn.

| NAMES | | RESIDENCES |
|---|---|---|
| LIZZIE B. SMITH........Mrs. Charles W. Boylston, | | Riverside, Conn. |
| JEANNIE R. STICKNEY.......Mrs. David I. Carson, | | Atlanta, Ga. |
| EMMA I. TARBOX.........................Died, 1874 | | |
| ELLIE L. TOWNSEND..........Mrs. Alvan T. Tracy, | | Washington, D. C. |
| NELLIE E. WATSON......Mrs. William Waldo Hyde, | | Hartford, Conn. |
| EMMA E. WENK...........Mrs. Frederic C. Pratt, | | Deep River, Conn. |
| LUCY S. WILLIAMS............................... | | Hartford, Conn. |

EVERETT ALEXANDER ........................... Rural, S. C.
JAMES S. BRYANT.......................Died, 1903
EDWIN H. FORBES, Ph.D., Yale.................... Torrington, Conn.
CHARLES J. FOX, M.D., N. Y. Univ. and Bellevue
   Hosp. Med. Coll. ............................ Willimantic, Conn.
ABNER HENDEE ................................. New Haven, Conn.
DWIGHT W. HUNTER, A.B., Yale, M.D., Columbia... New York, N. Y.
WILLIAM WALDO HYDE, A.B., Yale, LL.B., Boston
   Univ., Mayor of Hartford, 1892-4.............. Hartford, Conn.
HENRY K. MORGAN, JR............................ New York. N. Y.
ROBERT W. PATTON............................. Chicago, Ill.
EDWARD A. SHELDON...................Died, 1898
CHARLES H. SMITH, JR.................Died, 1894
WILLIAM F. WEISER............................. York, Pa.
HORACE B. WILLIAMS............................ East Hartford, Conn.

## 1873

VIAM INVENIEMUS AUT FACIEMUS

### MRS. CHARLES T. RUSS, Corresponding Secretary

EMILY W. BARBER.........Mrs. Seth P. Griswold, West Hartford, Conn.
AUGUSTA I. BELDEN.....................Died, 1886
ALICE A. BOWERS.............Mrs. Alice A. Clark, Hartford, Conn.
JENNIE M. BROWN.............................. Worcester, Mass.
IDA J. BURNHAM............................... Hartford, Conn.
ELIZABETH B. CAMP........Mrs. Charles T. Russ, Hartford, Conn.
KATE A. CORNISH.......Mrs. Thomas W. Saunders, Hartford, Conn.
HATTIE E. CORNWELL...................Died, 1894
GEORGIA A. CRANE........Mrs. Charles W. Skinner, Hartford, Conn.
MARY E. GILBERT.....................Died, 1874
ELLEN S. HAVENS............................. Hartford, Conn.
JESSIE F. HOLCOMB, Mrs. George M. Keefer
                     Died, 1888
MARTHA C. KILBOURN.....Mrs. Edward B. Hooker, Hartford, Conn.
ANNIE MORRIS...............Mrs. Alfred T. Perry, Marietta, Ohio
HARRIET E. PEASE.............................. Hartford, Conn.
E. JENNIE PECK............................... Bristol, Conn.
DORA G. PHELPS............................... Hartford, Conn.
MARY F. REARDEN.............................. Hartford, Conn.
HELEN Y. SMITH......Mrs. William W. Ellsworth, New York, N. Y.
ELLEN C. STANLEY.............................. East Hartford, Conn.
CARRIE E. WARNER.......Mrs. Ellsworth B. Strong, Portland, Conn.
MARY L. WARNER.............Mrs. James T. Pratt, Hartford, Conn.
UNA C. WHITTLESEY, Mrs. Charles P. Elliott
                     Died, 1896
ANNIE A. WILEY..........Mrs. Edward C. Frisbie, Hartford, Conn.

| NAMES | RESIDENCES |
|---|---|
| Eva R. Woodward.......Mrs. Horace M. Andrews, | Hartford, Conn. |
| Effie A. Worthington..Mrs. Charles L. McIntosh, | Milwaukee, Wis. |
| | |
| Henry C. Alvord, Rev., A.M., N. Y. Univ......... | South Weymouth, Mass. |
| James P. Andrews, A.B., LL.B., Yale.............. | Hartford, Conn. |
| Willis A. Briscoe, A.B., Yale.................... | Norwich, Conn. |
| Sidney W. Clark, Ph.B., Yale.................... | Hartford, Conn. |
| Frederick W. Davis, A.B., Yale.................. | Hartford, Conn. |
| Edward Deming ................................ | Hartford, Conn. |
| William H. Ely, A.B., Amherst.................. | New Haven, Conn. |
| F. Howard Ensign.............................. | East Hartford, Conn. |
| William E. Flanagan, Rev...................... | Baltimore, Md. |
| George E. Gilbert, A.B., Yale............Died, 1879 | |
| William H. Gillette............................ | Hartford, Conn. |
| William W. Hakes.............................. | Windsor, Conn. |
| Frederick A. Leavenworth, A.B., Princeton, LL.B., Columbia....... | Rochester, N. Y. |
| Henry Roberts, A.B., LL.B., Yale, Lieutenant-Governor of Connecticut, 1903-5, Governor of Connecticut, 1905-7 .............................. | Hartford, Conn. |
| Frank B. Smith................................. | Hartford, Conn. |
| Charles A. Watson, Ph.B., Yale................. | New York, N. Y. |
| George K. Welch, M.D., Columbia............... | Hartford, Conn. |
| Arthur Williams, A.B., Yale, Principal of Dwight School, New York, N. Y...................... | Mount Vernon, N. Y. |
| Charles E. Woodruff, LL.B., Yale............... | Springfield, Mass. |

## 1874

PALMA NON SINE PULVERE

Lillian A. Andrews, Corresponding Secretary

| | |
|---|---|
| Lillian A. Andrews........................... | Hartford, Conn. |
| Mary L. Barber................................ | Hartford, Conn. |
| Ida G. Belden............Mrs. Charles G. Lincoln, | Hartford, Conn. |
| Lillian M. Booth......................Died, 1900 | |
| Mary C. Burr................................. | Hartford, Conn. |
| Alice W. Chapman.........Mrs. Alfred A. Welles, | Glastonbury, Conn. |
| Julia L. Faxon............................... | Elmwood, Conn. |
| Martha A. Fowler............................. | Springfield, Mass. |
| Inez J. Fox..................Mrs. James J. Peard, | Hartford, Conn. |
| Mary W. Hamilton............................. | West Hartford, Conn. |
| Annie J. Hart........................Died, 1879 | |
| Katharine L. Haskell....Mrs. Charles S. Osborn, | Atchison, Kans. |
| Anna G. Hills............Mrs. George W. Pratt, | East Hartford, Conn. |
| Fannie I. Leonard........Mrs. Edward Manning, | Glastonbury, Conn. |
| Nellie M. McManus......Mrs. Michael F. Dooley, | Providence, R. I. |
| Christine E. Muller........Mrs. Henry A. Pierce, | Chicago, Ill. |
| Lena S. Northrop...........Mrs. Ludlow Barker, | West Hartford, Conn. |
| Mary C. Spring............Mrs. Ralph H. North, | Mount Airy, Pa. |
| Elizabeth Thacher.......Mrs. William S. Hinman, | Wichita, Kans. |
| Ellen E. Upson.......Mrs. Frank G. Woodworth, | Tougaloo, Miss. |
| Julia W. Upson, Mrs. Edward A. Cole..Died, 1887 | |
| Olive C. Welch..........Mrs. Everett P. Curtiss, | Hartford, Conn. |
| Elizabeth A. Whitney....Mrs. Walter L. Cheney, | Meriden, Conn. |

6

| NAMES | RESIDENCES |
|---|---|
| ABBY M. WILLIAMS....................Died, 1895 | |
| MARY E. YOUNG.............Mrs. Irving Emerson, | Hartford, Conn. |
| MAGGIE J. ZIEBELL.......Mrs. Thomas L. Johnston, | Hartford, Conn. |
| | |
| FRANK H. AMIDON......................Died, 1882 | |
| ROBERT D. ANDREWS, A.M., Colorado Coll......... | Boston, Mass. |
| CHARLES P. BACON, A.B., Cornell................. | New York, N. Y. |
| WILLIAM P. BELDEN, A.B., Yale.........Died, 1903 | |
| ARTHUR E. BOWERS, A.B., Yale................... | Manchester, Conn. |
| HORACE H. BUCK, REV., A.B., Amherst............ | Cheshire, Conn. |
| J. GILBERT CALHOUN, Ph.B., Yale................. | Hartford, Conn. |
| WILLIAM H. CHILDS............................. | New York, N. Y. |
| WALTER C. FAXON.............................. | Hartford, Conn. |
| THOMAS L. FISHER, REV., A.B., Amherst.......... | Ayer, Mass. |
| GEORGE BELL FRANCIS........................... | Brooklyn, N. Y. |
| CHARLES M. GILBERT, A.B., Yale........Died, 1881 | |
| DAVID HENNEY................................. | Upper Montclair, N. J. |
| EDWARD B. HOOKER, M.D., Boston Univ........... | Hartford, Conn. |
| HARRY S. KNAPP, U. S. N. Acad., 1878, Lieut. Com.. | U. S. Navy |
| CHARLES G. LINCOLN............................ | Hartford, Conn. |
| LEVERETT N. MOWRY............................ | Kearney, Nebr. |
| EVERETT S. WARNER, M.D., Columbia.............. | New York, N. Y. |
| FRANK C. WHITE......................Died, 1890 | |
| CHARLES O. WHITMORE, A.B., Yale................ | Hartford, Conn. |

### 1875

#### QUOD FACIMUS BENE FACIEMUS

CHARLES A. PEASE, Corresponding Secretary

| | |
|---|---|
| ANNA M. BEVIN......Mrs. Herbert C. Wadsworth, | Hartford, Conn. |
| MARY L. CATLIN...........Mrs. Frank C. Sumner, | Hartford, Conn. |
| ELIZABETH N. CHAPIN, Mrs. Roswell F. Blodgett | |
| Died, 1878 | |
| GRACE E. COOLEY, A. M., Brown, Ph.D., Univ. of Zürich, Associate Professor of Botany, Wellesley College ..................................... | Wellesley, Mass. |
| FANNY G. DARROW.............................. | Cambridge, Mass. |
| MINNIE FRANCIS............................... | Hartford, Conn. |
| FLORA J. GILLETTE..........Mrs. William Melrose, | Hartford, Conn. |
| MARY A. GLAZIER.........Mrs. Charles E. Chapin, | Greenwich, Conn. |
| NELLIE S. GOODRICH...........Mrs. George C. Eno, | Simsbury, Conn. |
| CAROLYN A. GOODWIN........................... | Hartford, Conn. |
| MARTHA E. HICKMOTT........................... | Hartford, Conn. |
| ELLA G. JOHNSON.............................. | Hartford, Conn. |
| NETTIE MYLECRAINE.........Mrs. John A. McCrea, | Fair Haven, N. Y. |
| MARY A. ROBINSON..........Mrs. Louis R. Cheney, | Hartford, Conn. |
| AGNES M. SEARS..............Mrs. Arthur B. Ryan, | Middletown, Conn. |
| GRACE E. SEYMOUR......Mrs. William S. Ingraham, | Bristol, Conn. |
| MARIA E. SLOCUM......Mrs. Cornelius W. Driscoll, | Hartford, Conn. |
| TUNIE F. SMITH............Mrs. Robert N. Seyms, | Hartford, Conn. |
| EFFIE P. SPRAGUE............................. | Hartford, Conn. |
| LOUISE R. STAMM.....Mrs. Joseph Buths, Died, 1893 | |
| MARY F. STILLMAN.....Mrs. Frederick A. Griswold, | Wethersfield, Conn. |
| HARRIETTE C. TERRY, Mrs. Theodore P. Prudden | |
| Died, 1886 | |

| NAMES | RESIDENCES |
|---|---|
| JULIA M. WALLACE............................... | Waterbury, Conn. |
| ELLA M. WARREN............Mrs. Henry J. Peavy, | Byron, Ga. |
| MARY R. WILLIAMS, Art Instructor in Smith College, | Northampton, Mass. |
| CARRIE E. WOODHOUSE, Mrs. William A. Fuller | |
| Died, 1900 | |
| LUCY M. WOODRUFF.............................. | Farmington, Conn. |

| | |
|---|---|
| ETHELBERT F. ALLEN.............................. | Kansas City, Mo. |
| WILLIAM D. ALLEN, Ph.B., Yale.................... | Chicago, Ill. |
| CHARLES H. J. BLISS.............................. | San Francisco, Cal. |
| CHARLES W. CANFIELD, Ph.B., Yale................ | New York, N. Y. |
| GEORGE H. CLARK, JR., A.B., Yale................. | Newark, N. J. |
| JOHN S. COWLES.........................Died, 1885 | |
| THOMAS COWLES.........................Died, 1882 | |
| GEORGE C. ENO.................................. | Simsbury, Conn. |
| ASA J. FARWELL, A.B., Yale....................... | Brooklyn, N. Y. |
| E. HART FENN................................... | Wethersfield, Conn. |
| EDWARD B. GAYLORD.............................. | Hartford, Conn. |
| CHARLES G. HUNTINGTON.......................... | Hartford, Conn. |
| FRANK E. HYDE, A.B., LL.B., Yale, U. S. Consul at | |
| Lyons, France, 1893-7......................... | Paris, France |
| CHARLES A. PEASE............................... | Hartford, Conn. |
| CHARLES W. ROBBINS............................. | Brewton, Ala. |
| WELLINGTON J. RODGERS.......................... | Los Angeles, Cal. |
| HERBERT H. SAUNDERS........................... | Hartford, Conn. |
| JOHN W. SHEPARD, A.B., Yale..................... | Brooklyn, N. Y. · |
| ALPHEUS H. SNOW, A.B., Yale, LL.B., Harvard..... | Washington, D. C. |

## 1876

### ΟΥ ΛΟΓΟΙ ΑΛΛΑ ΕΡΓΑ

#### CHARLES E. CHASE, Corresponding Secretary

| | |
|---|---|
| LEILA F. ADAMS............Mrs. Clayton Willard, | Wethersfield, Conn. |
| MINNIE BARTON........................Died, 1884 | |
| MINNIE L. BEAUMONT, Mrs. H. B. Williams | |
| Died, 1881 | |
| MARY R. CALHOUN............................... | Pontiac, Mich. |
| HATTIE J. COIT.............Mrs. Edward T. Platt, | New York, N. Y. |
| MARY E. COOK............Mrs. John M. Williams, | Manchester, Conn. |
| HATTIE E. COOKE.......Mrs. Philemon W. Robbins, | Hartford, Conn. |
| MARION L. DAVIS................................ | Hartford, Conn. |
| ETTA M. DOW.................................... | Hartford, Conn. |
| HELEN S. FOSTER............Mrs. Frank W. Smith, | St. Albans, Vt. |
| MARY E. GILBERT, Mrs. Willard H. Hunt.Died, 1898 | |
| HELEN E. HAWLEY.....................Died, 1883 | |
| MARGARET M. KANE............................. | Hartford, Conn. |
| ANNA R. KELLOGG......................Died, 1877 | |
| JULIA KELLOGG................Mrs. Claude Costen, | Oaky Streak, Ala. |
| MARY B. MATHER.......................Died, 1902 | |
| CORA A. PARDEE........Mrs. Charles W. Firebaugh, | New York, N. Y. |
| ANNIE L. PARSONS...Mrs. E. H. Talcott, Died, 1882 | |
| ANNIE M. PHELPS............Mrs. Hugh Harbison, | Hartford, Conn. |
| SOPHIA S. PRATT................................ | Wethersfield, Conn. |
| RACHEL W. ROOT...........Mrs. Henry C. Ewing, | Hartford, Conn. |

| NAMES | RESIDENCES |
|---|---|
| ELIZA J. ROULSTONE.............Mrs. James Moore, | Canandaigua, N. Y. |
| LUCY T. SMITH, Mrs. Frederick W. Davis, Died, 1881 | |
| ANNIE E. TRUMBULL............................ | Hartford, Conn. |
| EMMA L. WALDO................................ | Hartford, Conn. |
| IDA E. WELLES................................ | Hartford, Conn. |
| ADELAIDE S. WHEELOCK......................... | Middletown, Conn. |
| ISABELLE G. WHITE............................ | Hightstown, N. J. |
| NELLIE B. WILLARD............................ | Hartford, Conn. |
| LAURA C. WILLIAMS............................ | Hartford, Conn. |
| | |
| GEORGE M. ALLEN.............................. | Beloit, Wis. |
| CHARLES H. BARTLETT.......................... | Westfield, Mass. |
| LAWSON B. BIDWELL....................Died, 1891 | |
| ARTHUR E. BULL......................Died, 1900 | |
| CHARLES E. CHASE............................. | Hartford, Conn. |
| CHARLES F. GORMAN............................ | Hartford, Conn. |
| ANDREW G. HAMMOND, West Point, 1881, Major.... | U. S. Army |
| PAUL HANSELL........................Died, 1896 | |
| DANA W. KELLOGG, A.B., Yale...........Died, 1880 | |
| JOHN G. KELLOGG, A.B., Amherst........Died, 1903 | |
| GEORGE H. LITTLE............................. | Hartford, Conn. |
| THOMAS R. MORROW, A.B., LL.B., Yale............ | Kansas City, Mo. |
| WARD C. POWELL.............................. | Hartford, Conn. |
| WILLIAM E. SESSIONS.......................... | Bristol, Conn. |
| FRANK G. SMITH.............................. | Hartford, Conn. |
| FREDERICK M. SMITH, A.B., Yale, A.M., Harvard.... | Hartford, Conn. |
| HERBERT E. SMITH, Ph.B., Yale, M.D., Univ. of Pa., Professor of Chemistry, and Dean of the Medical School in Yale University............. | New Haven, Conn. |
| WILBUR H. SQUIRE............................. | Meriden, Conn. |
| MAX STERN, A.B., Yale, LL.B., Columbia.......... | New York, N. Y. |
| LOUIS A. TRACY.............................. | Hartford, Conn. |
| EDWIN C. WARD, A.B., Yale, LL.B., Columbia...... | Brooklyn, N. Y. |
| HEMAN CHARLES WHITTLESEY, A.B., Yale.......... | Middletown, Conn. |

## 1877

### ANIMO ET FIDE

### EMILY V. BARNARD, Corresponding Secretary

| | |
|---|---|
| ELIZABETH ABBE...Mrs. Richard Wright, Died, 1899 | |
| ANNIE ALFORD.............Mrs. Lucius G. Bartlett, | Boston, Mass. |
| FLORENCE N. ALVORD.......................... | Jamaica, N. Y. |
| EMILY V. BARNARD............................ | Hartford, Conn. |
| FANNIE E. BEAUMONT........Mrs. J. Frank Cowles, | East Hartford, Conn. |
| FANNY J. BIRCH..........Mrs. Thomas C. Leavens, | Newtonville, Mass. |
| ALICE BULLARD.............Mrs. Arthur F. Skeele, | Painesville, Ohio |
| HARRIET B. CARPENTER......Mrs. James F. Wattles, | Boston, Mass. |
| LIZZIE W. DENSLOW........Mrs. Oliver T. Mather, | Hartford, Conn. |
| ALICE FARNHAM............................... | Hartford, Conn. |
| ALICE N. FOWLER............................. | Hartford, Conn. |
| ANNA L. FRANCIS............................. | Glenbrook, Conn. |
| EMILIE GOODMAN.............Mrs. Richard Wright, | Newburyport, Mass. |
| ADELAIDE L. GRISWOLD.......Mrs. Willis M. Savage, | Wethersfield, Conn. |
| HATTIE HILLS................................ | Hartford, Conn. |

| NAMES | RESIDENCES |
|---|---|
| ADA W. HUNT...........................Died, 1881 | |
| MARY E. JOHNSON................................. | Hartford, Conn. |
| MARY B. LEWIS.................................... | Hartford, Conn. |
| ELLIE B. ROBBINS.........Mrs. Gilbert M. Griswold, | Hartford, Conn. |
| JANE E. ROBBINS, M.D., Woman's Med. Coll. of N. Y. Infirmary.................................... | New York, N. Y. |
| CARRIE L. SMITH, Mrs. Joseph C. Alvord. Died, 1899 | |
| MARGARETTE M. STEVENS.................Died, 1878 | |
| MARY B. SWIFT...Mrs. Arthur L. Gillett, Died, 1901 | |
| RUTH D. TRASK.............Mrs. Edward Adams, | Brooklyn, N. Y. |
| MARY L. UNDERWOOD......Mrs. Charles H. Daniels, | South Framingham, Mass. |
| ALICE E. WOLCOTT.........Mrs. Wilbur H. Squire, | Meriden, Conn. |
| EMMA WOLCOTT .................................. | Hartford, Conn. |
| ADDIE J. WOODFORD...Mrs. Willard M. Leavenworth, | Bloomfield, Conn. |
| D. NEWTON BARNEY, A.B., Yale.................... | Farmington, Conn. |
| PHILIP G. BARTLETT, A.B., Yale.................... | New York, N. Y. |
| WALTER D. BIDWELL, A.M., Williams, M.D., Harvard Died, 1896 | |
| EDWARD PAUL BRANDT, A.B., Yale......Died, 1882 | |
| GEORGE W. BURCH.............................. | Hartford, Conn. |
| ARTHUR W. COWLES, LL.B., National Univ......... | Washington, D. C. |
| ARLAN P. FRANCIS............................... | Newington Junction, Conn. |
| HARRY T. GATES........................Died, 1882 | |
| WILLIAM E. GATES............................... | Glastonbury, Conn. |
| ANDREW S. GAYLORD............................. | Terryville, Conn. |
| HENRY C. HALL, A.B., Amherst, LL.B., Columbia... | Colorado Springs, Colo. |
| HERMAN P. HEINE............................... | New London, Conn. |
| GEORGE C. KREUZER............................. | Hartford, Conn. |
| ARTHUR H. LYMAN............................... | Chicago, Ill. |
| HENRY W. MARTIN......................Died, 1878 | |
| WILLIAM J. McGURK, REV., A.M., St. John's Coll.... | South Manchester, Conn. |
| GEORGE P. McLEAN, A.M., Yale, Governor of Connecticut, 1901-3............................. | Simsbury, Conn. |
| FRANK E. MILLER, A.M., Trinity, M.D., Columbia... | New York, N. Y. |
| WARREN P. NEWCOMB, West Point, 1882, Capt. 5th Artillery ................................... | U. S. Army |
| ARTHUR M. PARENT.....................Died, 1902 | |
| EDWARD H. PEASE................................ | Chicago, Ill. |
| EPAPHRODITUS PECK, LL.B., Yale, Associate Judge Hartford County Court of Common Pleas, Instructor in Civil Procedure in Yale University.. | Bristol, Conn. |
| CHARLES H. PRENTICE..................Died, 1895 | |
| JAMES E. TUCKER............................... | Hartford, Conn. |
| RICHARD A. WHITE............................... | Greenwich, Conn. |

### 1878

ALIIS LAETUS, SAPIENS SIBI

ARCHIBALD A. WELCH, Corresponding Secretary

| | |
|---|---|
| MARY E. BARKER.........Mrs. Albert W. Scoville, | Hartford, Conn. |
| LOUISE L. BARTLETT............................. | Hartford, Conn. |
| KATE L. BIDWELL........Mrs. Arthur B. Clarkson, | Montreal, Canada |
| CAROLINE D. BISSELL....Mrs. Howard H. Garmany, | Hartford, Conn. |

| NAMES | RESIDENCES |
|-------|-----------|
| CARRIE E. BREWER........Mrs. Thomas E. Carroll, | Hartford, Conn. |
| LUCY F. BUCK.....................Died, 1882 | |
| CARRIE E. BUGBEY, Mrs. W. Charles Roberts | |
| Died, 1902 | |
| N. FLORENCE BULLOCK............................ | Hartford, Conn. |
| LOUISE D. BURNHAM..Mrs. Joseph M. Birmingham, | Hartford, Conn. |
| MARTHA L. CARPENTER....Mrs. Robert H. Roulston, | Hartford, Conn. |
| MINNIE J. CASE...........Mrs. James R. Anderson, | Wethersfield, Conn. |
| ALICE R. CRANE.......Mrs. Herman J. Maercklein, | Hartford, Conn. |
| NELLIE M. CUMMINGS......Mrs. David R. Hawley, | Farmington, Conn. |
| BELLE C. DAVIS.................................. | Hartford, Conn. |
| EVA DEUTSCH ................................. | Unknown |
| CATHERINE E. FLYNN.........Mrs. James H. Gunn, | East Hartford, Conn. |
| ISABELLE E. GOODRICH....Mrs. Frederick F. E. Buck, | West Hartford, Conn. |
| FLORENCE C. GROSS.........Mrs. John W. Hatstat, | Hartford, Conn. |
| MARY A. HARTLEY.....Mrs. Eugene H. Richmond, | Hartford, Conn. |
| EMELINE H. HAYDEN.......Mrs. Frank H. Bartlett, | New York, N. Y. |
| REGINA M. HUDSON........Mrs. Frederick P. Holt, | Hartford, Conn. |
| MARY L. HUNTINGTON............................ | Mansfield, Conn. |
| ELIZABETH C. JARVIS........Mrs. George W. Beach, | Hartford, Conn. |
| LILLIE C. KEEP.......Mrs. John B. Cone, Died, 1902 | |
| HATTIE S. KNIGHT, Mrs. William S. Hatch | |
| Died, 1891 | |
| FLORA MANDLEBAUM.........Mrs. Benjamin Haas, | Cincinnati, Ohio |
| HELEN T. McDOUGALL......Mrs. Albert E. Turner, | New York, N. Y. |
| BERTHA T. PIERCE..........Mrs. William·E. Peck, | New York, N. Y. |
| EMMA E. PIERSON.......Mrs. Willard A. Roraback, | Torrington, Conn. |
| IDA V. SHIRRELL................................. | Hartford, Conn. |
| ELIZABETH G. SISSON, Mrs. George W. Hubbard | |
| Died, 1897 | |
| MAY C. SPENCER................................ | Dorchester, Mass. |
| ADA E. STEELE..........Mrs. Horace B. Williams, | East Hartford, Conn. |
| ANNIE L. STEVENS........Mrs. William B. North, | New Haven, Conn. |
| KATE S. STILLMAN......................Died, 1879 | |
| ALICE SUMNER.................Mrs. Walter Camp, | New Haven, Conn. |
| CLARA M. SWEET, M.D., Boston Univ.............. | Springfield, Mass. |
| ANNIE H. TILDEN.....................Died, 1900 | |
| EMMA C. TUTTLE.......Mrs. Emma Tuttle James, | Roxbury, Mass. |
| ALICE L. WELCH...........Mrs. Andrew F. Gates, | Hartford, Conn. |
| ANNE M. WELLS................................. | Bridgewater, Mass. |
| HATTIE H. WHITE................................ | Manchester, Conn. |
| EMMA L. WILLIAMS............................. | South Manchester, Conn. |
| MARY W. WOLCOTT............Mrs. John Barstow, | Manchester, Vt. |
| CHARLES P. BERRY............................... | Carmi, Ill. |
| WALTER BLISS.................................. | Hartford, Conn. |
| GEORGE S. BOLTWOOD, A.B., LL.B., Yale............ | Grand Rapids, Mich. |
| MYRON H. BRIDGMAN............................ | Hartford, Conn. |
| WALTER G. CAMP.............................. | Hartford, Conn. |
| GURDON R. FISHER.....................Newton. | Highlands, Mass. |
| WILLIAM S. FOX................................ | Springfield, Mass. |
| SEYMOUR F. FRASICK, Ph.B., Yale................. | East Rockaway, N. Y. |
| ROWLAND H. GRISWOLD........................... | Erie, Pa. |
| THOMAS C. HAVENS............................. | Chicago, Ill. |
| WALTER E. HODGMAN............................ | Yonkers, N. Y. |
| FREDERICK E. HUNTER........................... | Thompsonville, Conn. |

| NAMES | RESIDENCES |
|---|---|
| TUN YEN LIANG................................ | Hupeh Province, China |
| CHARLES T. MARTIN............................ | Hartford, Conn. |
| WILLIAM H. H. MASON.......................... | Windsor, Conn. |
| FREDERICK M. MILLS....................Died, 1886 | |
| CHARLES N. MORRIS, REV., A.M., Yale, A.M., Trinity Coll., Toronto ............................ | Amesbury, Mass. |
| GEORGE W. MORRISON...................Died, 1887 | |
| CHARLES W. NEWTON........................... | Hartford, Conn. |
| WALTER G. PHELPS.....................Died, 1887 | |
| FRANK E. PRIOR.............................. | Los Angeles, Cal. |
| JAMES Q. RICE, A.B., Yale, LL.B., Columbian....... | New York, N. Y. |
| GEORGE DUDLEY SEYMOUR, LL.M., Columbian....... | New Haven, Conn. |
| WILLIAM SEYMOUR ............................ | Chicago, Ill. |
| EDWARD E. SMITH............................. | Hartford, Conn. |
| CHARLES G. STONE............................ | Hartford, Conn. |
| WALTER E. THORPE, M.D., N. Y. Homeopathic Med. Coll. and Hosp.............................. | Bristol, Conn. |
| ARTHUR L. ULRICH............................ | Hartford, Conn. |
| ARCHIBALD A. WELCH, A.B., Yale................ | Hartford, Conn. |
| EDWARD G. WELCH.....................Died, 1893 | |
| MARTIN WELLES, A.B., Yale, LL.B., M.L., Columbian, | Westfield, N. J. |
| EMMET S. WILLIAMS, A.B., Yale........Died, 1886 | |

## 1879

### Ζηλοῦτε τὰ κράτιστα

### CLARENCE H. WICKHAM, Corresponding Secretary

| | |
|---|---|
| MARY B. ABBOTT.................................. | San Diego, Cal. |
| SARAH J. ADGATE................................ | Farmington, Conn. |
| LILLIAN L. BISSELL............................. | Hartford, Conn. |
| LILLIAN M. BOGERT.........Mrs. John W. Strahan, | Hartford, Conn. |
| MARY E. BUCK..........................Died, 1886 | |
| HARRIET M. BUNDY.............................. | Hartford, Conn. |
| JOSIE M. BUTTERFIELD............Mrs. Albert Carr, | East Orange, N. J. |
| BERTHA A. CAMBRIDGE.......................... | Hartford, Conn. |
| E. LOUISE CAREY................................ | Hartford, Conn. |
| PHEBE A. DANIELS.............Mrs. A. G. Carter, | Bayonne, N. J. |
| CHARLOTTE W. DENNIS........Mrs. Thomas Little, | New York, N. Y. |
| MARY W. GRIDLEY.........Mrs. Charles M. Henney, | Hartford, Conn. |
| EVA I. HARRISON.......Mrs. Charles B. Thompson, | Mount Vernon, N. Y. |
| MARY B. HATCH.........Mrs. Russell G. Andrews, | Southington, Conn. |
| MARY C. HENNEY............................... | Hartford, Conn. |
| PHILENA HIBBARD, Mrs. Hawley Pettibone | |
| | Died, 1884 |
| GENEVIEVE B. KARR...Mrs. J. Aspinwall Hodge, Jr., | New York, N. Y. |
| HATTIE E. KELLOGG.............................. | Hartford, Conn. |
| FANNIE C. LUCAS............Mrs. Frank A. Grant, | Rocky Hill, Conn. |
| ISABEL L. MILL................................. | Hartford, Conn. |
| ADDIE RANSOM...........:..Mrs. William G. Baxter, | Hartford, Conn. |
| ANNA B. RICE.........Mrs. Lyman W. V. Kennon, | Twin Peaks, P. I. |
| ELIZABETH J. SHEPARD.........Mrs. C. L. Merrell, | Rockville, Conn. |
| EVA A. SMITH..............Mrs. Eva A. Daniels, | Hartford, Conn. |
| MARY E. TAINTOR........Mrs. Frederick W. Davis, | Hartford, Conn. |
| ELIZABETH H. TALCOTT, A.B., Smith.............:... | Elmwood, Conn. |

| NAMES | RESIDENCES |
|---|---|
| MARY WELCH....................Died, 1886 | |
| MARY C. WELLES, A.B., Smith, Ph.D., Yale, Instructor in Hartford Public High School............ | Newington, Conn. |
| LIZZIE H. WILLARD............................... | Wethersfield, Conn. |
| | |
| FRANK H. ADKINS............................... | Springfield, Mass. |
| JOHN R. AYER, A.B., Amherst.................... | Richmond, Mass. |
| LUCIUS BOLTWOOD, A.B., LL.B., Yale............. | Grand Rapids, Mich. |
| CHARLES M. BOSWELL..................Died, 1881 | |
| GEORGE E. BOWMAN, A.B., Yale................... | Boston, Mass. |
| CHARLES P. BOYLE............................... | Hartford, Conn. |
| JAMES M. BUNCE.......................Died, 1883 | |
| ALBERT CARR, A.B., Yale........................ | East Orange, N. J. |
| LOUIS R. CHENEY............................... | Hartford, Conn. |
| SAMUEL B. CHILDS, A.B., Yale, M.D., N. Y. Univ... | Denver, Colo. |
| MUN YEW CHUNG, Chargé d'affaires.............. | Madrid, Spain |
| L. CLERC DEMING, A.B., Yale.................... | New York, N. Y. |
| HARRY I. HORTON............................... | Hartford, Conn. |
| JOHN W. HUNTINGTON, A.B., Trinity.....Died, 1893 | |
| ALLYN C. LOOMIS, A.B., Yale...........Died, 1884 | |
| WILLIAM C. PEASE.............................. | Hartford, Conn. |
| THEODORE L. PHELPS............................ | Omaha, Nebr. |
| JAMES E. PRIOR, A.B., Holy Cross, M.D., Baltimore Univ. ................................. | Boston, Mass. |
| MARK T. ROBBINS............................... | Lee, Mass. |
| FRANK W. ROOD................................. | Columbus, Ohio |
| DENNIS F. RYAN.......................Died, 1901 | |
| HERBERT W. THOMPSON.......................... | Hartford, Conn. |
| CLARENCE B. TREAT, Instructor in St. John's School. | Santa Barbara, Cal. |
| SHOU KIE TSAI................................. | Tientsin, China |
| EDWARD M. WELCH.............................. | New York, N. Y. |
| CLARENCE H. WICKHAM.......................... | Manchester, Conn. |
| KAI KAH WONG, Imperial Chinese Commission..... | St. Louis, Mo. |
| FRANK D. WOODRUFF............................. | New York, N. Y. |

## 1880 .

### EXTREMOS PUDEAT REDIISSE

### CHARLES G. CASE, Corresponding Secretary

| | |
|---|---|
| LUCY A. BARBOUR............................... | Hartford, Conn. |
| GRACE C. BIDWELL.............................. | Hartford, Conn. |
| EMMA L. BINGHAM..........Mrs. John R. Atkins, | Chicago, Ill. |
| JANE L. BROWNELL, A.M., Bryn Mawr, Associate Principal of private school.................... | Bryn Mawr, Pa. |
| ELIZABETH J. CAIRNS........................... | Hartford, Conn. |
| MARY E. CASTLE............................... | Brooklyn, N. Y. |
| ELIZABETH B. CLARK............................ | Wethersfield, Conn. |
| EUNICE A. CLARK.............Mrs. Webb Souers, | Des Moines, Iowa |
| ALICE E. ELY..Mrs. Frederick D. Jewett, Died, 1891 | |
| ALICE L. FRENCH.............................. | Waterbury, Conn. |
| ANNIE GOODMAN.............Mrs. John F. Plumb, | New Milford, Conn. |
| GRACE HALL .................................. | Westfield, Mass. |
| CAROLINE F. HAMILTON, A.B., Smith, M.D., N. Y... | Aintab, Turkey |
| ELLEN S. HANSON.......Mrs. Archibald G. Loomis, | New York, N. Y. |

| NAMES | RESIDENCES |
|---|---|
| SADIE B. HILLHOUSE.......Mrs. William Hillhouse, | Meadville, Pa. |
| CARRIE E. HOLLISTER................................ | Hartford, Conn. |
| FRANCES B. HUDSON.......Mrs. William M. Storrs, | Hartford, Conn. |
| HATTIE O. HUNT.....Mrs. William Whitney Ames, | Montclair, N. J. |
| ISABELLA D. HUNTER.......Mrs. Wilbur F. Gordy, | Springfield, Mass. |
| KATHERINE M. HURLBURT, A.B., Smith............. | Columbia University |
| JULIA A. JOHNSON...........Mrs. Bernard Burns, | Hartford, Conn. |
| ELLA L. KILBOURNE....................Died, 1892 | |
| EMMA J. MALONE.................................. | Hartford, Conn. |
| JULIA N. MITCHELL............................. | Cincinnati, Ohio |
| HARRIET E. PIERCE.............................. | Plainville, Conn. |
| ANNA G. ROCKWELL.............................. | New Britain, Conn. |
| MARY E. SAUNDERS.............................. | Hartford, Conn. |
| ALICE SCHWAB...........Mrs. Simon C. Metzger, | Hartford, Conn. |
| ADELAIDE L. SMITH.............................. | Hartford, Conn. |
| ELIZABETH SMITH.............Mrs. J. R. Thornton, | Alexandria, La. |
| ALICE D. SNOW...........Mrs. Charles D. Burrill, | Morristown, N. J. |
| ROSA E. WARNER.......................Died, 1884 | |
| AGNES D. WEST................................. | Norfolk, Va. |
| CHARLOTTE E. WHITE.......Mrs. Frank N. Sharpe, | Hartford, Conn. |
| LAURA C. WILSON..............Mrs. W. B. Gibbs, | Navasota, Tex. |

| | |
|---|---|
| CHARLES McL. ANDREWS, A.M., Trinity, Ph.D., Johns Hopkins, Professor of History in Bryn Mawr College ......................................... | Bryn Mawr, Pa. |
| BENJAMIN S. BARROWS, Ph.B., Yale, M.D., N. Y. Univ. .............................................. | Hartford, Conn. |
| EDWIN H. BINGHAM.............................. | Hartford, Conn. |
| HOWARD F. BOARDMAN.............................. | Hartford, Conn. |
| GEORGE D. BUCK.......................Died, 1882 | |
| STEPHEN BULKLEY .............................. | Brooklyn, N. Y. |
| CHARLES G. CASE. .............................. | Hartford, Conn. |
| WILLIAM E. COLLINS, A.M., Williams....Died, 1893 | |
| ALBERT D. CROWELL.....................Died, 1892 | |
| LORENZO DANIELS ............................. | New York, N. Y. |
| WILLIAM C. DEMING, M.D., Columbia............. | Westchester, N. Y. |
| WILLIAM S. FOSTER, REV., A.M.,Wesleyan, Died, 1899 | |
| CHARLES M. GLAZIER........................... | West Hartford, Conn. |
| GEORGE G. HALL................................. | Louisville, Ky. |
| GEORGE C. HILLS................................. | Brooklyn, N. Y. |
| FRANK E. JOHNSON, A.M., Trinity................ | Hartford, Conn. |
| C. HARTLEY MORPIN, Principal of Colored School... | Boonville, Ind. |
| JAMES R. MORRISON.....................Died, 1889 | |
| WILLIAM B. NOBLE.............................. | East Hartford, Conn. |
| FRANK I. PRENTICE.............................. | Hartford, Conn. |
| WILLIAM R. SEDGWICK, M.D., N. Y. Univ.......... | Cambridge, Mass. |
| JOHN J. SEINSOTH.............................. | Hartford, Conn. |
| FRANK R. STODDARD.....................Died, 1891 | |
| R. OGDEN TYLER................................. | Chicago, Ill. |
| ROBERT A. WADSWORTH.......................... | Hartford, Conn. |
| GEORGE P. WARDELL, A.M., Wesleyan.............. | Ocean Grove, N. J. |
| HARVEY R. WARREN .............................. | Los Angeles, Cal. |
| JOHN WELDON, M.D., N. Y. Univ................. | Willimantic, Conn. |

## 1881

SECUNDIS MONERE INCITARE ADVERSIS

HARRY D. OLMSTED, Corresponding Secretary

MARY F. BLISS............Mrs. Charles H. Phillips, Jamestown, N. Dak.
GRACE BROWNELL.........Mrs. Epaphroditus Peck, Bristol, Conn.
HARRIET M. BROWNELL, A.B., Bryn Mawr, Instructor
   in Collegiate School at Passaic, N. J........... Bristol, Conn.
FANNIE R. CALHOUN..........Mrs. Ralph Clarkson, Chicago, Ill.
MARTHA B. CHAPIN............................... Springfield, Mass.
HATTIE L. CHARTER........Mrs. Wilber P. Bunnell, New Britain, Conn.
FRANCES E. CHICKERING........................... Washington, D. C.
MARY E. COLEMAN............Mrs. John N. Welles, Wethersfield, Conn.
ELLANORA COWPERTHWAITE, A.B., Stanford........ Helena, Mont.
MARY DANFORTH............Mrs. Charles A. Pease, Hartford, Conn.
CLARA M. DENISON............................... Hartford, Conn.
MARY L. DICKINSON.........Mrs. Henry M. Smith, Newtown, Conn.
GRACE W. GALLAUDET......Mrs. Francis L. Kendall, Washington, D. C.
HATTIE E. GILBERT............................... Coventry, Conn.
SELMA F. HANSEL.............Mrs. George B. Gill, Medford, Mass.
CHARLOTTE IVES............Mrs. William J. Ulrich, Meriden, Conn.
ISABEL JORDAN.........Mrs. George Philip Endress, Bennington, Vt.
MARGARET L. KNAPP................................ Hartford, Conn.
ESTHER DE LEEUW.......Mrs. Adolph Oppenheimer, New York, N. Y.
GERTRUDE O. LEWIS, Principal of Litchfield County
   Training School for Nurses.................... Winsted, Conn.
FANNIE M. LINCOLN.......Mrs. Robert H. Hamill, Summit, N. J.
LIZZIE V. MANGAN.........Mrs. Roger W. Stinson, Hartford, Conn.
MARY H. MANLEY.........Mrs. Samuel A. Beddall, Tamaqua, Pa.
JANET S. McCRONE.......Mrs. William F. English, East Windsor, Conn.
C. ALMIRA MILLS................................. Windsor, Conn.
NELLIE T. MULHALL.............................. Hartford, Conn.
LILLIAN L. NEWTON........Mrs. Wilbur M. Stone, Brooklyn, N. Y.
ELIZABETH A. POST............................... Hartford, Conn.
JULIA E. PRATT, Instructor in Hampton Institute... Hampton, Va.
MARY R. REDFIELD..........Mrs. William E. Porter, New York, N. Y.
CAROLINE T. ROBBINS, M.S., Wesleyan............. Wethersfield, Conn.
AUGUSTA S. SCHAEFER........Mrs. Dennie L. Farr, Holyoke, Mass.
HATTIE R. SEYMOUR....................Died, 1886
HARRIET L. SWIFT............................... Rochester, N. Y.
MARY C. TAYLOR................................. Wethersfield, Conn.
MARY A. T. TRACY............................... Hartford, Conn.
GRACE UPSON..............Mrs. Robert A. Mahan, Marianna, Ark.
MARTHA L. WADSWORTH........................... Hartford, Conn.
JOSEPHINE A. WHITNEY.......Mrs. Harry R. Knox, Hartford, Conn.
CORA WOLCOTT............Mrs. Irving W. Havens, Collinsville, Conn.
ANNIE C. WOOD................................. Hartford, Conn.


DANIEL D. BIDWELL, A.B., Yale.................... East Hartford, Conn.
ROBERT D. BONE................................. Hartford, Conn.
MIRON J. CASE.................................. West Hartford, Conn.
G. HERBERT CHENEY.............................. New York, N. Y.
WAN KWEI CHIENG............................... Foo Chow, China
EDWIN F. DIMOCK............................... Brookline, Mass.
THOMPSON C. ELLIOTT, A.B., Amherst.............. Walla Walla, Wash.
FREDERICK W. FRANCIS, A.B., Yale................ Brooklyn, N. Y.

| NAMES | RESIDENCES |
|---|---|
| ALFRED W. FRENCH, B.S., Mass. Inst. of Technology, | Piqua, Ohio |
| WILLIAM H. HALLOCK, A.B., Amherst....Died, 1894 | |
| CLAIR S. HUTCHINSON............................ | Hartford, Conn. |
| HIRAM B. LOOMIS, A.B., Trinity, Ph.D., Johns Hopkins, Principal of Bernhard Moos School, Chicago, Ill....................................... | Glen Ellyn, Ill. |
| HARRY D. OLMSTED............................... | East Hartford, Conn. |
| LEWIS W. RIPLEY................................ | Glastonbury, Conn. |
| LUCIUS F. ROBINSON, A.B., Yale.................... | Hartford, Conn. |
| WALTER A. SADD, Ph.B., Yale...................... | Chattanooga, Tenn. |
| FRANK R. SHIPMAN, REV., A.B., B.D., Yale......... | Andover, Mass. |
| CHARLES L. WAY, A.B., Yale....................... | Boston, Mass. |
| WILLIAM R. WHITMORE............................ | Springfield, Mass. |
| WILLIAM E. WILLIAMS.................Died, 1886 | |
| CHARLES F. WILSON.............................. | Brooklyn, N. Y. |

## 1882

POSSUNT QUIA POSSE VIDENTUR

MRS. CHARLES R. HANSEL, Corresponding Secretary

MARY B. ALLEN, Mrs. Frederick W. Turner
Died, 1887

| | |
|---|---|
| LEILA E. ANDERSON............................. | Hartford, Conn. |
| JULIA R. BARNES............................... | Plainville, Conn. |
| NELLIE M. BERRY........Mrs. Charles W. Newton, | Hartford, Conn. |
| GRACE E. BLISS................................ | Hartford, Conn. |
| MARY L. BLISS.................Mrs. Walter Bliss, | Longmeadow, Mass. |
| SARA A. BOYLE...............(Sister M. Amatus), | New Haven, Conn. |
| CALISTA V. BROCKETT........Mrs. Julian R. Holley, | Bristol, Conn. |
| MARY M. BULKELEY.....Mrs. Edward S. Van Zile, | Hartford, Conn. |
| MARY A. BURNHAM....Mrs. Morrison C. Hamilton, | Hartford, Conn. |
| ADA E. BURT................................... | Hartford, Conn. |
| CLARA D. CAPRON.............................. | Hartford, Conn. |
| LOUISE CASTLE ............................... | Brooklyn, N. Y. |
| E. HELENA CHASE.............................. | Springfield, Mass. |
| FANNY M. CLARK........Mrs. Robert W. Robbins, | Wethersfield, Conn. |
| LEAH J. CONE............Mrs. Eugene P. Darrow, | New Brunswick, N. J. |
| MAY H. CONKLIN............Mrs. John M. Crouse, | Utica, N. Y. |
| HARRIET G. DAY, A.B., Smith, Mrs. Charles R. Hansel ....................................... | Hartford, Conn. |
| ADELAIDE DEMING, Instructor in Art at Pratt Institute, Brooklyn, N. Y......................... | Westchester, N. Y. |
| SARAH A. DOOLEY........Mrs. Joseph A. Kilbourn, | Hartford, Conn. |
| JOSEPHINE FELDHUSEN...................Died, 1889 | |
| MARY A. GLEASON........Mrs. William G. Church, | Hartford, Conn. |
| L. BELLE GORTON.............................. | Hartford, Conn. |
| MARGARET M. J. GRIFFIN.................Died, 1896 | |
| ALICE W. HITCHCOCK......Mrs. Harry F. L. Orcutt, | Charlottenburg, Germany |
| MARY A. HUBBARD..........Mrs. Gideon C. Segur, | Hartford, Conn. |
| LUCY M. JONES...........Mrs. Edward F. Meeker, | Bridgeport, Conn. |
| LAURA M. MATHER............................. | Hartford, Conn. |
| MATILDA S. McKEGG, Mrs. John Johnston.Died, 1890 | |
| ANNIE M. PILLION, Mrs. James G. Rowe.Died, 1901 | |
| CARRIE L. PRATT.........Mrs. Frederick R. Going, | Cranford, N. J. |

| NAMES | RESIDENCES |
|---|---|
| JENNIE M. ROULSTONE.....Mrs. Charles W. Cooper, | Oakville, Conn. |
| CORA J. SEAVER.................................... | Hartford, Conn. |
| SARAH E. STANLEY.........Mrs. Frank E. Jenkins, | Atlanta, Ga. |
| ALICE U. STERLING, Mrs. Robert E. Dunston | |
| | Died, 1888 |
| CLOTILDE M. STERN..............Mrs. Julius Lewy, | New York, N. Y. |
| JOSEPHINE STILES ............................... | Hartford, Conn. |
| SARAH E. STONE................................... | Wilson, Conn. |
| BERTHA E. TAYLOR................................ | Wethersfield, Conn. |
| BELLE THOMPSON..........Mrs. William F. Fuller, | Hartford, Conn. |
| FRANCES G. WELCH......Mrs. Bernard T. Williams, | Hartford, Conn. |
| CORA M. WESLEY.................................. | Providence, R. I. |
| NETTIE L. WHITNEY............................... | Hartford, Conn. |
| ADDIE I. WILCOX.........Mrs. J. Frederick Burpee, | Hartford, Conn. |
| CARRIE B. WOODFORD, Mrs. Edward B. Pratt | |
| | Died, 1893 |

| | |
|---|---|
| HENRY S. ADAMS................................. | Brooklyn, N. Y. |
| ERNEST L. CALDWELL, A.B., Yale, Instructor in Morgan Park Academy........................... | Morgan Park, Ill. |
| FRANCIS R. COOLEY, A.B., Yale.................... | Hartford, Conn. |
| WILLIAM B. DAVIDSON............................. | Hartford, Conn. |
| THOMAS MILLS DAY, JR., A.B., LL.B., Yale......... | Plainfield, N. J. |
| EDWARD C. FELLOWES, REV., A.B., B.D., Yale........ | Derby, Conn. |
| ROBERT S. GRISWOLD.............................. | Hartford, Conn. |
| FELIX S. HAAS.........................Died, 1901 | |
| CHARLES C. HARRIS............................... | Wethersfield, Conn. |
| EDWARD B. HATCH, A.B., Trinity................... | Hartford, Conn. |
| JAMES W. HATCH.....................Died, 1887 | |
| JOHN W. HERRICK............................... | Unknown |
| JAMES HOW...........................Died, 1901 | |
| EDWIN Y. JUDD, Ph.B., Yale....................... | West Hartford, Conn. |
| JAMES B. KENNEDY............................... | Unknown |
| EDWARD T. LEE, A.B., Harvard, LL.B., Columbian.. | Chicago, Ill. |
| EDWARD E. LYMAN................................ | Stratford, Conn. |
| EDWARD M. NEY.................................. | Hartford, Conn. |
| ALFRED H. PEASE................................. | Hartford, Conn. |
| MORRIS PENROSE ................................ | Cleveland, Ohio |
| ALBERT E. PHELPS................................ | Windsor, Conn. |
| ARTHUR S. PHELPS, REV., A.B., B.D., Yale.......... | Ontario, Cal. |
| ARTHUR L. SHIPMAN, A.B., LL.B., Yale............ | Hartford, Conn. |
| EDGAR C. STILES, A.B., Yale...................... | West Haven, Conn. |
| HENRY K. W. WELCH.............................. | Hartford, Conn. |
| HENRY C. WHITE................................. | Hartford, Conn. |
| ALMERON W. WICKHAM........................... | New Haven, Conn. |

## 1883

Νῦν Πόνος Ὑστέρον Νίκη

ARTHUR PERKINS, Corresponding Secretary

| | |
|---|---|
| CARRIE R. ADAMS..........Mrs. Charles C. Harris, | Wethersfield, Conn. |
| NELLIE E. ADAMS.....................Died, 1896 | |
| NETTIE R. ADAMS.........Mrs. Horace H. Pelton, | Brooklyn, N. Y. |
| NELLIE C. BARBER............................... | Warehouse Point, Conn. |

| NAMES | RESIDENCES |
|---|---|
| EMMA J. BOARDMAN.........Mrs. Emma B. Howe, | Hartford, Conn. |
| LUCY M. BRACE.............Mrs. Joshua W. Allen, | Hartford, Conn. |
| PAULINE BROWNE ................................ | Hartford, Conn. |
| HARRIET C. CADWELL....Mrs. Harriet C. Humphrey, | Winsted, Conn. |
| LIZZIE L. COLVER...............Mrs. John S. Porter, | Prague, Austria |
| MINNIE G. COSTELLO...........Mrs. John T. Dunn, | Hartford, Conn. |
| MARY J. DOUGHERTY......Mrs. Edward H. Tierney, | Holyoke, Mass. |
| ADELE A. DUNHAM, Mrs. Frank R. Childs | |
| Died, 1886 | |
| MARY P. FOSKETT, A.B., Smith, Mrs. George C. Boswell ..................................... | Bayshore, N. Y. |
| MARY E. GARVAN...........Mrs. John A. Jackson, | New York, N. Y. |
| KATE R. GOWDY..........Mrs. George McC. Grant, | Melrose, Conn. |
| GRACE A. GROSVENOR.......Mrs. George H. Woodis, | Worcester, Mass. |
| LOUISE S. HAAS.................................. | Hartford, Conn. |
| FRANCESKA A. HENKE............................ | Hartford, Conn. |
| GRACE H. HOLBROOK.........Mrs. Henry C. White, | Hartford, Conn. |
| NELLIE G. HOLBROOK.........Mrs. Calvin F. Barber, | Brooklyn, N. Y. |
| ANNIE E. HOLCOMBE.............................. | Windsor, Conn. |
| ANNA S. JONES...........Mrs.. William M. Brown, | Titusville, Fla. |
| MARY S. LEE...........................Died, 1892 | |
| JULIA Y. MATHER....:Mrs. Frederick H. Robertson, | Wichita, Kans. |
| HELEN McCLUNIE................................ | Hartford, Conn. |
| BERTHA V. McCORMICK........................... | Windsor, Conn. |
| MARTHA J. NARAMORE, Associate Principal of Ossining School................:............. | Ossining, N. Y. |
| HELEN M. PIERCE................:............... | Plainville, Conn. |
| JENNIE A. PRATT, Instructor in Hartford Public High School ...............................South | Glastonbury, Conn. |
| MARY E. ROBBINS, Assistant Professor of Library Science in Simmons College.................. | Boston, Mass. |
| MARY S. ROBBINS, Mrs. William F. Forby.Died, 1898 | |
| LUCY T. ROBINSON...........Mrs. Sidney T. Miller, | Detroit, Mich. |
| JULIA A. SCOTT................................. | Hartford, Conn. |
| ADELAIDE E. SHEW, Mrs. James E. Tucker | |
| Died, 1901 | |
| HARRIET A. SLABOSZEWSKI....................... | Hartford, Conn. |
| MARY M. SMITH.......................Died, 1887 | |
| CHARLOTTE M. SPIERS........................... | New York, N. Y. |
| JOSEPHINE M. STEBBINS..................Died, 1895 | |
| LILLIAN A. STONE............Mrs. Harry E. Rice, | Boston, Mass. |
| HELEN F. SYKES................................. | Hartford, Conn. |
| HARRIETTA M. TYLER......Mrs. William P. Barber, | West Hartford, Conn. |
| EMILY C. UPHAM, A.B., Smith, M.D., Woman's Med. Coll., Philadelphia, Pa....................... | Boston, Mass. |
| GEORGIANA WATSON........Mrs. Edward B. Hatch, | Hartford, Conn. |
| SARAH WELCH.........................Died, 1884 | |
| MARY A. WELLS.........Mrs. Hosmer P. Redfield, | Hartford, Conn. |
| C. LOUISE WILLIAMS, B.S., Smith................. | Hartford, Conn. |
| | |
| CHARLES ADAMS, A.B., Yale..................... | Brooklyn, N. Y. |
| JOSHUA W. ALLEN, A.B., Yale..........Died, 1897 | |
| HOWARD E. BIDWELL............................ | East Hartford, Conn. |
| HOMER W. BRAINARD, A.B., Harvard, Instructor in Public High School.......................... | Hartford, Conn. |

| NAMES | RESIDENCES |
|---|---|
| HENRY B. BROWNELL, A.B., Yale, LL.M., Georgetown Univ..................................... | New Brighton, N. Y. |
| WALTER B. CHENEY..........................South | Manchester, Conn. |
| ALBERT S. COOK, A.B., Yale....................... | Hartford, Conn. |
| FREDERIC W. HART, REV., A.B., Yale............... | Denver, Colo. |
| BERT D. HUNTINGTON........................... | Newburyport, Mass. |
| ARTHUR E. MILLER............................... | Meriden, Conn. |
| EDWARD E. MOSELEY............................. | Hartford, Conn. |
| ARTHUR PERKINS, A.B., LL.B., Yale............... | Hartford, Conn. |
| WILLIAM L. PHELPS, A.B., Yale, A.M., Harvard, Ph.D., Yale, Professor of English Literature in Yale Univ..................................... | New Haven, Conn. |
| FREDERICK S. PICKETT, A.B., Yale, M.D., Columbia.. | Cleveland, Ohio |
| JOHN S. PORTER, REV., A.B., Williams............. | Prague, Austria |
| SAMUEL B. ROBBINS, Ph.B., Yale.................. | Great Falls, Mont. |
| WILLIAM J. SAMES............................... | Laredo, Tex. |

## 1884

### NON NOBIS SOLUM

ANNIE L. HOLCOMB, Corresponding Secretary

| | | |
|---|---|---|
| CAROLINE G. ADAMS.........Mrs. Everett E. Dow, | Hartford, Conn. |
| FLORENCE E. ADAMS.....Mrs. Florence E. Rogers, | New York, N. Y. |
| JENNIE L. BAILEY...........Mrs. Walter G. Camp, | Hartford, Conn. |
| JOSEPHINE BARCHFELD ........................... | Hartford, Conn. |
| GRACE C. BARNETT..........Mrs. George N. Smith, | Hartford, Conn. |
| GRACE C. BROOKS............................... | Hartford, Conn. |
| GRACE C. BURDICK.....Mrs. Charles H. Eldridge, | Mount Vernon, N. Y. |
| JENNIE S. CASE................................. | North Canton, Conn. |
| HARRIET A. CLARK.............................. | Hartford, Conn. |
| KATE F. CLIFFORD...........Mrs. Joseph H. Cahill, | Hartford, Conn. |
| MARY F. CONROY...........(Sister Mary Benedict), | Hartford, Conn. |
| SARAH C. DAY.................................. | Hartford, Conn. |
| EDITH C. FOSTER.............Mrs. Oscar A. Phelps, | Hartford, Conn. |
| HATTIE M. FOSTER.............................. | Hartford, Conn. |
| ALMA L. GILBERT............................... | Hartford, Conn. |
| GRACE GOODRICH..........Mrs. William B. Dwight, | Hartford, Conn. |
| L. CHRISTINE GRIFFIN........................... | West Hartford, Conn. |
| ALICE HANSELL.........Mrs. Francis H. Hastings, | Hartford, Conn. |
| NELLIE M. HAVEN.......................Died, 1893 | |
| ANNIE L. HOLCOMB.............................. | Hartford, Conn. |
| ANNIE L. HUBBARD.........Mrs. Burton S. Loomis, | Windsor, Conn. |
| ALICE F. HUMPHREY........Mrs. George D. Seely, | Washington, D. C. |
| HELEN L. JOHNSON......................Died, 1904 | |
| ROSE I. JOHNSON............................... | Hartford, Conn. |
| AMY L. KEENEY.............Mrs. Amy K. Hadsell, | Hockanum, Conn. |
| BERTHA H. KLINGER............................. | Hartford, Conn. |
| KATE J. LOSTY.........................Died, 1888 | |
| LUCY O. MATHER, Instructor in Public High School, | Hartford, Conn. |
| AGNES C. MORRISON..........Mrs. James J. Quinn, | Hartford, Conn. |
| BERTHA E. PATZ................................. | Hartford, Conn. |
| ISABEL B. PRIOR................................ | Waterbury, Conn. |
| ELLA A. ROBINSON.......Mrs. Frederick W. White, | Hartford, Conn. |
| GERTRUDE H. ROGERS.........................South | Manchester, Conn. |

| NAMES | RESIDENCES |
|---|---|
| JESSIE E. SAUNDERS............................... | Hartford, Conn. |
| EMMA N. SCHWAB.......Mrs. Frederick J. Curnick, | New York, N. Y. |
| CARRIE L. SEYMOUR............................... | Hartford, Conn. |
| HARRIET L. SEYMOUR............................. | Hartford, Conn. |
| MARY L. SMITH, Mrs. Henry H. Dickinson | |
| Died, 1887 | |
| ADA J. SPRAGUE..........Mrs. Frederick F. Kramer, | Denver, Colo. |
| CARRIE L. STUDLEY...........Mrs. Charles Kellogg, | Great Barrington, Mass. |
| STELLA J. WHEELER..........Mrs. Stella J. Post, | Worcester, Mass. |
| FLORA N. WILLES...........Mrs. George Simmons, | Unknown |
| MARY WILLIAMS.........Mrs. William H. Corbin, | Hartford, Conn. |

| | |
|---|---|
| DAVID P. BANCROFT, M.D., N. Y. Univ....Died, 1891 | |
| CLARENCE A. BARBOUR, REV., A.B., Brown, D.D., | |
| Univ. of Rochester............................. | Rochester, N. Y. |
| JONATHAN C. BIDWELL........................... | Hartford, Conn. |
| GEORGE M. BROWN............................... | Boston, Mass. |
| HERBERT S. BULLARD, Ph.B., LL.B., Yale........... | Hartford, Conn. |
| PHILIP D. BUNCE, A.B., Yale, M.D., Columbia...... | Hartford, Conn. |
| BURTON O. CASE................................. | Chicago, Ill. |
| THOMAS S. CHENEY...................Died, 1898 | |
| WILLIAM C. CHENEY......................South | Manchester, Conn. |
| ROBERT B. CONE................................. | New York, N. Y. |
| FRANK W. CORBIN..................Died, 1886 | |
| WILLIAM H. CORBIN, A.B., Yale................... | Hartford, Conn. |
| WILLIAM B. DWIGHT............................. | Hartford, Conn. |
| THOMAS B. ENDERS, A.B., Yale, M.D., Columbia.... | West Hartford, Conn. |
| JOHN R. FENN.................................. | West Hartford, Conn. |
| HARRY P. FOSTER.....................Died, 1901 | |
| GEORGE B. FOWLER, A.B., LL.B., Yale.............. | Detroit, Mich. |
| CHARLES A. HOW................................. | Hannibal, Mo. |
| THOMAS K. KENNEDY, A.M., Holy Cross........... | Hartford, Conn. |
| ARCHIBALD E. LORD.............................. | Waterbury, Conn. |
| FRANCIS C. PRATT, Ph.B., Yale.................... | Hartford, Conn. |
| GEORGE N. SEYMOUR, A.B., Amherst............... | Elgin, Nebr. |
| GEORGE W. SMITH......................South | Manchester, Conn |
| FRANK J. SPENCER............................... | Bloomfield, Conn. |
| FRANK E. STONE................................ | Hartford, Conn. |
| CHARLES L. TOLLES............................. | Hartford, Conn. |
| LEWIS S. WELCH, A.B., Yale...................... | New Haven. Conn. |
| J. WILLIS WILSON............................... | Pittsburg, Pa. |

## 1885

GRADATIM

DAVID G. SMYTH, Corresponding Secretary

| | |
|---|---|
| JENNIE E. BERRY...........Mrs. Ernest G. Hatch, | Buffalo. N. Y. |
| ANNIE B. BIDWELL.........Mrs. Clarence F. Catlin. | Hartford. Conn. |
| JULIA E. BIGELOW..........Mrs. Joseph H. Fiilow, | West Norwalk, Conn. |
| MARION W. BOND............................... | Hartford, Conn. |
| FLORENCE K. BUCK...Mrs. Jacob Humphrey Greene, | Hartford, Conn. |
| JENNIE S. CADY.............Mrs. William A. King. | Willimantic, Conn. |
| LIZZIE A. CLEARY........................Died, 1888 | |
| ELSIE A. CURTISS, A.B., Oberlin, Mrs. Herbert K. | |
| Job ......................................... | Kent, Conn. |

| NAMES | RESIDENCES |
|-------|------------|

SUVIA DAVISON.....Mrs. Lewis B. Paton, Died, 1904
MINNIE F. EAVES................................... Hartford, Conn.
MARGARET B. FOLEY, B.L., Smith.................... Hartford, Conn.
HARRIET J. FORD................Mrs. James Gray, Springfield, Mass.
CARRIE L. GLADWIN.........Mrs. Marry P. Fowler, Hartford, Conn.
THERESA V. GUINAN (Sister Mary Joseph Dominic)
          Died, 1892
MARY G. HAGUE.............Mrs. Henry S. Moore, Southington, Conn.
SARA A. HANNA.................................... Seattle, Wash.
EVA H. HART...................................... Burnside, Conn.
MARY A. HOLBROOK..........Mrs. Arthur S. Hyde, Hartford, Conn.
HARRIET E. HOLCOMB.......Mrs. William A. Peck, Jersey City, N. J.
GERTRUDE JUDD.................Mrs. Edgar A. Field, Hartford, Conn.
NELLIE MAY................Mrs. Harman Johnson, New Britain, Conn.
MARY A. McCANN................................... Hartford, Conn.
CECILE MIELLEZ.............Mrs. Rodney S. Dennis, New York, N. Y.
JESSIE I. NEVERS.............Mrs. Hubert D. Tracy, Hartford, Conn.
HATTIE I. OLIN...........Mrs. Norman C. Barwise, Denver, Colo.
ANNIE M. PAGRAM................................... Hartford, Conn.
CARRIE S. PRATT...........Mrs. George H. Barton, West Hartford, Conn.
JENNIE P. ROWLEY...............Mrs. John Owen, Hartford, Conn.
ANGIE J. RUSSELL.........Mrs. William H. Rhodes, Hartford, Conn.
MARY H. SEYMOUR......Mrs. Luther M. Woodford, Allegheny, Pa.
FANNIE J. SLOANE.........Mrs. Herman L. Bolles, Hartford, Conn.
JENNIE A. SMALLEY.......Mrs. Edward G. Bassett, Plainville, Conn.
EMMA H. SMITH..........Mrs. Emma H. Putney, Hartford, Conn.
LILA A. SPELMAN..........Mrs. William H. Rowe, Bristol, Conn.
MARTHA K. STARR................................... Hartford, Conn.
CHARLOTTE B. STEELE...Mrs. Adrian R. Wadsworth, Farmington, Conn.
NELLIE H. STEVENS..........Mrs. Carlyle C. Cook, Hartford, Conn.
NELLIE K. STEVENS................................. Old Saybrook, Conn.
J. GERTRUDE STORRS......Mrs. Frederick J. Perkins, Hartford, Conn.
MARY N. TYLER, A.B., Wellesley, Mrs. Frederick H.
     Jones ......................................... Wakefield, Mass.
EDITH VERY ...................................... Hartford, Conn.
ELIZABETH M. WELLS...Mrs. Theodore W. Hannum, Wethersfield, Conn.


B. REEVE ABBE, JR., A.B., Yale, M.D., Columbia
          Died, 1898
CHARLES M. BROOKS............................... Naugatuck, Conn.
CHARLES R. BURNHAM, LL.B., Yale................. Hartford, Conn.
ARTHUR S. CARLETON.............................. Albany, N. Y.
CHARLES M. CLARK................................ Waterbury, Conn.
WILLIAM P. CONKLIN.............................. Hartford, Conn.
WOLCOTT W. ELLSWORTH, REV., A.B., Yale.......... Johnstown, N. Y.
JOSEPH R. ENSIGN, A.M., Yale.................... Simsbury, Conn.
FREDERICK FITZ GERALD, U. S. Consul at Cognac,
     France, 1895-7.............................. New York, N. Y.
GEORGE H. GILMAN, A.B., Yale.................... Hartford, Conn.
JOHN C. GRIGGS, A.B., Yale, Ph.D., Leipzig, Pro-
     fessor of Vocal Music in Vassar College, Pough-
     keepsie, N. Y............................... Yonkers, N. Y.
JOHN W. HIGGINS................................. Unknown
EDWARD W. HOOKER............................... Hartford, Conn.
LELAND HOWARD, Ph.B., Yale...........Died, 1890

| NAMES | RESIDENCES |
|---|---|
| JOSEPH S. HUNTINGTON | Old Lyme, Conn. |
| ROBERT W. HUNTINGTON, JR., A.B., Yale | Hartford, Conn. |
| OLIVER K. ISHAM, M.D., N. Y. Univ | Hartford, Conn. |
| GEORGE C. KIMBALL, Ph.B., Yale | Hartford, Conn. |
| FREDERICK S. MANDLEBAUM, M.D., Bellevue Hosp. Med. Coll. | New York, N. Y. |
| WILLIAM R. MATSON, A.B., Yale | Hartford, Conn. |
| ETHELBERT A. MOORE | New Britain, Conn. |
| DANIEL S. MORRELL | Hartford, Conn. |
| GEORGE H. PRATT | Waterbury, Conn. |
| HENRY S. ROBINSON, A.B., Yale | Hartford, Conn. |
| EDMUND J. RYAN, A.M., Mt. St. Mary's, Professor of Mathematics in Mt. St. Mary's College | Mt. St. Mary's, Md. |
| FREDERICK A. SCOTT, A.B., LL.B., Yale | Terryville, Conn. |
| FREDERICK F. SMALL | West Hartford, Conn. |
| DAVID G. SMYTH, A.B., Brown, Instructor in Public High School | Hartford, Conn. |
| CHARLES W. STILES, A.M., Ph.D., Leipzig, M.S., Wesleyan, Chief of Division of Zoölogy, U. S. Public Health and Marine Hospital Service | Washington, D. C. |
| LEWIS A. STORRS, A.B., Yale | Hartford, Conn. |
| RUEL C. TUTTLE, A.M., Trinity | Windsor, Conn. |

## 1886

### Καλὸν τὸ ἆθλον

MARIAN H. JONES, Corresponding Secretary

| | |
|---|---|
| ANNA H. ANDREWS, Ph.B., Wesleyan, Instructor in Public High School | Hartford, Conn. |
| ELIZABETH P. ANDREWS | Wethersfield, Conn. |
| EDITH L. ARMS | Hartford, Conn. |
| HELEN J. BIRKENMAYER | Hartford, Conn. |
| GERTRUDE V. BLAKE............Mrs. John F. Blake, | Hartford, Conn. |
| FANNIE F. BROWN | Hartford, Conn. |
| BESSIE R. BURNELL | Hartford, Conn. |
| BERTHA C. CAPRON.......Mrs. Samuel B. Robbins, | Great Falls, Mont. |
| LEILA B. CHAPMAN.....Mrs. Julius Eugene Kinney, | Denver, Colo. |
| ANNIE L. CORBIN.............Mrs. J. Allen Wiley, | Hartford, Conn. |
| ALICE T. CUMMINGS | Hartford, Conn. |
| MARY DORSEY...........................Died, 1893 | |
| GRACE A. ENSIGN, Mrs. James G. Harvey, Died, 1900 | |
| MARY A. ENSIGN.............Mrs. Gerrish Newell, | Arlington, N. J. |
| ADELIA C. FAY.......Mrs. Z. Freeman Westervelt, | Rochester, N. Y. |
| EMMA K. FOSKETT | Meriden, Conn. |
| ZULETTE K. GILBERT.......Mrs. John M. Parker, Jr., | Hartford, Conn. |
| LILLIE GOLDSMITH | Hartford, Conn. |
| MABEL E. GOODRICH........Mrs. George H. Gilman, | Hartford, Conn. |
| NELLIE E. GRISWOLD.......Mrs. William S. Walker, | Newington, Conn. |
| MINNIE E. HARRISON......Mrs. Walter D. Barrows, | Hartford, Conn. |
| JESSIE V. HENDRICK | Forestville, Conn. |
| CARRIE E. HILLS | Hartford, Conn. |
| MARIAN H. JONES, B.L., Smith | Hartford, Conn. |
| MARY CLISSOLD KNAPP | Hartford, Conn. |
| ANNIE M. LAWLER........Mrs. George F. Johnson, | Hartford, Conn. |

7

| NAMES | RESIDENCES |
|---|---|
| MABELLE S. MARSH.....Mrs. Edward W. Bowdoin, | Hartford, Conn. |
| E. FLORENCE NEWBERRY............................ | South Windsor, Conn. |
| BELLE M. PARSONS................................ | Hartford, Conn. |
| ELIZA H. PRENTICE................................ | Hartford, Conn. |
| GRACE D. SMITH..........Mrs. Charles R. Childs, | Hartford, Conn. |
| MARTHA A. STODDARD......Mrs. Edward B. Nichols, | Minneapolis, Minn. |
| JULIA A. ULRICH...........Mrs. William J. Barber, | Harwinton, Conn. |
| HANNAH C. WELLS............................... | Wethersfield, Conn. |
| FANNIE M. WHITEHOUSE................Died, 1889 | |
| CARRIE P. WINTER, A.B., Oberlin, A.M., Univ. of Illinois...................Mrs. Charles A. Kofoid, | Berkeley, Cal. |
| FRANCES L. WOODFORD, B.S., Wellesley, Mrs. John P. Bankson ............................. | Ardmore, Pa. |
| LUCY D. WOODRUFF............................. | Hartford, Conn. |
| | |
| LOUIS L. BEACH, D.D.S., Philadelphia Dental Coll.. | Bristol, Conn. |
| REGINALD BIRNEY................................ | Hartford, Conn. |
| AMASA D. CHAFFEE, A.B., Yale, M.D., Columbia.... | New York, N. Y. |
| ARTHUR P. DAY, A.B., LL.B., Yale................ | Hartford, Conn. |
| RODNEY S. DENNIS......................Died, 1904 | |
| FREDERICK H. ELLSWORTH, Ph.B., Yale............. | New Haven, Conn. |
| HORACE H. ENSWORTH, B.S., Mass. Inst. of Tech.... | Hartford, Conn. |
| WILLIAM A. GAYLORD............................ | Worcester, Mass. |
| MARTIN L. GILMAN............................... | Buckland, Conn. |
| FRANK W. GRAVES............................... | New York, N. Y. |
| CLIFFORD S. GRISWOLD, A.B., Trinity............... | Groton, Mass. |
| BARUCH ISRAELI, A.B., Yale, M.D., Georgetown Univ., | Washington, D. C. |
| CLARENCE E. JONES.............................. | New Hartford, Conn. |
| HERBERT I. LADD................................ | Bristol, Conn. |
| CHARLES T. LAMB................................ | Worcester, Mass. |
| WILLIAM H. LEETE, A.B., Yale.................... | Thompsonville, Conn. |
| WILLIAM K. LUX................................ | Hartford, Conn. |
| EDWARD McP. McCOOK, A.B., Trinity.............. | Fort Bayard, N. Mex. |
| CHARLES R. NASON.............................. | Hartford, Conn. |
| ROGER S. NEWELL, Ph.B., LL.B., Yale............. | Bristol, Conn. |
| FREDERICK W. PITKIN............................ | Manchester Green, Ct. |
| GEORGE W. RAYNES, A.B., Yale................... | Charlestown, Mass. |
| EDWARD M. SHELTON, A.B., Yale................. | Burlington, Iowa |
| GEORGE A. SHEPARD, M.D., Jefferson Med. Coll..... | New York, N. Y. |
| EDWIN H. TUCKER.............................. | Hartford, Conn. |
| MARSHALL J. TULLER............................ | Hartford, Conn. |
| FRANCIS P. WEBB............................... | New York, N. Y. |
| EDWIN STANLEY WELLES......................... | Newington, Conn. |
| DAVID N. WILLIAMS............................. | Portland, Conn. |
| GEORGE D. WRIGHT.....................Died, 1896 | |

## 1887

AUDE ALIQUID DIGNUM

EDWARD H. ABBOT, Corresponding Secretary

| | |
|---|---|
| AMY L. BARBOUR, A.B., Smith, Ph.D., Yale, Instructor in Greek in Smith College, Northampton, Mass.................................... | Hartford, Conn. |
| EMILY L. BATTERSON............................. | Hartford, Conn. |

| NAMES | RESIDENCES |
|---|---|
| MAUD I. BENNETT, Mrs. Addison L. Green | |
| Died, 1901 | |
| HELEN A. BOWLES, Mrs. Andrew J. Kidder, Jr. | |
| Died, 1901 | |
| M. GRACE BROWN......Mrs. Harry W. Douthwaite, | Hartford, Conn. |
| ALICE T. BULKELEY................................ | Litchfield, Conn. |
| LILLIE B. CARPENTER..........Mrs. George A. Hill, | Syracuse, N. Y. |
| JEAN G. CASWELL................................. | West Hartford, Conn. |
| SUSIE R. CHARTER........Mrs. Edward P. Mather, | Nashville, Tenn. |
| CLARA M. CONE.................................. | Hartford, Conn. |
| MARY R. FENN............Mrs. Willard D. Brown, | Lexington, Mass. |
| MARY C. FOX.................................... | Hartford, Conn. |
| HATTIE GILLETTE................................. | Hartford, Conn. |
| SUSIE A. GRISWOLD.............................. | Hartford, Conn. |
| ELLA M. HARRISON, Mrs. Frederick D. Berry | |
| Died, 1902 | |
| MARGARET A. HOREY............................. | Hartford, Conn. |
| GERTRUDE A. HYDE.........Mrs. Arthur D. Newton, | Hartford, Conn. |
| MARTHA L. JARVIS............Mrs. Charles E. Taft, | Hartford, Conn. |
| BLANCHE LEAVITT, Ph.B., Boston Univ............. | Newport, R. I. |
| ISABEL E. LORD................................. | Brooklyn, N. Y. |
| MARY MARCHANT ............................... | Hartford, Conn. |
| MARY ST. L. MULLER.....Mrs. William G. Morrow, | San Francisco, Cal. |
| NETTIE L. MUNROE.........Mrs. William D. Camp, | Hartford, Conn. |
| LAURA B. PEASE................................. | Hartford, Conn. |
| LILLIAN A. RICHARDSON.......................... | Newport, N. H. |
| MARY M. RIDDLE..............Mrs. Herman Page, | Chicago, Ill. |
| LILLIAN E. SHEPARD, A.B., Smith, Mrs. Herbert O. | |
| Bowers ...................................... | Manchester, Conn. |
| MABEL A. SILSBY.......Mrs. Frederick M. Harlow, | Hartford, Conn. |
| FANNIE G. STONE.........Mrs. Charles McManus, | Hartford, Conn. |
| ROSE W. STORRS................................. | Hartford, Conn. |
| CLARA E. TUTTLE..........Mrs. Clara T. Hubbard, | Hartford, Conn. |
| JULIA A. WELCH.......................Died, 1892 | |
| KATE S. WILCOX, Mrs. Frederick T. Simpson | |
| Died, 1899 | |
| JULIA S. WILLIAMS.............................. | Hartford, Conn. |
| MARY A. WILLIAMS........Mrs. Henry R. Hayden, | East Hartford, Conn. |
| HELEN L. WOLCOTT, A.B., Smith, Instructor in Hart- | |
| ford Public High School..................... | Wethersfield, Conn. |
| | |
| EDWARD H. ABBOT............................... | West Hartford, Conn. |
| ALBERT R. BAKER, A.B., Yale...................... | Boston, Mass. |
| HERBERT O. BOWERS, A.B., LL.B., Yale............ | Manchester, Conn. |
| CHARLES E. BRAINARD...................Died, 1889 | |
| EVERETT P. BREWER............................. | East Hartford, Conn. |
| JOHN H. BUCK, A.B., Yale........................ | Hartford, Conn. |
| JOHN L. BUNCE, A.B., Yale....................... | Hartford, Conn. . |
| HERBERT CARLETON, A.M., Carleton................ | St. Louis Park, Minn. |
| HENRY R. CHENEY.........................South | Manchester, Conn. |
| WILLIAM R. C. CORSON, A.B., Yale................. | Hartford, Conn. |
| FRANK H. ELMORE, A.B., Williams................ | Providence, R. I. |
| HARRISON B. FREEMAN, JR., A.B., LL.B., Yale...... | Hartford, Conn. |
| ROBERT C. GLAZIER.............................. | Hartford, Conn. |
| RALPH M. GRANT, A.B., Wesleyan................. | East Windsor Hill, Ct. |
| JOSEPH B. HALL, M.D., Yale..................... | Hartford, Conn. |

| NAMES | RESIDENCES |
|---|---|
| G. BURTON HAWLEY | Indianapolis, Ind. |
| FREDERICK R. HOISINGTON, B.S., Trinity | Philadelphia, Pa. |
| ARTHUR W. HOWARD, M.D., N. Y. Univ | Wethersfield, Conn. |
| HARRY HOWARD, A.B., Trinity.......Died, 1895 | |
| HERMAN H. KIBBEY, A.M., Dartmouth | Swanton, Vt. |
| FREDERICK S. KIMBALL, A.B., Yale | Hartford, Conn. |
| EDWARD H. LATIMER | Gales Ferry, Conn. |
| EDWARD F. MARTIN | Hartford, Conn. |
| ELISHA R. RICH | New York, N. Y. |
| THOMAS B. SMITH, A.B., Trinity, M.D., Harvard... | Lowell, Mass. |
| FREDERIC C. STRONG | Winsted, Conn. |
| ARTHUR B. UNDERWOOD | Newark, N. J. |
| NATHAN A. WEED | Pittsburg, Pa. |
| CHARLES H. WELDON | Hartford, Conn. |
| WILLIAM F. WHITMORE | West Hartford, Conn. |
| HENRY L. WILLIAMS, A.B., Yale, M.D., Univ. of Pa. | Minneapolis, Minn. |

## 1888

### MAJORUM INITIA RERUM

ELIZABETH FAY, Corresponding Secretary

| | |
|---|---|
| LENA M. ADAMS, A.M., Wesleyan, Mrs. John P. Rand | Worcester, Mass. |
| LILLIE M. BULLOCK.........Mrs. Frank G. Paulisch, | Hartford, Conn. |
| ANNE K. BUNCE.......Mrs. Howell Cheney, South | Manchester, Conn. |
| EMELINE S. CHAPMAN.....Mrs. James W. Johnson, | Los Angeles, Cal. |
| JULIA A. DICKERSON | Hartford, Conn. |
| MABEL B. DILLINGHAM....Mrs. Loomis A. Newton, | Hartford, Conn. |
| MYRAH EATON........Mrs. Frederick B. Seymour, | Hartford, Conn. |
| ELIZABETH FAY | Hartford, Conn. |
| NELLIE T. FLYNN........Mrs. Charles J. Reardon, | Hartford, Conn. |
| CORDELIA M. FRAYER | Hartford, Conn. |
| ELIZABETH B. FREEMAN.....Mrs. Everett W. Lewis, | Hyde Park, Mass. |
| FRANCES H. FREEMAN.....Mrs. James A. Turnbull, | Hartford, Conn. |
| EDNA S. GILBERT | Hartford, Conn. |
| F. ZULETTE GOODRICH......Mrs. Thomas L. Masson, | Glen Ridge, N. J. |
| BERTHA H. GRISWOLD.......Mrs. Albert S. Arnold, | Wethersfield, Conn. |
| KATHARINE G. GROU | West Hartford, Conn. |
| SARA W. HILLS, Mrs. Frank M. Hartshorne Died, 1898 | |
| ELIZA J. HOLCOMB | Windsor, Conn. |
| OLGA C. HOLLAND..........Mrs. George H. Pratt, | Waterbury, Conn. |
| CHARLOTTE L. HUBBARD | Claremont, N. H. |
| KATE M. HUNTTING.......Mrs. Frederick E. Fuller, | East Hartford, Conn. |
| ANNE M. JOHNSON.................Died, 1894 | |
| MATILDA A. JOHNSON | Philadelphia, Pa. |
| HELEN G. KARR............Mrs. Lucius C. Ryce, | Plainfield, N. J. |
| CLARA M. KLINGER | Hartford, Conn. |
| ANNIE W. LAMB | Hartford, Conn. |
| BERTHA G. LANE..........Mrs. William R. Smith, | Meriden, Conn. |
| MARY L. LEWIS............Mrs. Walter E. Marsh, | Bridgeport, Conn. |
| MARY LYON...............Mrs. Chester B. Albree, | Allegheny, Pa. |
| KATHARINE H. MARSH....Mrs. Ralph W. Reinhold, | New York, N. Y. |

| NAMES | RESIDENCES |
|---|---|
| ELIZA L. McCOOK...........Mrs. Logan H. Roots, | Hankow, China |
| ANNIE R. McDONNELL............................ | Hartford, Conn. |
| ANNE W. MOORE................................. | Hartford, Conn. |
| MADALINE K. MORSE............................. | Boston, Mass. |
| HELEN C. NICHOLS..........Mrs. Harry A. Smith, | Hartford, Conn. |
| PAULINE I. PHELPS............................. | Bloomfield, Conn. |
| LUCY B. PRATT, Instructor in St. Margaret's School, | Waterbury, Conn. |
| HARRIET ROBBINS, A.B., Bryn Mawr, Instructor in Hartford Public High School................. | Wethersfield, Conn. |
| HELEN M. ROBERTS.......Mrs. William K. Ackley, | East Hartford, Conn. |
| ELIZABETH H. SHIPMAN...Mrs. Charles O. Shaffer, | Bolton, Conn. |
| FANNIE E. SPENCER........Mrs. Charles R. Nason, | Hartford, Conn. |
| ANNIE I. WHITE............. Mrs. James J. Burd, | Utica, N. Y. |
| ADA M. WOODFORD.........Mrs. Edwin H. Tucker, | Hartford, Conn. |
| | |
| HARRY A. G. ABBE, REV., A.B., Yale, B.D., Hartford Theological Seminary ...................... | Nyack, N. Y. |
| FREDERIC C. BIDWELL.......................... | Bloomfield, Conn. |
| WILLIAM C. CAPRON............................ | Great Falls, Mont. |
| HOWELL CHENEY, A.B., Yale.............. South | Manchester, Conn. |
| KNIGHT D. CHENEY, JR., A.B., Yale............. | New York, N. Y. |
| MARK CHENEY.................................. | So. Manchester, Conn. |
| ROBERT CLARK, A.M., Amherst................... | Cedar Grove, N. J. |
| ROBERT W. CURTIS, B.S., Trinity, Ph.D., Yale, Assistant Professor of Chemistry in Univ. of Kansas, | Lawrence, Kans. |
| CLIVE DAY, A.B., Ph.D., Yale, Assistant Professor of History in Yale University................. | New Haven, Conn. |
| ALFRED J. ENSIGN.............................. | East Hartford, Conn. |
| CHARLES J. FAY, A.B., Yale, LL.B., Columbia...... | New York, N. Y. |
| WILBUR J. FILLEY.............................. | Hartford, Conn. |
| EDWARD A. FLANNERY, REV., S.T.B., Coll. of Saint Thomas Aquinas, Genoa, Italy................. | Hazardville, Conn. |
| EDWIN R. GILBERT............................. | Boston, Mass. |
| HAROLD B. GOODRICH, A.M., Harvard............. | Boston, Mass. |
| RALPH C. GOODWIN............................. | Cambridge, Mass. |
| MAITLAND F. GRIGGS, A.B., Yale, LL.B., N. Y. Law School ...................................... | New York, N. Y. |
| WALLACE B. GRISWOLD.......................... | Lincoln, Nebr. |
| JOSEPH J. HIGGINS, M.D., Columbia.............. | New York, N. Y. |
| JOHN H. HILLS................................. | East Hartford, Conn. |
| GEORGE S. HURLBUT............................. | Stamford, Conn. |
| WILLIAM F. KELEHER............................ | Hartford, Conn. |
| WILLIAM S. KINGSBURY, B.S., Trinity, M.D., Yale.. | Glastonbury, Conn. |
| PAUL KLIMPKE, A.M., Yale, Instructor in Taft School ...................................... | Watertown, Conn. |
| HENRY N. LEE, A.B., Harvard................... | Chicago, Ill. |
| GEORGE L. LUX................................ | Hartford, Conn. |
| L. P. WALDO MARVIN, A.B., LL.B., Yale........... | Hartford, Conn. |
| HOWARD A. MIDDLETON......................... | Broad Brook, Conn. |
| GEORGE J. MORGAN............................ | Brooklyn, N. Y. |
| ROBERT E. S. OLMSTED, A.B., Amherst............ | New York, N. Y. |
| WILLIAM H. PELTON, Ph.B., Yale................ | Hartford, Conn. |
| GEORGE H. PINNEY............................. | Glastonbury, Conn. |
| CLIFFORD W. PORTER, M.D., N. Y. Homeopathic Med. Coll. and Hosp.....................Died, 1897 | |
| HARRY M. REYNOLDS............................ | Hartford, Conn. |

| NAMES | RESIDENCES |
|---|---|
| HOMER C. ROBERTS | East Hartford, Conn. |
| KNIGHT E. ROGERS | South Manchester, Conn. |
| ARTHUR M. ROWLEY | Hartford, Conn. |
| WILLIAM R. ROYCE | Philadelphia, Pa. |
| CHARLES O. SHAFFER | New York, N. Y. |
| JAMES E. STEELE | Springfield, Mass. |
| HARLAN H. TAINTOR, A.B., Yale | Died, 1893 |
| RALPH D. TULLER | Hartford, Conn. |
| WILLIAM M. WEAVER, M.D., Yale | Hartford, Conn. |
| ABRAM C. WILLIAMS, A.B., M.D., Yale | Springfield, Mass. |

## 1889

### Aἰὲν ἀριστεύειν

JANE W. STONE, Corresponding Secretary

| | |
|---|---|
| CORNELIA T. ADAMS...Mrs. James Frederic Hunter, | New Haven, Conn. |
| NELLIE B. ANDREWS, Instructor in Institution for the Deaf ....................Washington | Heights, N. Y. |
| MARY W. ARMS | Hartford, Conn. |
| CAROLINE M. BAUER | Kensington, Conn. |
| EDITH M. BENNETT......Mrs. Ernest W. Brigham, | Newton Center, Mass. |
| MARY A. BIDWELL, Mrs. Burr M. Weeden, Died, 1897 | |
| ELIZA A. BILL | Hartford, Conn. |
| ROSA L. BILL............Mrs. Mortimer L. Bristol, | West Hartford, Conn. |
| HATTIE A. BRAGG | Hartford, Conn. |
| ALICE L. BRODIE........Mrs. J. William Marsland, | New Britain, Conn. |
| KITTIE E. COOMBS......Mrs. Alexander M. Jackson, | Hartford, Conn. |
| CARRIE B. CURTIS.........Mrs. Augustus L. Moss, | Sandusky, Ohio |
| VALSORINE F. D'ARCHE (Sister D'Arche) | Montreal, Canada |
| GERTRUDE E. DICKENSON....Mrs. William A. Shew, | Hartford, Conn. |
| FLORENCE G. EDWARDS | Kingston, N. Y. |
| JEANIE M. FINLAY.....................Died, 1892 | |
| ANNA B. GEER | Hartford, Conn. |
| BERTHA S. GIDDINGS, A.B., Mills College, California, Mrs. Herbert N. Bevier | San Francisco, Cal. |
| MARY P. GILLETTE | Hartford, Conn. |
| EDITH G. GRISWOLD, Mrs. Francis E. Brouwer-Ancher, | Hartford, Conn. |
| SUSIE S. GRISWOLD.........Mrs. Richard W. Rice, | Windsor, Conn. |
| JENNIE M. HATCH | New York, N. Y. |
| GRACE M. HILLS | Hartford, Conn. |
| LILLIE M. HUNTTING | East Hartford, Conn. |
| CHARLOTTE M. KELLOGG.....Mrs. Howard P. Bourn, | Melrose Highlands, Mass. |
| ALICE G. LUX.................Mrs. Irving C. Treat, | Hartford, Conn. |
| EVA L. MARSHALL.........Mrs. Charles M. Bugbee, | Springfield, Mass. |
| SUSAN I. McCLAY.........Mrs. Cyrus C. Williams, | Hartford, Conn. |
| ELIZABETH H. MORGAN | Hartford, Conn. |
| CORNELIA A. MORRIS | Hartford, Conn. |
| GEORGIA M. MOSELEY........Mrs. Frank A. Warner, | Hartford, Conn. |
| HATTIE H. NEVERS......Mrs. Elisha Hart Pember, | Hartford, Conn. |
| ELMA A. NICHOLS.........Mrs. Frederick A. Ladd, | West Somerville, Mass. |
| MARY P. O'FLAHERTY, A.B., Wesleyan, Instructor in High School | Holyoke, Mass. |

| NAMES | RESIDENCES |
|---|---|
| FLORA B. OWEN........Mrs. Chauncey B. Andrews, | Hartford, Conn. |
| MARY A. PALMER................................ | Manchester, Conn. |
| JULIE S. REILLY............Mrs. George C. Bailey, | Hartford, Conn. |
| ANNA C. ROBBINS.......Mrs. Wilfred W. Savage, | Wethersfield, Conn. |
| NELLIE S. RYAN................................ | Hartford, Conn. |
| MINNIE J. SHEEDY.............................. | Hartford, Conn. |
| MARY S. STARR................................ | Hartford, Conn. |
| MINNIE STERN..................Mrs. Felix Lyon, | Hartford, Conn. |
| CLARA L. STONE............................... | Wilson, Conn. |
| JANE W. STONE............................... | Hartford, Conn. |
| LIZZIE J. THURSTON....Mrs. Romilly F. Humphries, | South Norwalk, Conn. |
| MAY L. WATERS..........Mrs. Arthur L. Wheeler, | Bryn Mawr, Pa. |
| JENNIE B. WATSON............................. | Hartford, Conn. |
| HELEN L. WEBB, Mrs. L. Averell Carter..Died, 1896 | |
| CLARA E. WELLS............................... | Hartford, Conn. |
| MARY P. WHEELER............................. | Hartford, Conn. |
| | |
| FRANKLIN J. ABBE, A.B., Yale................... | Worcester, Mass. |
| EDWIN S. ALLEN, B.S., Trinity.................. | Hartford, Conn. |
| WILLIAM R. BEGG, A.B., Yale, LL.B., Univ. of Minn. | St. Paul, Minn. |
| GEORGE N. BELL, M.D., Yale.................... | Hartford, Conn. |
| FREDERICK F. BENNETT, A.B., Yale.............. | Holyoke, Mass. |
| C. SANFORD BULL, A.B., Yale................... | Waterbury, Conn. |
| LOUIS F. BUTLER............................... | Hartford, Conn. |
| CHARLES P. CARTER........................... | Glastonbury, Conn. |
| CHARLES B. CHANDLER.................Died, 1893 | |
| CHARLES W. CONKLIN........................... | Buffalo, N. Y. |
| WILLIAM E. CONKLIN, A.B., Trinity.............. | Wallingford, Conn. |
| JAMES W. DAVIS................................ | Brooklyn, N. Y. |
| FRANK H. ENO.................................. | Simsbury, Conn. |
| EDMUND J. FAIRFIELD........................... | Cleveland, Ohio |
| DENISON GALLAUDET............................ | Ogden, Utah |
| EDSON F. GALLAUDET, A.B., Yale, Ph.D., Johns Hopkins ........................................ | Dayton, Ohio |
| SAMUEL F. P. GLADWIN.................Died, 1890 | |
| WILLARD J. GOULD.............................. | Southington, Conn. |
| T. JARVIS LEWIS............................... | East Hartford, Conn. |
| ARCHIE H. LOOMIS............................. | New York, N. Y. |
| RALPH R. LOUNSBURY, A.B., Yale, LL.B., Chicago Coll. of Law................................. | Chicago, Ill. |
| IRVING P. LYON, A.B., Yale, M.D., Johns Hopkins.. | Buffalo, N. Y. |
| WILLIAM E. MIDDLETON.................Died. 1903 | |
| ARTHUR W. NORTON............................. | Manchester, Conn. |
| FRANCIS PARSONS, A.B., LL.B., Yale.............. | Hartford, Conn. |
| AUSTIN H. PEASE.............................. | Coxsackie, N. Y. |
| ALFRED H. PRATT.........................South | Glastonbury, Conn. |
| JOHN T. ROBINSON, A.B., Yale................... | Hartford, Conn. |
| CLARENCE M. RODGERS.......................... | Hartford, Conn. |
| JOHN J. SCOTT................................ | Hartford, Conn. |
| FRANKLIN H. SEARLE........................... | Hartford, Conn. |
| WILLIAM H. SMITH............................. | Hartford, Conn. |
| WILLIAM E. SWIFT, B.S., Mass. Inst. of Technology, | Washington, D. C. |
| ARTHUR R. THOMPSON, A.B., Yale................ | Hartford, Conn. |
| WALTER H. VORCE............................. | St. Albans, Vt. |

| NAMES | RESIDENCES |
|---|---|
| LEMUEL A. WELLES, A.M., Yale, LL.B., N. Y. Law School ........................................ | New York, N. Y. |
| ARTHUR L. WHEELER, A.B., Ph.D., Yale, Professor of Latin in Bryn Mawr College.............. | Bryn Mawr, Pa. |
| PHILIP K. WILLIAMS, Ph.B., Yale................. | Glastonbury, Conn. |
| HOWARD W. YEOMANS............................ | Cleveland, Ohio |

## 1890

### CERTUM EST PROGREDI

MRS. CHARLES LINCOLN TAYLOR, Corresponding Secretary

| | |
|---|---|
| MARIAN A. ATKINS.........Mrs. J. Elmer Daniels, | Middletown, Conn. |
| DAISY F. BARBOUR............................. | Hartford, Conn. |
| MABEL L. CARLETON.......Mrs. Edwin B. Nichols, | Gambier, Ohio |
| ANNA W. CLARK.............Mrs. Albert Morgan, | Wethersfield, Conn. |
| CAROLINE C. CLARK, Ph.B., Wesleyan, Mrs. Edward M. Barney ................................... | Pawtucket, R. I. |
| LENA H. CLARK.........Mrs. Edmund J. Fairfield, | Cleveland, Ohio |
| ELSIE J. DRESSER.............................. | Hartford, Conn. |
| HILMA C. FERNQUIST...........Mrs. Philip Ayley, | Unknown |
| EDITH M. FOULDS............Mrs. Calvin Weidner, | Manchester, Conn. |
| JULIA E. FOWLER.........Mrs. Charles E. Whiting, | Hartford, Conn. |
| LILLYS M. GOODRICH.......Mrs. Frank H. Crygier, | Hartford, Conn. |
| CARRIE F. HAMILTON........................... | Hartford, Conn. |
| ELLA C. HARRINGTON........Mrs. Edwin S. Cowles, | Hartford, Conn. |
| KATHERINE L. HILLS, Instructor in Public High School ...................................... | Hartford, Conn. |
| JEANNETTE B. HUNTER........................... | Thompsonville, Conn. |
| ALICE W. JACOBS.............................. | Hartford, Conn. |
| ANNIE M. KEYES............................... | Hartford, Conn. |
| LOUISE H. KINSMAN............................ | Hartford, Conn. |
| LENA I. KNOX...........Mrs. Lena I. Merrill, | Hartford, Conn. |
| EVA M. NORTH, A.B., Mt. Holyoke, Mrs. D. Howard Craver ....................................... | Ogdensburg, N. Y. |
| FLORENCE O. PRATT........Mrs. William L. Ledger, | Hartford, Conn. |
| MARY A. RILEY............................... | Hartford, Conn. |
| MARY C. ROBERTS............................. | Hartford, Conn. |
| CHARLOTTE K. RONALD.......................... | Hartford, Conn. |
| PAULINE L. RYDER........Mrs. William H. Witter, | Hartford, Conn. |
| JOSEPHINE H. SCHWAB.......................... | Hartford, Conn. |
| EMMA E. SHAFFER............................. | Hartford, Conn. |
| FRANCES S. SHEDD............................ | Wethersfield, Conn. |
| BERTHA H. SMITH.....Mrs. Charles Lincoln Taylor, | Hartford, Conn. |
| MINNIE J. SMITH............................. | Hartford, Conn. |
| MARY B. SPERRY............Mrs. Harold Pattison, | Hartford, Conn. |
| JULIA STERN.........Mrs. Abraham L. Thalheimer, | Hartford, Conn. |
| MINERVA E. TYLER.......Mrs. Hubert W. Chapman, | Greensburg, Pa. |
| MABEL F. WHITE.......Mrs. Arthur G. Holbrook, | Coldwater, Mich. |
| ROBERTA E. WHITING........Mrs. Louis L. Driggs, | Washington, D. C. |
| ALICE S. WILLIAMS........................... | Hartford, Conn. |
| | |
| ALEXIS P. BARTLETT, A.B., Yale, LL.B., N. Y. Law School ...................................... | New York, N. Y. |
| H. LEONARD BEADLE........................... | Hartford, Conn. |
| HARRY A. BEADLE, REV., A.B., Bowdoin........... | Franklin, Conn. |

| NAMES | RESIDENCES |
|---|---|
| HERBERT E. BELDEN | Hartford, Conn. |
| CLINTON S. BISSELL, A.B., Yale | Litchfield, Conn. |
| HOWARD H. BURDICK, B.S., Mass. Inst. of Technology, | Hartford, Conn. |
| HARRY F. CONE | Hartford, Conn. |
| D. HOWARD CRAVER, REV., A.B., Union | Ogdensburg, N. Y. |
| EDWARD B. EATON | Hartford, Conn. |
| GEORGE W. ELLIS, A.B., Trinity | Hartford, Conn. |
| ERNEST B. ELLSWORTH, Ph.B., Yale | Hartford, Conn. |
| EDWARD J. GARVAN, A.B., LL.B., Yale | Hartford, Conn. |
| EDWIN C. GILLETTE, REV., A.B., Williams | Canaan, Conn. |
| HOWARD R. GRISWOLD | Hartford, Conn. |
| HERBERT E. MARSTON | New York, N. Y. |
| JOHN J. MCLAUGHLIN, REV., S.T.D., Propaganda, Rome | Meriden, Conn. |
| HERBERT C. NEWBERRY Died, 1892 | |
| EDWIN B. NICHOLS, A.B., Wesleyan, A.M., Harvard, Professor of Romance Languages in Kenyon College | Gambier, Ohio |
| LOUIS M. PARSONS | Brooklyn, N. Y. |
| DECIUS L. PIERSON, A.B., Yale Died, 1897 | |
| JOSEPH H. PRATT, Ph.D., Yale | Chapel Hill, N. C. |
| CLYDE P. SMITH | Hartford, Conn. |
| HOWARD FRANKLIN SMITH, A.B., M.D., Yale | Hartford, Conn. |
| EDWARD L. STEELE, A.B., Wesleyan, LL.B., Yale | Hartford, Conn. |
| HARRY C. STURTEVANT Died, 1890 | |
| F. BENONI SWEET, M.D., Yale | Springfield, Mass. |
| GEORGE M. TOWNSEND, A.B., Yale | Los Angeles, Cal. |
| ELBERT L. WEAVER | Hartford, Conn. |
| GEORGE H. YOST, A.B., Stanford | Palo Alto, Cal. |

## 1891

### ULTRA ASPICIMUS

WILFRED W. SAVAGE, Corresponding Secretary

| | | |
|---|---|---|
| OLIVE M. ALLEN | Mrs. William P. Robertson, | Hartford, Conn. |
| ADA B. BAILEY | | Hockanum, Conn. |
| PAULINE M. BAUER | | Kensington, Conn. |
| MARY J. BLAKE | | Hartford, Conn. |
| LEILA H. BLAKESLEE | | Hartford, Conn. |
| S. LILLIAN BRIGGS | Mrs. William H. Barron, Jr., | Danielson, Conn. |
| MARION B. BROWNE | | Hartford, Conn. |
| GERTRUDE A. BURDICK | Mrs. Robert G. Lipsey, | New York, N. Y. |
| NELLIE S. CAREY | Mrs. Frank P. Reynolds, | Hartford, Conn. |
| M. ISABEL CODY | | Hartford, Conn. |
| EDNA D. CONKLIN | Mrs. Charles F. Sumner, Jr., | Bolton, Conn. |
| ALICE M. CROCKER | | Hartford, Conn. |
| GERTRUDE E. DAVIS Died, 1895 | | |
| SARAH R. EVERETT | | Worcester, Mass. |
| ELIZABETH F. GARVAN Died, 1898 | | |
| CHRISTINE F. GLEN | | Hartford, Conn. |
| MARY A. GOODMAN, B.L., Smith | | Hartford, Conn. |
| MABEL S. GROU | | West Hartford, Conn. |
| LILLA M. HARRIS | Mrs. Lewis H. Russell, | Hartford, Conn. |
| NANCY L. HOISINGTON, B.L., Smith | | Port Kennedy, Pa. |

| NAMES | RESIDENCES |
|---|---|
| MARY J. LALLY.................................... | Hartford, Conn. |
| ROSE A. MORIARTY................................. | New Haven, Conn. |
| HARRIET E. NOBLE................................. | Hartford, Conn. |
| ESTHER PRATT............Mrs. J. Howard Gaylord, | West Brookfield, Mass. |
| EDITH K. RICHARDS................................ | Hartford, Conn. |
| H. LOUISE ROBERTS........Mrs. Frederick E. Judd, | Pendleton, Oregon |
| MARY S. ROBINSON................................. | Hartford, Conn. |
| EDITH P. SAWYER.......Mrs. Charles L. W. Pettee, | Hartford, Conn. |
| LOTTA L. SLESINGER......Mrs. Dwight L. Burnham, | East Hartford, Conn. |
| LEILA M. SMART.................................. | Hartford, Conn. |
| AMIE I. SMITH, A.B., Cornell, A.M., Yale, Mrs. Elisha R. Wolcott............................ | Wethersfield, Conn. |
| MARY B. SPELLACY......................Died, 1903 | |
| LILLIAN G. TALCOTT......Mrs. Clement H. Brigham, | Hartford, Conn. |
| MAY F. TAYLOR.................................. | Hartford, Conn. |
| NELLIE E. TEN EYCK............................. | West Hartford, Conn. |
| ALLYS E. TYLER................................. | Wethersfield, Conn. |
| MARGARET WARNER, A.B., Bryn Mawr.............. | Hartford, Conn. |
| MAUD E. WELLS, A.B., Wesleyan, Mrs. Edgar Weeks, | Marlboro, Mass. |
| KATE P. WHEELOCK.............................. | Hartford, Conn. |
| HARRIETT E. WILLIS........Mrs. Stephen R. Smith, | Hartford, Conn. |
| ALICE L. WORTHINGTON.....Mrs. Charles G. Smith, | New York, N. Y. |
| MARY C. WRIGHT................................. | Hartford, Conn. |
| | |
| ALBERT BALLERSTEIN............................. | Hartford, Conn. |
| COLLINS W. BENTON............................. | Hartford, Conn. |
| CLEMENT H. BRIGHAM........................... | Hartford, Conn. |
| FREDERICK K. CASWELL.......................... | Schenectady, N. Y. |
| SHERWOOD A. CHENEY, 1st Lieut., Engineer Corps, U. S. Army.................................. | Washington, D. C. |
| HARVEY W. CORBIN.............................. | Hartford, Conn. |
| MATTHEW E. COUGHLIN.......................... | Hartford, Conn. |
| CHARLES H. CULLEN............................. | New York, N. Y. |
| EDWARD B. FIELD.............................. | Hartford, Conn. |
| LOUIS S. FITCH............................... | Hartford, Conn. |
| EVERETT M. FRANCIS............................ | Hartford, Conn. |
| FREDERIC R. GALACAR, A.B., Yale.................. | Boston, Mass. |
| FRANK C. GILL................................ | Hartford, Conn. |
| JOSEPH C. GUINAN, M.D., Bellevue Hosp. Med. Coll., | Wallingford, Conn. |
| WILBUR T. HALLIDAY........................... | Hartford, Conn. |
| CLARENCE F. HAYNES........................... | Chicago, Ill. |
| CLARENCE E. JAGGAR........................... | Worcester, Mass. |
| WILLIAM J. LYNCH, M.D., Coll. of Physicians and Surgeons, Baltimore, Md...........Died, 1902 | |
| PHILIP J. MCCOOK, A.B., Trinity, LL.B., Harvard... | New York, N. Y. |
| ERNEST J. MILLER............................. | Warehouse Point, Conn. |
| JOHN K. MOORE, REV., A.B., B.D., Yale............ | Elizabethtown, N. Y. |
| CHARLES F. NORRIS....................Died, 1892 | |
| FREDERICK E. OLMSTED, Ph.B., Yale.............. | Washington, D. C. |
| HENRY H. PEASE............................... | Hartford, Conn. |
| WILBERT L. PERRY............................. | Hartford, Conn. |
| F. ERNEST PRATT.............................. | New York, N. Y. |
| ASHMEAD G. RODGERS........................... | Niagara Falls, N. Y. |
| GEORGE H. RYDER, Ph.B., Wesleyan, M.D., Harvard. | Worcester, Mass. |
| WILFRED W. SAVAGE, Ph.B., Yale................. | Wethersfield, Conn. |
| JOHN J. SINNOTT.............................. | Hartford, Conn. |

| NAMES | RESIDENCES |
|---|---|
| HARRY K. TAYLOR, A.B., Yale..................... | Cleveland, Ohio |
| THOMAS G. VAIL.................................. | Hartford, Conn. |
| J. MAYHEW WAINWRIGHT, A.B., Trinity, M.D., Columbia ....................................... | New York, N. Y. |
| ALANSON H. WIGHTMAN........................... | West Hartford, Conn. |

## 1892

### MAJORA IN POSSE

#### WALTER H. CLARK, Corresponding Secretary

| | |
|---|---|
| MARY L. BANKS.........Mrs. Edward H. Wilkins, | Middletown, Conn. |
| MABELL A. BARNARD....................Died, 1893 | |
| GRACE L. BAYLISS.........Mrs. George A. Sumner, | Hartford, Conn. |
| CAROLINE S. BELDEN........Mrs. James E. Brooks, | Glen Ridge, N. J. |
| MARY M. BENNETT............................... | Hartford, Conn. |
| FLORENCE B. BRYDEN.......Mrs. George E. Meech, | Middletown, Conn. |
| SUSIE A. BUCKINGHAM....Mrs. Alston B. Moulton, | Washington, D. C. |
| MINNIE L. BUDDE............................... | Hartford, Conn. |
| CLARA A. BURNAP........Mrs. George A. Harmon, | Suffield, Conn. |
| CLARA M. BUTLER.........Mrs. Chauncey B. Lamb, | Hartford, Conn. |
| MATILDA S. CALDER, B.S., Mt. Holyoke, Mrs. John Lawrence Thurston ......................... | Hartford, Conn. |
| ELIZABETH S. CARTER......Mrs. Frank W. Whiton, | Hartford, Conn. |
| FLORENCE M. CONE.............................. | Hartford, Conn. |
| AGNES A. COOK............Mrs. Elbert L. Weaver, | Hartford, Conn. |
| CARRIE E. CUMMINGS.....Mrs. William W. Lester, | Hartford, Conn. |
| NELLIE E. DERBY..........Mrs. Ernest M. Morgan, | Plainville, Conn. |
| MARY E. DIBBLE................................ | Hartford, Conn. |
| GERTRUDE F. DUFFY........Mrs. Eugene H. House, | East Hartford, Conn. |
| EDITH T. ELLSWORTH........Mrs. John D. Parker, | West Hartford, Conn. |
| EVA L. EMMONS...........Mrs. Wallace M. Berry, | Hartford, Conn. |
| MAY S. FINNEY, Ph.B., Wesleyan, Mrs. Bernard S. Wilford ...................................... | Branford, Conn. |
| AGNES B. FORBES........Mrs. George F. Womrath, | New York, N. Y. |
| JENNIE P. FORBES.........Mrs. William G. Hawes, | Brooklyn, N. Y. |
| MARY F. GALVIN............................... | Hartford, Conn. |
| JULIA E. GILMAN, B.L., Smith, Mrs. Walter H. Clark, | Hartford, Conn. |
| ALICE B. GLAZIER.............................. | New York, N. Y. |
| F. MAY GRAVES............Mrs. Henry R. Wright, | Hartford, Conn. |
| ELEANOR T. GREEN.............................. | Great Barrington, Mass. |
| CAROLINE A. GRISWOLD.....Mrs. George G. Bulkley, | Lancaster, Pa. |
| MARY G. HUNTINGTON.......Mrs. Henry W. Storrs, | Meriden, Conn. |
| ESTELLE A. G. JACKSON......Mrs. Alfred J. Norton, | Cambridge, Mass. |
| ANNIE J. F. KENNEDY........................... | Hartford, Conn. |
| GRACE C. KIMBALL, B.L., Smith, Mrs. Lyman W. Griswold ..................................... | Greenfield, Mass. |
| EDITH M. KING................Mrs. Ralph B. Ives, | Hartford, Conn. |
| MAUD E. LATHAM..........Mrs. Harry A. Pellett, | Readville, Mass. |
| MARY A. MALOY................................ | Hartford, Conn. |
| MARY E. McCARTHY............................. | Hartford, Conn. |
| NORA J. McEVOY............................... | Hartford, Conn. |
| LOUISA M. PICKLES.....Mrs. Clifford T. Strickland, | Brooklyn, N. Y. |
| MARY C. O. PIERSON..Mrs. Horace B. Cheney, South | Manchester, Conn. |
| EDITH E. RICKER..........Mrs. Charles A. Gilbert, | Hartford, Conn. |

| NAMES | RESIDENCES |
|---|---|
| IRMAGARDE ROSSITER............................... | Hartford, Conn. |
| JULIA G. SELDEN...........Mrs. Thomas J. Kelley, | Hartford, Conn. |
| MABELLE R. SEXTON.........Mrs. Fred W. Bartlett, | Hartford, Conn. |
| JULIA G. SIMONDS..........Mrs. Edward L. Steele, | Hartford, Conn. |
| ELIZABETH E. SINNOTT............................ | Hartford, Conn. |
| LOUISE D. SMITH................................. | Hartford, Conn. |
| VIOLET B. SMITH................................. | Hartford, Conn. |
| HARRIETT B. SPRAGUE............................. | Hartford, Conn. |
| ELISABETH W. STONE, B.L., Smith, Instructor in Public High School.............................. | Hartford, Conn. |
| FLORENCE M. STURTEVANT......................... | Hartford, Conn. |
| SUSIE C. THOMPSON........Mrs. Harry E. Marvel, | Boston, Mass. |
| S. KATHERINE THURSTON..Mrs. William H. Rowley, | Hartford, Conn. |
| HATTIE F. WARNER..........Mrs. Robert L. Beebe, | South Windham, Conn. |
| OLA M. WATROUS..........Mrs. James L. Russell, | Boston, Mass. |
| JESSIE W. WEEKS................................. | Hartford, Conn. |
| MABEL C. WEEKS................................. | Hartford, Conn. |
| CLARA E. VON WETTBERG, A.B., Wellesley, Mrs. John A. Degen ...................................... | Manilla, P. I. |
| LILLIAN E. WHEELER.....Mrs. Herbert J. Wyckoff, | Chelsea, Vt. |
| HATTIE G. WHITMORE........Mrs. John O. Enders, | West Hartford, Conn. |
| CLARA B. WILKINSON............................. | Hartford, Conn. |
| ELLA M. WILLIAMS............................... | Hartford, Conn. |
| FLORELLA W. WILSON...Mrs. Florella W. Wheelock, | Hartford, Conn. |
| MARIBEL A. YALE..........Mrs. Clarence Belcher, | Hartford, Conn. |
| | |
| BENJAMIN ADAMS, A.B., Yale..................... | Brooklyn, N. Y. |
| W. RODERICK ADAMS, LL.B., M.L., D.C.L., Yale..... | New York, N. Y. |
| SAMUEL M. ALVORD, A.B., Yale, Instructor in Public High School.............................. | Hartford, Conn. |
| JAMES ANGUS ................................... | New York, N. Y. |
| PHILIP H. BAILEY, A.B., Yale..................... | London, Eng. |
| WARREN T. BARTLETT............................. | Hartford, Conn. |
| ARTHUR P. BENNETT............................. | Hartford, Conn. |
| GEORGE E. BULKLEY, A.B., Yale.................... | Hartford, Conn. |
| MARSHALL A. BUTLER............................ | Meriden, Conn. |
| ERNEST H. CADY, Ph.B.,Yale...................... | West Hartford, Conn. |
| BERNARD J. CARR, M.D., Coll. of Physicians and Surgeons, Baltimore, Md................Died, 1904 | |
| FREDERICK S. CHAPMAN, Ph.B., Yale................ | Richmond Hill, N. Y. |
| WARD CHENEY, A.B., Yale, 1st Lieut., 4th Infantry, U. S. A. Killed at Imus, Philippine Islands, 1900 | |
| WALTER H. CLARK, A.B., LL.B., Yale.............. | Hartford, Conn. |
| GEORGE H. COE, Ph.B., Yale...................... | Schenectady, N. Y. |
| BENJAMIN G. ELLSWORTH......................... | Hartford, Conn. |
| SAMUEL FERGUSON, B.S., Trinity, E.E., A.M., Columbia, A.M., Trinity......................... | Schenectady, N. Y. |
| GEORGE G. FORBES.......................Died, 1902 | |
| RICHARD J. GOODMAN, A.B., LL.B., Yale............ | Hartford, Conn. |
| JAMES W. GUNNING, A.B., Trinity................ | Hartford, Conn. |
| FRANKE S. HAVENS, A.B., Ph.D., Yale.............. | Hartford, Conn. |
| SAMUEL H. HAVENS............................... | Hartford, Conn. |
| HAROLD G. HOLCOMBE, A.B., Yale.................. | Hartford, Conn. |
| WILLIAM J. JUDGE, REV........................... | Meriden, Conn. |
| ROBERT C. KNOX................................. | Hartford, Conn. |
| CHAUNCEY B. LAMB.............................. | Hartford, Conn. |

| NAMES | RESIDENCES |
|---|---|
| CHARLES T. MITCHELL............................. | Hartford, Conn. |
| JAMES F. O'LEARY, A.B., Villanova Coll., M.D., Univ. of Buffalo............................. | Hartford, Conn. |
| WARREN P. PALMER....................Died, 1903 | |
| HENRY A. PERKINS, A.B., Yale, E.E., A.M., Columbia, Professor of Physics in Trinity College.... | Hartford, Conn. |
| FRANK L. PINNEY, U. S. N. Acad., 1898, Lieut...... | U. S. Navy |
| JOSEPH A. PRESTON............................... | Hartford, Conn. |
| LAURENCE F. PRICE............................... | Warehouse Point, Conn. |
| HENRY H. ROBINSON, Ph.B., C.E., Ph.D., Yale, Instructor in Geology in Yale University......... | New Haven, Conn. |
| ALBERT G. SAWTELLE............................. | Hartford, Conn. |
| ROBERT M. SPENCER............................. | Toledo, Ohio |
| JAMES TERRY, Ph.B., Yale........................ | Hartford, Conn. |
| CHARLES B. WOLCOTT............................ | Plantsville, Conn. |
| BURTON K. WOODWARD........................... | Troy, N. Y. |

## 1893

### MEREAMUS SUCCESSUM

### ERNEST A. WELLS, Corresponding Secretary

| | |
|---|---|
| MARIAN C. ABBE.................................. | Springfield. Mass. |
| MARY E. BALL..............Mrs. Dwight W. Knox, | Hartford, Conn. |
| EDITH E. BARTLETT............................. | Hartford, Conn. |
| MARY A. BEARDSLEY............................. | Hartford, Conn. |
| ALICE D. BELDEN.........Mrs. Alexander N. Cook, | Brooklyn, N. Y. |
| M. ELEANOR BISSELL, B.L., Smith.................. | Hartford, Conn. |
| MYRA E. BLISS................................... | Hartford, Conn. |
| HELEN BROWN, B.L., Smith....................... | Hartford, Conn. |
| ALICE E. BURR...........Mrs. A. N. Williams, | Hartford, Conn. |
| MARCIA S. CARPENTER........Mrs. Frank E. Stone, | Hartford, Conn. |
| M. MAY CARROLL................................ | East Hartford, Conn. |
| LILLIAN C. CONE................................. | Hartford, Conn. |
| MARY J. COURTICE..........Mrs. Samuel H. Berry, | Hartford, Conn. |
| ELIZABETH L. DAVENPORT....................... | New Brighton, N. Y. |
| GRACE N. DUSTAN, A.B., Smith, Mrs. Joseph S. Rawson ......................................... | Ardmore, Pa. |
| KITTIE L. EMMONS............................. | Hartford, Conn. |
| ANNIE D. EVANS..........Mrs. Richard P. Lyman, | Hartford, Conn. |
| FLORENCE L. FISHER.......Mrs. Cloyd M. Chapman, | Brooklyn, N. Y. |
| BERNICE E. FRANCIS.......Mrs. Everett C. Willson, | Hartford, Conn. |
| LAURA J. GALACAR, B.L., Smith.................... | Springfield, Mass. |
| EDITH M. GIDDINGS............................. | Hartford, Conn. |
| MABEL A. GROVER......Mrs. Charles G. Huntington, | Hartford, Conn. |
| EDITH S. HALE.................................. | Hartford, Conn. |
| A. ELIZABETH HANMER.......................... | Wethersfield, Conn. |
| ALICE M. HILLS.........Mrs. Arthur Guy Hinkley, | Hartford, Conn. |
| LAURA A. HOTCHKISS............................ | New York, N. Y. |
| LUCY O. HUNT, B.L., Smith...................... | Hartford, Conn. |
| JANET S. HUNTTING............................. | Hartford, Conn. |
| EMMA M. JARMAN................................ | East Hartford, Conn |
| MARY H. JOHNSON, B.L., Smith.................. | New York, N. Y. |
| WINIFRED K. KENNEY............................ | Hartford, Conn. |
| SARAH E. LANE..............Mrs. Ernest N. Way, | Hartford, Conn. |
| LAURA T. LANMAN.....Mrs. Thomas Dudley Riggs, | Stevenson, Md. |
| EDITH A. MATHER..........Mrs. Joseph P. Tuttle, | Hartford, Conn. |

| NAMES | RESIDENCES |
|---|---|
| MARY L. MONAHAN................................... | Hartford, Conn. |
| EDITH L. MOORE............Mrs. George M. Miller, | Hartford, Conn. |
| FLORENCE L. MORRELL.......Mrs. Henry G. Duffield, | Princeton, N. J. |
| MARY J. REILLY..................................... | Hartford, Conn. |
| EDITH S. RICHARDS.......Mrs. George T. Pearsons, | New York, N. Y. |
| SARAH R. ROBERTS..........Mrs. Charles W. Gray, | Portsmouth, N. H. |
| WINIFRED A. RYAN................................ | Hartford, Conn. |
| MABEL L. SHACKLEY.............................. | West Hartford, Conn. |
| ALICE M. SLATE..........Mrs. Malcolm A. Norton, | West Hartford, Conn. |
| EDNA C. SMITH.................................... | Hartford, Conn. |
| LOUISE SPENCER.............Mrs. William R. Begg, | St. Paul, Minn. |
| HENRIETTA E. STONE..........Mrs. Robert E. Todd, | Chicago, Ill. |
| ALICE V. SURRIDGE.......................Died, 1899 | |
| LORETTA G. SWIFT.................Mrs. John Smith, | Manchester, Conn. |
| ABBIE M. SYKES..............Mrs. Alfred C. Clark, | Hartford, Conn. |
| HARRIET M. THOMPSON...Mrs. Alfred M. Hitchcock, | Hartford, Conn. |
| LILA WARD...............Mrs. Robert L. McLain, | Hartford, Conn. |
| M. MARGARET WARNER............................. | Hartford, Conn. |
| LAURA A. WEAVER.......................Died, 1904 | |
| CLARA E. WEED.................................... | Hartford, Conn. |
| FLORENCE C. WELLES............................. | Wethersfield, Conn. |
| KATHARINE WELLES............................... | New York, N. Y. |
| CHARLOTTE F. WHITE, B.L., Smith.................. | Manchester, Conn. |
| MARY E. WILCOX.............Mrs. Elmer H. Fogg, | Hartford, Conn. |
| GEORGIA M. WITHERELL...Mrs. Clinton S. Woodward, | Hartford, Conn. |
| | |
| HERBERT B. AUGUR, A.B., Yale..................... | Portland, Oregon |
| CARROLL C. BEACH, B.S., Trinity, M.D., Boston Univ. | Hartford, Conn. |
| ROBERT L. BEEBE................................... | South Windham, Conn. |
| M. TOSCAN BENNETT, A.B., LL.B., Yale............ | Hartford, Conn. |
| EDWARD S. BRACKETT, A.B., M.D., Yale............. | Providence, R. I. |
| HOWARD DE W. BRAINARD.......................... | New York, N. Y. |
| JOHN W. CHAPMAN................................. | Hartford, Conn. |
| RICHARD O. CHENEY, JR., Ph.B., Yale.........South | Manchester, Conn. |
| LUZERNE S. COWLES, B.S., Mass. Inst. of Technology, | Boston, Mass. |
| LOUIS A. CRESSY................................... | Hartford, Conn. |
| GUSTAVUS F. DAVIS................................ | Hartford, Conn. |
| FRANCIS J. DUFFEY, M.D., Columbia, F.R.C.S., King's Coll., London, Eng............................ | New York, N. Y. |
| HENRY D. ELMORE................................. | Hartford, Conn. |
| FREDERICK L. EMMONS, A.B., Yale................. | East Hartland, Conn. |
| FRANCIS P. GARVAN, A.B., Yale, LL.B., N. Y. Law School ........................................ | New York, N. Y. |
| CHARLES W. GROSS, A.B., Yale, LL.B., Harvard.... | Hartford, Conn. |
| PATRICK J. HEFFERNAN........................... | St. Louis, Mo. |
| FRANK E. HOWARD, Ph.B., Yale................... | Hartford, Conn. |
| WARD S. JACOBS, Ph.B., Yale, M.E., Cornell........ | Hartford, Conn. |
| CHESTER B. KELLOGG.............................. | Brooklyn, N. Y. |
| JAMES W. LAWRENCE.............................. | Hartford, Conn. |
| HENRY E. LUX.................................... | Hartford, Conn. |
| GEORGE S. McCOOK, A.B., Trinity.........Died, 1900 | |
| DANIEL F. MURPHY, A.B., Harvard................. | New York, N. Y. |
| CHARLES E. PECK, Ph.B., Yale.................... | Hartford, Conn. |
| HENRY J. PILLION, D.D.S., N. Y. Coll. of Dentistry.. | Hartford, Conn. |
| EDWARD L. SMITH, A.B., LL.B., Yale.............. | Hartford, Conn. |
| FRANK H. STOCKER, M.D., N. Y. Homeopathic Med. Coll. and Hosp.................................. | Hartford, Conn. |

| NAMES | RESIDENCES |
|---|---|
| MARTIN C. STOKES | Hartford, Conn. |
| ELLSWORTH M. TAYLOR | New York, N. Y. |
| ALBERT P. TULLER, A.B., Yale | Morristown, N. J. |
| DAVID C. TWICHELL, A.B., Yale, M.D., Columbia | Saranac Lake, N. Y. |
| EDWARD T. WARE, REV., A.B., Yale, B.D., Union Theol. Sem., Chaplain and Dean in Atlanta Univ., | Atlanta, Ga. |
| HARRY L. WELLES | Wethersfield, Conn. |
| ERNEST A. WELLS, A.B., Yale, M.D., Johns Hopkins, | Hartford, Conn. |
| JAMES D. WELLS | Wethersfield, Conn. |

## 1894

### EN AVANT

#### HORACE B. CLARK, Corresponding Secretary

| | |
|---|---|
| KATE E. ADAMS, A.B., Mt. Holyoke, Mrs. Warren E. Wheeler | Pleasant Hill, Tenn. |
| GRACE A. ARMS | Hartford, Conn. |
| FANNIE D. BACON | Hartford, Conn. |
| KATHERINE M. BACON........Mrs. George H. Coe, | Schenectady, N. Y. |
| DAISY C. BARBER | Hartford, Conn. |
| CLARA B. BUCK.....................Died, 1897 | |
| SALLY T. BULKELEY.....Mrs. Richard H. Macauley, | Detroit, Mich. |
| MABELLE BURNHAM...Mrs. Edward R. Woodhouse, | Wethersfield, Conn. |
| HELEN B. CALDER, A.B., Mt. Holyoke | Hartford, Conn. |
| JOSEPHINE L. CAMP | Hartford, Conn. |
| MARGARET A. CARROLL | Hartford, Conn. |
| MARY E. CHAMBERLIN....Mrs. Charles E. Hubbard, | Hartford, Conn. |
| LOUISE C. CLAPP...........Mrs. Frank W. Loomis, | Hartford, Conn. |
| LUCY M. CLARK.........Mrs. Winfred G. Carleton, | West Somerville, Mass. |
| MARY W. CLARKE | Hartford, Conn. |
| ELIZABETH M. COSTELLO | Hartford, Conn. |
| KATHRYN E. DECKER | Wethersfield, Conn. |
| FLORENCE DEMING | Hartford, Conn. |
| WINIFRED M. ECKHARDT.Mrs. Hubbard W. Calhoun, | Hartford, Conn. |
| MARION ENGELKE.........Mrs. Herbert G. Bissell, | Hartford, Conn. |
| FLORENCE M. FITTS.............Mrs. André Tridon, | New York, N. Y. |
| LOUISE R. FREEMAN.......Mrs. Harry J. Matthews, | Cockeysville, Md. |
| MARTHA W. GRAVES.......Mrs. Edward W. Bush, | Hartford, Conn. |
| MIRIAM C. GRISWOLD......Mrs. Charles L. Johnson, | Hartford, Conn. |
| EFFIE M. HILLS | West Haven, Conn. |
| JANE R. HILLS, B.L., Smith..Mrs. Guy E. Beardsley, | Hartford, Conn. |
| LAURA K. HILLS | Farmville, Va. |
| MARGARETTA B. HOGAN | Hartford, Conn. |
| GRACE S. HUNT...........Mrs. John W. Chapman, | Dorchester, Mass. |
| ELLA HUNTTING | Columbia University |
| GERTRUDE J. JOHNSON | Hartford, Conn. |
| GRACE W. LANDON | Hartford, Conn. |
| SALLY P. LAW, A.B., Bryn Mawr.............Johns | Hopkins University |
| ANNE L. MALTBIE | Granby, Conn. |
| PAULINE S. MAYER.......Mrs. Julius M. Rosenfeld, | New York, N. Y. |
| MAIDA L. MINER | Hartford, Conn. |
| ALICE L. MOORE...........Mrs. Robert B. Gooden, | Ventura, Cal. |
| BRIDGET T. MULCAHY | Hartford, Conn. |

| NAMES | RESIDENCES |
|---|---|
| ELEANOR NEWELL, Ph.B., Wesleyan................ | Hartford, Conn. |
| T. MAY NORRIS........................... | Hartford, Conn. |
| HANNAH P. O'FLAHERTY, A.B., Wesleyan......... | Hartford, Conn. |
| MARY A. Z. O'NEIL............................ | Hartford, Conn. |
| SARAH A. PERKINS......Mrs. Edmund A. Merriam, | Torrington, Conn. |
| ANTOINETTE R. P. PIERSON..............Died, 1903 | |
| E. MAUDE PURINTON........................... | Hartford, Conn. |
| ALICE I. REEVE.............................. | Los Angeles, Cal. |
| EDITH L. RISLEY, B.S., Wesleyan, Instructor in Public High School........................... | Hartford, Conn. |
| FRANCES G. SIMONDS......!............Died, 1900 | |
| SARAH T. SPRAGUE........................... | Hartford, Conn. |
| LILLIAN M. SQUIRES.......................... | Hartford, Conn. |
| M. ADELLA STEELE.........Mrs. William L. Linke, | Hartford, Conn. |
| LILLIAN M. TAYLOR........................... | Hartford, Conn. |
| MABEL E. TYLER............................ | Bloomfield, Conn. |
| ISABEL M. WALBRIDGE, Ph.B., Wesleyan............ | West Hartford, Conn. |
| CLARA A. WHITE............................. | Hartford, Conn. |
| RUTH D. WHITE, A.B., Smith...Mrs. A. H. Benton, | Chicopee, Mass. |
| CLARA A. WHITON.........Mrs. Selden W. Hayes, | Hartford, Conn. |
| ALICE L. WILCOX............................ | Hartford, Conn. |
| AURILLA R. WITHAM.......................... | Hartford, Conn. |
| MARY L. WOLCOTT......Mrs. Henry Robinson Buck, | Hartford, Conn. |
| ELIZABETH C. WRIGHT, A.B., Wesleyan, Instructor in Public High School......................... | Hartford, Conn. |
| M. CAROLINE ZACHER......................... | Hartford, Conn. |
| | |
| WILLIAM C. BARTHOLOMEW...................... | Hartford, Conn. |
| FRANCIS P. BERGEN, B.S., Mass. Inst. of Technology, | Chicago, Ill. |
| HERBERT G. BISSELL.......................... | Hartford, Conn. |
| CARDELLA D. BROWN.......................... | Lynn, Mass. |
| JOHN F. CALLAHAN, REV....................... | Bridgeport, Conn. |
| CLIFFORD D. CHENEY, A.B., Yale.............South | Manchester, Conn. |
| HORACE B. CLARK, A.B., Yale................... | Hartford, Conn. |
| HAROLD L. CLEASBY, A.M., Trinity, A.M., Ph.D., Harvard ............................... | Berlin University |
| GASTON H. EDWARDS, Ph.B., M.S., M.D., Yale....... | Brooklyn, N. Y. |
| LEONARD A. ELLIS, B.S., Trinity................. | Hartford, Conn. |
| WILLIAM G. ERVING, A.B., Yale, M.D., Johns Hopkins ............................... | Washington, D. C. |
| CHARLES F. FIELDS, A.B., Brown.................. | Theological Seminary, Rochester, N. Y. |
| CHARLES R. FISHER........................... | Hartford, Conn. |
| JOHN S. GARVIE............................. | St. Louis, Mo. |
| FREDERICK P. GEER..........................South | Manchester, Conn. |
| PHILIP L. HOTCHKISS......................... | Hartford, Conn. |
| WILLIAM W. HUNN........................... | Hartford, Conn. |
| WARREN B. JOHNSON, A.B., LL.B., Yale........... | Enfield, Conn. |
| WOOLSEY McA. JOHNSON, A.B., Trinity........... | Hartford, Conn. |
| JOSEPH E. JOYCE, REV., A.B., Holy Cross, D.D., Propaganda, Rome............................. | Bridgeport, Conn. |
| FRANKLIN M. KELLOGG, B.S., Mass. Inst. of Technology ............................... | Brooklyn, N. Y. |
| SAMUEL A. MARSHALL, A.B., Yale, M.D., Johns Hopkins ............................... | New York, N. Y. |
| MAURICE F. McAULIFFE, REV................... | Hartford, Conn. |

| NAMES | RESIDENCES |
|---|---|
| J. Henry McManus | Hartford, Conn. |
| Thomas P. Mulcahy, Rev. | Derby, Conn. |
| Edward D. O'Brien | Hartford, Conn. |
| Edward C. Perkins, A.B., Yale | Kingston, N. Y. |
| Paul J. J. Preu | Brooklyn, N. Y. |
| Howard A. Price | Warehouse Point, Conn. |
| Alfred E. Richards, A.M., Yale, Instructor in Modern Languages in Lehigh University | Bethlehem, Pa. |
| James Robinson Smith, A.M., Yale | Cheshire, Conn. |
| Wayne E. Smith | Hartford, Conn. |
| H. Robbins Stillman | Richmond Hill, N. Y. |
| Albert M. Sturtevant, A.B., Trinity, A.M., Harvard, Instructor in German in Harvard Univ. | Cambridge, Mass. |
| Charles Lincoln Taylor | Hartford, Conn. |
| Franklin G. Welles | Wethersfield, Conn. |
| John T. Welles, A.B., Yale | Wethersfield, Conn. |
| Arthur C. Williams, A.B., Yale | Hartford, Conn. |

## 1895

### VIRTUTE NON VERBIS

### Frances A. McCook, Corresponding Secretary

| | |
|---|---|
| Jane V. Bacon | Wethersfield, Conn. |
| Mary W. Bacon......Mrs. Eugene M. Daughn, | Hartford, Conn. |
| Annie P. Balmer | Hartford, Conn. |
| Helen M. Barchfeld | Hartford, Conn. |
| Rosa L. Barrows | Hartford, Conn. |
| Alice M. Bartlett......Mrs. Frederic H. Forbes, | Hartford, Conn. |
| Grace R. Beardsley | Hartford, Conn. |
| Mabel L. Bosworth | Hartford, Conn. |
| Grace A. Bradley......Mrs. James E. Steele, | Springfield, Mass. |
| Alice Brigham, Ph.B., Wesleyan | Hartford, Conn. |
| Lottie E. Brokaw | Hartford, Conn. |
| Elizabeth L. Burdick | Unknown |
| Lena A. Burwell | Hartford, Conn. |
| Nellie T. Cody | Hartford, Conn. |
| Helen C. Crowe......Mrs. George L. Burnham, | Hartford, Conn. |
| Ida B. Dibble......Mrs. Wilbert S. Latter, | Worcester, Mass. |
| Elizabeth C. Dickenson | Hartford, Conn. |
| Mary E. Duggan, A.B., Smith | Hartford, Conn. |
| Nellie F. V. Edwards | Atlantic City, N. J. |
| Jane C. Flynn | Hartford, Conn. |
| Bessie L. Franklin | Hartford, Conn. |
| Florence S. Frisbie | Hartford, Conn. |
| Mabel F. Galacar......Mrs. Marvin C. Birnie, | Springfield, Mass. |
| Clara M. Glazier | Hartford, Conn. |
| Gertrude I. Graves......Died, 1898 | |
| Lillian I. Harding | Hartford, Conn. |
| Florence Harris......Mrs. Victor H. Bruce, | Atlanta, Ga. |
| Berdena J. Hart......Mrs. James W. Ward, | Hartford, Conn. |
| Christine Hart......Mrs. Robert A. Wadsworth, | Hartford, Conn. |
| Gertrude R. Hart......Mrs. Louis S. Coe, | New York, N. Y. |
| Emma W. Hawkins...Mrs. Clayton P. Chamberlin, | Hartford, Conn. |
| M. Ida Hawley......Died, 1900 | |
| Fannie B. Howe......Mrs. Alfred W. Mucklow, | Hartford, Conn. |

8

| NAMES | RESIDENCES |
|---|---|
| CAROLINE T. HUNTINGTON......................... | Hartford, Conn. |
| ANNA L. HURLBURT................................ | Hartford, Conn. |
| JENNIE E. HYDE.........Mrs. Russell C. Northam, | Hartford, Conn. |
| NELLIE M. IGO.................................... | Pittsburg, Pa. |
| ANNIE L. IVES.............Mrs. Thomas B. Booth, | Newton Center, Mass. |
| ANNA R. JOHNSON............................... | Hartford, Conn. |
| CATHERINE D. KENNEDY.......................... | Hartford, Conn. |
| ALICE C. KIMBALL................................ | Wethersfield, Conn. |
| IDA M. KLINGER........................Died, 1900 | |
| EDITH M. LUX............Mrs. Harold F. Conant, | Boston, Mass. · |
| KITTIE L. MAGUIRE.......Mrs. Arthur A. McLeod, | Hartford, Conn. |
| CLARA F. MALLORY, A.B., Mt. Holyoke | |
| New England Conservatory of Music, | Boston, Mass. |
| CARRIE L. MASLEN......Mrs. Frederic H. Kenyon, | Hartford, Conn. |
| BELLE MAYER.........Mrs. Dana W. Bartholomew, | Hartford, Conn. |
| MARY S. R. MAYO................................ | Hartford, Conn. |
| ANNIE L. McCARTHY............................. | Hartford, Conn. |
| FRANCES A. McCOOK............................. | Hartford, Conn. |
| ELIZABETH A. McGOVERN...Mrs. Bartley McGovern, | Glengevlin, Ireland |
| ETHEL A. McLEAN............Mrs. Wilfred Kurth, | Brooklyn, N. Y. |
| MATHILDE MOMMERS........................South | Manchester, Conn. |
| MARGARET A. MULLEN............................. | Fitchburg, Mass. |
| AMY E. OLMSTED.........Mrs. Luzerne S. Cowles, | Allston, Mass. |
| KATHERINE B. OWEN.............................. | Columbia University |
| ALICE V. PATTISON............Mrs. Joseph Merritt, | Hartford, Conn. |
| LUCY B. PIERCE.............Mrs. George D. Snow, | Comstock's Bridge, Ct. |
| ANNIE L. PRATT.............Mrs. George E. Jewett, | Chicago, Ill. |
| MARY C. RYAN................................... | Hartford, Conn. |
| LOUISE M. SEYMS................................ | Hartford, Conn. |
| CLARA L. SHEA.................................. | Hartford, Conn. |
| CECIL P. G. SHEPHERD........................... | New York, N. Y. |
| DAISY M. SMITH................................. | Hartford, Conn. |
| MARGARETHA SPORER............................. | Hartford, Conn. |
| EMMA L. STANDISH.............................. | Wethersfield, Conn. |
| ELIZABETH S. STEELE, B.L., Smith................. | Hartford, Conn. |
| MARIA F. STOKES................................ | Hartford, Conn. |
| MARGARET M. SULLIVAN.......................... | Hartford, Conn. |
| LEONTINE McA. THOMSON.......Mrs. James Terry, | Hartford, Conn. |
| MAY L. WEEKS.............Mrs. Morgan Johnson, | Hartford, Conn. |
| SUSAN W. WIGHTMAN............................. | West Hartford, Conn. |
| ETHEL L. WILLIAMS.............................. | Hartford, Conn. |
| RENA B. WILLIAMS.......Mrs. Frederick T. Moore, | East Hartford, Conn. |
| LOUISE K. ZURHORST......Mrs. Frederick W. Smith, | Brooklyn, N. Y. |
| | |
| GERALD S. BARBER......................Died, 1896 | |
| CLIFFORD H. BELDEN, C.E., Cornell................ | Hartford, Conn. |
| ELMER C. BENEDICT............................. | Hartford, Conn. |
| EDWARD L. BIRKERY.............................. | Hartford, Conn. |
| HENRY J. BLAKESLEE, M.S., Trinity................ | Hartford, Conn. |
| JAMES W. BOOTH................................ | Hartford, Conn. |
| JOHN H. W. BRINLEY............................ | Newington Junction, Ct. |
| ROBERT D. BROWN, Ph.B., Yale.................... | Emeryville, Cal. |
| EDWIN P. BURDICK, B.S., Mass. Inst. of Technology, | London, Eng. |
| GUY M. CARLETON, A.B., Yale..................... | Hartford, Conn. |
| HERBERT M. CASE, B.S., Mass. Inst. of Technology.. | Cincinnati, Ohio |
| GEORGE H. C. ENSWORTH......................... | New York, N. Y. |

| NAMES | RESIDENCES |
|---|---|
| Eugene D. Field.................................. | Hartford, Conn. |
| Arthur D. Francis............................... | Hartford, Conn. |
| James L. Howard, Jr., Ph.B., Yale................ | Hartford, Conn. |
| Edward R. Ingraham, Ph.B., Yale............... | Hartford, Conn. |
| Edward J. Kennedy............................. | Hartford, Conn. |
| Thomas F. Lawrence, A.B., Yale................ | Hartford, Conn. |
| John J. McKone................................ | Hartford, Conn. |
| Winthrop B. Moore....................Died, 1899 | |
| Harleigh Parkhurst, Ph.B., Yale, E.E., Univ. of Minn. ....................................... | Walpole, N. H. |
| Joseph R. Peckham, Rev......................... | Meriden, Conn. |
| Alfred E. Roberts, A.B., Wesleyan, A.M., Columbia, | New York, N. Y. |
| William P. Sage, Ph.B., Yale................... | Hartford, Conn. |
| David L. Sears.................................. | Hartford, Conn. |
| Henry R. Shipman, A.B., Yale, A.M., Ph.D., Harvard, Instructor in Dartmouth College.......... | Hanover, N. H. |
| Ralph W. E. Sizer.............................. | Bridgewater, Mass. |
| Norman C. Spencer, Ph.B., Yale................ | Hartford, Conn. |
| Charles R. Swift, Jr., A.B., Yale................ | Lake Forest, Ill. |
| William H. Warner, A.B., Colorado Coll., A.B., Yale ....................................... | New Haven, Conn. |
| Frederic B. Wright ............................ | Hartford, Conn. |
| Morrison B. Yung, Ph.B., Yale, M.E., Columbia.... | Santiago, Cuba |
| Edmund L. Zacher.............................. | Hartford, Conn. |

## 1896

### PERSEVERANDO VINCES

### Frank E. Hale, Corresponding Secretary

| | |
|---|---|
| Mabel Allen...........................Died, 1902 | |
| M. Louise Allen............Mrs. Leon P. Brown, | Hartford, Conn. |
| Mary F. Anderson.............................. | Calhoun, Ala. |
| Rosabelle V. Bacon....Mrs. Arthur W. P. Malins, | Hartford, Conn. |
| Marion L. Barrett.............................. | Hartford, Conn. |
| Grace E. Beckwith......Mrs. J. Marshall Basney, | Hartford, Conn. |
| Elizabeth R. Bill...........Mrs. Frank A. Fish, | Keene, N. H. |
| Mary E. Billings...........Mrs. William B. Green, | East Orange, N. J. |
| Mary E. Birmingham........................... | Hartford, Conn. |
| L. Gertrude Boutelle.......................... | Hartford, Conn. |
| Clara Brigham...........Mrs. Arthur P. Bennett, | Hartford, Conn. |
| H. Eleanor Brigham............................ | Hartford, Conn. |
| Loraine S. Brown...........Mrs. David Calhoun, | Hartford, Conn. |
| Daisy M. Bulkley.............................. | Hartford, Conn. |
| Harriette J. Burnell......Mrs. George T. Kendall, | Memphis, Tenn. |
| Alice M. Burt................................. | Hartford, Conn. |
| Eliza N. Case................................. | Bloomfield, Conn. |
| Helen E. Case................................. | New Haven, Conn. |
| Lottie M. Champlin............................ | Hartford, Conn. |
| Mary H. Clark................................. | Hartford, Conn. |
| Grace A. Coe.................................. | Hartford, Conn. |
| Gertrude V. Coleman........................... | Hartford, Conn. |
| Clara L. Conklin.........Mrs. Harry L. Hilton, | Hartford, Conn. |
| Frances W. Cummings, A.B., Smith.............. | New York, N. Y. |

| NAMES | RESIDENCES |
|---|---|
| EDITH C. CURTIS.........Mrs. Howard S. Borden, | New York, N. Y. |
| ELIZABETH A. CURTIS......Mrs. Cranston Brenton, | Hartford, Conn. |
| MAY L. DENISON................................... | Hartford, Conn. |
| CLARA L. DUDLEY......Mrs. Frederick W. Mathews, | Newton Center, Mass |
| GRACE C. ELDRIDGE......Mrs. Ralph E. McCausland, | Hartford, Conn. |
| EMMA B. ELMER.................................. | Hartford, Conn. |
| BELLE EMERSON............Mrs. E. H. Huntington, | Winchester, Mass. |
| BESSIE M. FLETCHER........Mrs. J. McD. A. Lacy, | Marion, Va. |
| ALICE E. FLYNN................................... | Hartford, Conn. |
| EDNA L. FOLEY, B.L., Smith....................... | Hartford, Conn. |
| ETHEL M. GARVIN, A.B., Vassar................... | Wolfboro, N. H. |
| GERTRUDE L. GOODENOUGH, A.B., Mt. Holyoke | |
| Simmons College, | Boston, Mass. |
| HARRIET L. GOODWIN, A.B., Smith................. | Hartford, Conn. |
| MARION E. GOTT....................Pratt Institute, | Brooklyn, N. Y. |
| ANNIE L. GRISWOLD......Mrs. Seymour H. White, | Wethersfield, Conn. |
| HELENA A. GROU.................................. | West Hartford, Conn. |
| MABEL E. HARDING............................... | Hartford, Conn. |
| EDNA M. HARRIS.................................. | Meriden, Conn. |
| GRACE A. HIGGINS.........Mrs. George D. Spencer, | Hartford, Conn. |
| C. CORDELIA HILLIARD......Mrs. Lucius B. Barbour, | Hartford, Conn. |
| EMILY MARGUERITE HOLCOMBE.................... | Hartford, Conn. |
| ALICE L. HOVEY.................Mrs. T. E. Stenger, | Jenkintown, Pa. |
| ELIZABETH HYDE................................. | Hartford, Conn. |
| MARY L. JACKSON................................ | Hartford, Conn. |
| EDITHA L. JACOBS................................ | Hartford, Conn. |
| ELIZABETH M. KEANE............................. | Hartford, Conn. |
| FLORENCE H. KELLOGG............................ | Hartford, Conn. |
| EDENA L. MARSH.........Mrs. George W. Fleming, | Williamsport, Pa. |
| MARY E. McDONNELL............................. | Hartford, Conn. |
| MARIE T. McLEAN............................... | Hartford, Conn. |
| HELEN L. McMANUS.............................. | Hartford, Conn. |
| NELLIE B. M. McMULLEN......Mrs. P. G. Kimball, | Boston, Mass. |
| GRACE A. NASON................................. | Hartford, Conn. |
| ELSIE L. NEY.............................. ..... | Hartford, Conn. |
| ELLEN P. O'FLAHERTY, M.D., Cornell.............. | Hartford, Conn. |
| ANNA A. QUINN.......................Died, 1899 | |
| MAMELLA QUINN................................. | Hartford, Conn. |
| EDITH P. REID.................................. | Hartford, Conn. |
| BERTHA T. ROBBINS.............................. | Wethersfield, Conn. |
| SADIE F. ROSENTHAL......Mrs. Theodore R. Eisner, | New York, N. Y. |
| LEONICE C. M. STURMDORF....Mrs. Alban B. Limpus, | Teddington, Eng. |
| ALICE R. TAYLOR.............................South | Glastonbury, Conn. |
| WINIFRED R. TEEL, A.B., Mt. Holyoke.............. | New Britain, Conn. |
| MARY L. WARREN, D.D.S., Phila. Dental Coll...... | Hartford, Conn. |
| GEORGIANA WELLES......Mrs. Norman C. Spencer, | Hartford, Conn. |
| ANNA G. WESTCOTT.............................. | Hartford, Conn. |
| MARGARET M. WHITE............................. | Hartford, Conn. |
| ESTHER I. WHITTELSEY, Mrs. Frederick C. Burnham, | Hartford, Conn. |
| GRACE WOLCOTT ................................ | Hartford, Conn. |
| JESSAMINE B. WOODS............................. | Hartford, Conn. |
| MAY H. WORTHINGTON....Mrs. William R. Penrose, | Hartford, Conn. |
| | |
| GEORGE M. BAKER, A.B., Yale, Instructor in German | |
| in Yale University............................ | New Haven, Conn. |

| NAMES | RESIDENCES |
|---|---|
| LUCIUS B. BARBOUR, A.B., Yale | Hartford, Conn. |
| S. RUSSELL BARTLETT, A.B., Yale, B.S., Mass. Inst. of Technology | Greenville, S. C. |
| MORGAN B. BRAINARD, A.B., LL.B., Yale | Hartford, Conn. |
| LYMAN D. BROUGHTON | Hartford, Conn. |
| HENRY G. BRYANT | New York, N. Y. |
| WINTHROP BUCK, A.B., Yale | Saybrook, Conn. |
| BENJAMIN BUDGE | Hartford, Conn. |
| LOUIS B. CHAPMAN......Cornell Univ. Med. Coll., | New York, N. Y. |
| MORTON S. CRESSY, A.B., Yale, LL.B., Harvard | Zion City, Ill. |
| HARRY I. CROSS, B.S., Worcester Polytechnic | Alta, Cal. |
| STANLEY W. EDWARDS, A.B., LL.B., Yale | Hartford, Conn. |
| LOUIS A. GOODELL | Hartford, Conn. |
| HORACE R. GRANT | West Hartford, Conn. |
| ARTHUR H. GRAVES, A.B., Yale, Instructor in Forest Botany in Yale University | New Haven, Conn. |
| FRANK E. HALE, A.B., Ph.D., Yale | Brooklyn, N. Y. |
| ROWLAND B. HILLS......Died, 1899 | |
| FREDERICK C. INGALLS, B.S., Trinity | U. S. Navy |
| CORTLANDT F. LUCE, A.B., Yale | New Brighton, N. Y. |
| L. WILLIAM LYMAN | Hartford, Conn. |
| OWEN F. T. McCABE | Hartford, Conn. |
| CHARLES H. MINER | Brooklyn, N. Y. |
| FREDERICK C. MORCOM | Cincinnati, Ohio |
| HOWARD F. PEASE | Denver, Colo. |
| CHARLES A. RELYEA | Hartford, Conn. |
| ERNEST L. SIMONDS, A.B., Trinity | Hartford, Conn. |
| WILLIAM H. SLOANE | Hartford, Conn. |
| ANSON W. SMITH, Instructor in Pratt Institute | Brooklyn, N. Y. |
| CLARENCE H. SMITH | Hartford, Conn. |
| ANDREW G. STEELE | Hartford, Conn. |
| EDWARD C. STONE, A.B., Yale | Trinity College |
| SIMON L. TOMLINSON, A.B., Trinity......Died, 1901 | |
| JOSEPH R. WATSON | New York, N. Y. |
| HAROLD B. WHITMORE | West Hartford, Conn. |

## 1897

### FRAM

F. RAYMOND STURTEVANT, Corresponding Secretary

| | |
|---|---|
| MABEL H. ADAMS | Wethersfield, Conn. |
| FLORENCE A. BARBOUR, Mrs. Arthur R. Van De Water, | New York, N. Y. |
| JEANNETTE B. BARTHOLOMEW, B.L., Smith, Mrs. Wilson W. Robotham | Unionville, Conn. |
| NORMA B. BENNETT | Trenton, N. J. |
| ELLA N. BRACKETT, Mrs. William C. Prentiss Died, 1900 | |
| NEVA A. BROKAW | Hartford, Conn. |
| HELEN E. BROWN, B.L., Smith | Hartford, Conn. |
| EVA M. BUFFINGTON | Hartford, Conn. |
| GRACE W. BUNCE | Hartford, Conn. |
| ELSIE BURDICK | Boston University |
| FLORENCE G. CADY | Boston, Mass. |

| NAMES | RESIDENCES |
|---|---|
| MARY E. CADY......................................... | Hartford, Conn. |
| BESSIE G. CARLETON, A.B., Vassar.................. | New York, N. Y. |
| KATRINA CHRISTIANSEN...Mrs. William E. Bennett, | Springfield, Mass. |
| MARY J. COOK.............Mrs. Frank E. Newton, | Hartford, Conn. |
| GEORGETT E. DONLEY....................Died, 1899 | |
| MARY J. DOWLING................................. | Hartford, Conn. |
| GERTRUDE M. DRESSER............................. | Hartford, Conn. |
| ISABELLE G. DRISCOLL..Mrs. Andrew J. Broughel, Jr., | Hartford, Conn. |
| ELIZABETH P. DUFFY.............................. | Hartford, Conn. |
| ELLEN H. DUGGAN, B.L., Smith.................... | Hartford, Conn. |
| CLAUDIA E. EHBETS............................... | Hartford, Conn. |
| ALICE W. ENGLISH, Ph.B., Wesleyan............... | Reading, Mass. |
| GENEVIEVE F. GARVAN............................. | Hartford, Conn. |
| L. MABEL GRANT................................. | Hartford, Conn. |
| LEILA C. GRISWOLD.........Mrs. Elmer C. Benedict, | Hartford, Conn. |
| LOUISE J. GUINAN............................... | Hartford, Conn. |
| MARY E. HART.................................. | Springfield, Mass. |
| MYRTLE R. HART...........Mrs. Ashley D. Leavitt, | Willimantic, Conn. |
| IDA L. HATHEWAY............................... | Hartford, Conn. |
| GRACE M. HOXIE................................. | Hartford, Conn. |
| ELLEN A. HUNTINGTON, A.B., Univ. of Illinois, Instructor in Domestic Science in Univ. of Wisconsin ......................................... | Madison, Wis. |
| NELLIE M. HURLBURT....Mrs. Clarence E. Whitney, | Hartford, Conn. |
| EFFIE M. JOHNSTON..........Mrs. Arthur W. Fish, | Hartford, Conn. |
| ORA F. LAMB...............Mrs. Arthur L. Brown, | Hartford, Conn. |
| ANNIE LORENZ................................... | Hartford, Conn. |
| ANNIE B. LYMAN................................ | Hartford, Conn. |
| PAULINE A. LYMAN.............................. | Hartford, Conn. |
| ROSALINE MAIRSON.............................. | Hartford, Conn. |
| MAY MATTHEWS ................................. | Hartford, Conn. |
| AMIE MAYER..................Mrs. Leon F. Cohen, | New York, N. Y. |
| ELLA E. MCINTOSH.............................. | Hartford, Conn. |
| FIDELIA M. MCKINNEY........................... | Hartford, Conn. |
| ELIZABETH NEWTON....Mrs. Charles Dwight Allen, | Hartford, Conn. |
| MARY I. O'BRIEN............................... | Hartford, Conn. |
| KATHRYN C. G. O'NEIL.......................... | Hartford, Conn. |
| MARY G. OSBORN................................ | Hartford, Conn. |
| IDA E. L. PATZ................................ | Hartford, Conn. |
| CLARA M. PIERCE.........Mrs. Herbert C. Erving, | Hartford, Conn. |
| KATHRYN POWERS............................... | Hartford, Conn. |
| MARY C. RABS...............Mrs. John F. Nolan, | Hartford, Conn. |
| FLORENCE L. READETT.......................... | Hartford, Conn. |
| EDITH E. RISLEY.............................. | West Hartford, Conn. |
| HELEN ROBERTS............................... | Hartford, Conn. |
| EDITH H. ROSENTHAL.......................... | Hartford, Conn. |
| KATHARINE N. SEYMS.......................... | Hartford, Conn. |
| ELSIE C. SKINNER......Mrs. Henry R. Tomlinson, | Hartford, Conn. |
| NELLIE C. SMITH............................. | Hartford, Conn. |
| HELEN A. WEED, A.B., Syracuse Univ............ | East Springfield, N. Y. |
| IDA J. WELLS................................ | Hartford, Conn. |
| ADDIE E. WOODWARD........................... | Hartford, Conn. |
| | |
| CHARLES D. ALLEN........................... | Hartford, Conn. |
| WALTER B. ALLEN, A.B., Yale.................. | Hartford, Conn. |

| NAMES | RESIDENCES |
|---|---|
| Robert W. Barbour............................ | Homestead, Pa. |
| Francis W. H. Bill............................. | Hartford, Conn. |
| Frederic R. C. Boyd, B.S., Mass. Inst. of Technology, | Lynn, Mass. |
| Daniel E. Brainard............................ | Hartford, Conn. |
| Charles A. Breed.............................. | Hartford, Conn. |
| William P. Calder, B.S., Wesleyan............... | Hartford, Conn. |
| Burton H. Camp, A.B., Wesleyan, Instructor in Wesleyan University ......................... | Middletown, Conn. |
| William H. Clemons, B.S., Wesleyan, Instructor in English in Princeton University.............. | Princeton, N. J. |
| Harold B. Colton, A.B., Yale.................... | Hartford, Conn. |
| Carl W. Davis, A.B., Yale....................... | Harrisburg, Pa. |
| John A. Decker, Jr., A.B., Wesleyan............. | Hartford, Conn. |
| Raymond F. Driscoll............................ | Hartford, Conn. |
| Malcolm M. Eckhardt, Ph.B., Yale.............. | Derby, Conn. |
| Leon N. Futter, A.B., Columbia, LL.B., N. Y. Law School ........................................ | New York, N. Y. |
| James L. Goodwin, A.B., Yale................... | Hartford, Conn. |
| James B. Henney, A.B., Harvard, LL.B., N. Y. Law School ............................... | New York, N. Y. |
| Augustus C. Hirth....................Died, 1899 | |
| J. Robinson Hollister........................... | West Hartford, Conn. |
| David Kempner, LL.B., Yale.................... | Hartford, Conn. |
| William M. Maltbie, A.B., Yale................. | Yale University |
| Walter A. Mitchell, A.B., Trinity, Instructor in Columbia University ......................... | New York, N. Y. |
| J. G. DeWitt Morrell, Ph.B., M.E., Yale, E.E., Princeton ...................................... | Hartford, Conn. |
| John F. Morris................................. | Hartford, Conn. |
| John Olmsted ................................. | Portland, Oregon |
| Charles C. Russ, A.B., Yale..................... | Yale University |
| Henry C. Russ, A.B., Yale...................... | Johns Hopkins Univ. |
| Thomas W. Russell, A.B., Yale.................. | Hartford, Conn. |
| Charles T. Smart, B.S., Trinity, West Point, 1904, Lieut......................................... | U. S. Army |
| Ernest W. Smith, A.B., Yale.................... | Hartford, Conn. |
| Edwin A. Strong................................ | New York, N. Y. |
| F. Raymond Sturtevant, A.B., Trinity, A.B., Harvard ......................................... | Harvard University |
| Robert J. F. Sullivan.......................... | Hartford, Conn. |
| James S. Taintor, A.B., Yale.................... | Hartford, Conn. |
| Howard F. Taylor, A.B., Yale................... | University of Chicago |
| Burton P. Twichell, A.B., Yale.................. | Yale University |
| Ralph O. Wells, A.B., Yale, LL.B., Harvard...... | Hartford, Conn. |
| Heywood H. Whaples, A.B., Yale................ | Hartford, Conn. |
| Alonzo P. White............................... | Hartford, Conn. |

### 1898

### Κάλλιστα ζητώμεθα

Mary F. Whiton, Corresponding Secretary

| | |
|---|---|
| Effie M. Abrams............................... | Hartford, Conn. |
| Laura M. Barber............................... | Detroit, Mich. |
| Maud F. Bowman........Mrs. Henry D. Bartram, | New York, N. Y. |

| NAMES | RESIDENCES |
|---|---|
| GENEVIEVE M. CALNEN | Hartford, Conn. |
| BESSIE M. CLEASBY | Hartford, Conn. |
| CLARA S. CONRADS......Mrs. Robert H. Ellsworth, | West Hartford, Conn. |
| ALICE L. CURTIS, B.L., Smith.....Mrs. Leon L. Mott, | Hartford, Conn. |
| ANNA M. DUNNING.......Mrs. Francis E. Field, | Hartford, Conn. |
| MINNIE O. ENGEL | Hartford, Conn. |
| THERESA C. FLANNERY | Hartford, Conn. |
| KATE M. FLETCHER | Washington, D. C. |
| EFFIE S. GRAVES...................Died, 1903 | |
| MARY E. HASKELL | Hartford, Conn. |
| MARCELLA K. HELION | Hartford, Conn. |
| BERTHA P. HOBSON | Meriden, Conn. |
| NELLIE E. HOOD | Hartford, Conn. |
| MARY E. HUBBARD | Hartford, Conn. |
| MABEL H. JAMESON | Hartford, Conn. |
| FLORA M. KING | Hartford, Conn. |
| BERTHA J. LYONS | Hartford, Conn. |
| F. ELIZABETH MACK, Instructor in Hartford Public High School | Windsor, Conn. |
| GRACE E. MAHL............Mrs. George M. Baker, | New Haven, Conn. |
| KATHERINE V. McLAUGHLIN | Hartford, Conn. |
| ISABEL L. F. PALMER | Hartford, Conn. |
| HATTIE E. PHELPS | Hartford, Conn. |
| KATHRYN R. RICHARDS | Hartford, Conn. |
| ANNE W. RISLEY | West Hartford, Conn. |
| HELEN B. RIST.....................Died, 1903 | |
| ELISE A. ROBERTS | Hartford, Conn. |
| LOUISE G. RYAN.....................Died, 1902 | |
| ISABEL D. SEELYE........Mrs. Philip K. Williams, | Glastonbury, Conn. |
| FLORENCE L. SEXTON | Hartford, Conn. |
| THERESA A. SHEEHAN | Hartford, Conn. |
| FLORENCE SIMMONS | Hartford, Conn. |
| MAY E. SLOAN | Hartford, Conn. |
| MARY B. STANLEY | West Hartford, Conn. |
| FLORENCE P. SYKES.......Mrs. Edwin S. Mugford, | Hartford, Conn. |
| OLA M. TUCKER...............Mrs. William Clift, | Brooklyn, N. Y. |
| ALICE B. WARFIELD, A.B., Smith | Hartford, Conn. |
| GRACE B. WATKINSON, A.B., Smith | Hartford, Conn. |
| MARY F. WHITON | West Hartford, Conn. |
| EDITH C. WILLIAMS | East Hartford, Conn. |
| ALICE L. WOOLLEY | Hartford, Conn. |
| | |
| HENRY E. ADAMS, M.D., Yale | Hartford, Conn. |
| JOHN E. AHERN | Hartford, Conn. |
| GEORGE E. AVERY | Hartford, Conn. |
| RALPH BALLERSTEIN | New York, N. Y. |
| CLARENCE L. BARKER | Brooklyn, N. Y. |
| ALBERT A. BASKERVILLE | Hartford, Conn. |
| M. HENRY BERGEN, A.B., Yale | New York, N. Y. |
| NEWTON C. BRAINARD, A.B., Yale | Hartford, Conn. |
| HENRY T. BRAY, M.D., Univ. of Vermont | New Britain, Conn. |
| HENRY E. CHAPMAN, JR | Chicago, Ill. |
| WILLIAM DAVIS BOWERS CLARK.......Died, 1899 | |
| EDMUND JANES CLEVELAND, A.B., Trinity | Episcopal Theological School, Cambridge, Mass. |

| NAMES | RESIDENCES |
|---|---|
| RICHARD H. COLE, A.B., Yale | Hartford, Conn. |
| JOSEPH F. COOLEY | Hartford, Conn. |
| JAMES E. COWLISHAW | Hartford, Conn. |
| GEORGE E. DAVIS, A.B., Yale, Instructor in St. Paul's School | Concord, N. H. |
| EDWIN C. DICKENSON, LL.B., Yale | Hartford, Conn. |
| WALTER H. FARMER, B.S., Mass. Inst. of Technology, | Nashua, N. H. |
| JOHN P. FITCH | Manchester, Conn. |
| BENEDICT D. FLYNN | Hartford, Conn. |
| EDWARD W. FRISBIE, A.B., Yale | Hartford, Conn. |
| ALBERT L. HARDENDORFF | North Amherst, Mass. |
| LAURENT HEATON, A.B., Yale | Poughkeepsie, N. Y. |
| LUCIUS H. HOLT, A.M., Yale | Yale University |
| W. BRIAN HOOKER, A.M., Yale, Instructor in English in Columbia University | New York, N. Y. |
| ALVAN W. HYDE, A.B., Yale | Harvard University |
| ESAIAS ISRAELI | New York, N. Y. |
| EDWIN L. KING | Hartford, Conn. |
| JOSEPH R. LACY | Hartford, Conn. |
| NEWTON W. LARKUM | Hartford, Conn. |
| RICHARD C. LINCOLN, Ph.B., Yale | Hartford, Conn. |
| HERBERT S. MACBRIDE | Died, 1905 |
| CHARLES W. MARSH | New York, N. Y. |
| CHARLES S. MARSTON, M.E., Columbia | Arlington, N. J. |
| ANSON T. McCOOK, A.B., Trinity | Harvard University |
| EDMUND S. MERRIAM, A.B., Trinity | Göttingen University |
| KARL P. MORBA, A.B., Trinity, Instructor in Choate School | Wallingford, Conn. |
| EVERETT H. MORSE | Hartford, Conn. |
| ROBERT B. NEWELL, A.B., Wesleyan | Hartford, Conn. |
| THOMAS J. O'BRIEN | Hartford, Conn. |
| J. FRANK O'CALLAHAN, A.B., Yale | Columbia University |
| GEORGE F. OLMSTED | East Hartford, Conn. |
| HUBERT P. PECK | Hartford, Conn. |
| JAMES A. PREU | Hartford, Conn. |
| JAMES D. PRICE | Warehouse Point, Ct. |
| CHARLES A. ROBERTS, A.B., Yale | Yale University |
| ROBERT L. ROWLEY, M.D., Yale | Hartford, Conn. |
| FRANK A. SEWARD | Hartford, Conn. |
| SAMUEL W. SHAILER | New Britain, Conn. |
| ALLEN E. SMITH, Ph.B., Yale | Hartford, Conn. |
| GEORGE C. ST. JOHN, A.B., Harvard, Instructor in the Adirondack-Florida School | Simsbury, Conn. |
| CHARLES H. STORRS | Hartford, Conn. |
| BARTLETT G. YUNG, A.B., Yale | New York, N. Y. |

## 1899

### CERTUM FINEM PETE

### ELIOT R. CLARK, Corresponding Secretary

| | |
|---|---|
| MARY B. ALTON | Hartford, Conn. |
| AGNES K. BABCOCK | Mrs. Franklin L. Knox, Hartford, Conn. |
| HETTIE G. BAKER | Hartford, Conn. |
| KATHERINE G. BIRMINGHAM | Hartford, Conn. |

| NAMES | RESIDENCES |
|---|---|
| AGNES G. BRITTON | Hartford, Conn. |
| BESSIE N. BROCKWAY, A.B., Smith | Hartford, Conn. |
| MARY C. CARROLL | Hartford, Conn. |
| ETHEL CARTER..........Mrs. H. Clifford Wheeler, | Winsted, Conn. |
| VIOLA M. CASEY | Hartford, Conn. |
| ALICE V. CHAPIN | Hartford, Conn. |
| ELSIE H. CLEVELAND | Rocky Hill, Conn. |
| VIOLA I. COLLINS | Hartford, Conn. |
| ELIZABETH W. CURTISS | Hartford, Conn. |
| CLARA B. DEMING | Hartford, Conn. |
| ANNIE Z. DONOVAN | Hartford, Conn. |
| LILLIAN R. DUFFEY, A.B., Columbia | Brooklyn, N. Y. |
| ANNA M. DUGGAN | Hartford, Conn. |
| ELLEN C. DWYER | Hartford, Conn. |
| HANNAH M. EGAN.....................Died, 1904 | |
| MAUDE B. ELLIS..............Mrs. Harry S. Hall, | New York, N. Y. |
| CARRIE A. GAUTHIER, A.B., Smith | New York, N. Y. |
| FLORA E. GAUTHIER | Hartford, Conn. |
| ELENE E. GEER | New York, N. Y. |
| EMMA T. GILLETTE | Hartford, Conn. |
| ETHEL E. GREEN, A.B., Mt. Holyoke | Hartford, Conn. |
| M. HELENE GREEN | Hartford, Conn. |
| ALICE R. GRISWOLD, A.B., Mt. Holyoke | Hartford, Conn. |
| ANNETTE M. HILLS | West Hartford, Conn. |
| CLARA B. HINCKLEY..........Mrs. Harold L. Pope, | Hartford, Conn. |
| EVA M. HOADLEY..........Mrs. John K. Groesbeck, | Hartford, Conn. |
| GRACE L. HOLADAY | Springfield, Mass. |
| ISABEL K. HOOKER | Hartford, Conn. |
| HELEN E. HOWARD | Hartford, Conn. |
| MAY L. JACOBS | Wellesley College |
| ANNA M. KASSENBROOK | Hartford, Conn. |
| FLORENCE C. KENEY......Mrs. Frederick C. Neilson, | Hartford, Conn. |
| MARY A. LANDRIGAN | Hartford, Conn. |
| ANNA L. LANGDON | Hartford, Conn. |
| ANNA E. LAWSON | Hartford, Conn. |
| IDA M. E. LORENZEN.......Mrs. Samuel C. Cooper, | Hartford, Conn. |
| MARY E. MAHON | Hartford, Conn. |
| MARJORIE V. MATSON | Hartford, Conn. |
| NELLIE I. McKEOWN........Mrs. Prescott H. White, | Hartford, Conn. |
| MAUDE J. MIX | Brooklyn, N. Y. |
| ELLA L. MYERS | Hartford, Conn. |
| MARY E. NOBLE | Hartford, Conn. |
| KATHERINE T. NORTHAM | Hartford, Conn. |
| ADA I. NORTON, A.B., Smith | Hartford, Conn. |
| ALICE M. OLSEN | Hartford, Conn. |
| M. MARGUERITE PERSSE | Hartford, Conn. |
| FLORENCE M. PINNEY | Hartford, Conn. |
| LILLIAN L. POTTER | Hartford, Conn. |
| AMY L. PRATT | South Glastonbury, Conn. |
| ELIZABETH T. PYNE | Hartford, Conn. |
| ELSIE W. REID | Hartford, Conn. |
| JESSAMINE ROCKWELL | West Hartford, Conn. |
| MARY L. SEXTON | Hartford, Conn. |
| GRACE M. SPEAR.........Mrs. Richard C. Lincoln, | Hartford, Conn. |
| MARION G. TALLMAN | Hartford, Conn. |
| OLIVE WARE, A.B., Smith | Hartford, Conn. |

| NAMES | RESIDENCES |
|---|---|
| ALICE W. WARNER, A.B., Smith | Wethersfield, Conn. |
| GRACE L. WATERS....Mrs. George H. Bartholomew, | Hartford, Conn. |
| HELEN WATSON | Boston, Mass. |
| ALICE C. WELCH | Hartford, Conn. |
| DAISY A. WILSON | Hartford, Conn. |
| | |
| PERRIE M. ARNOLD, B.S., Mass. Inst. of Technology, | Hartford, Conn. |
| ALEXANDER BALGLEY | Brooklyn, N. Y. |
| ALLEN C. BRAGAW, A.B., Yale | New York Law School |
| RALPH H. BURDETT | Hartford, Conn. |
| JAMES N. H. CAMPBELL, A.B., Yale | Yale University |
| WILLIAM L. CARTER | Hartford, Conn. |
| FRANK C. CHAMPLIN | Buffalo, N. Y. |
| RUSSELL CHENEY, A.B., Yale | South Manchester, Conn. |
| ELIOT R. CLARK, A.B., Yale | Johns Hopkins Univ. |
| FRANCIS W. COLE, A.B., Yale | Harvard University |
| CHARLES M. CROSS, M.E., Cornell | Lynn, Mass. |
| CHARLES A. CULLEN | Hartford, Conn. |
| DONALD A. DUNHAM, A.B., Yale | Hartford, Conn. |
| JOHN M. ELLIS, M.E., Cornell | New York, N. Y. |
| JOHN W. FINDON | University of Maryland |
| LOUIS L. GRANT | South Windsor, Conn. |
| ELISHA E. HILLIARD | Hartford, Conn. |
| JOSEPH E. HIRTH | Hartford, Conn. |
| THOMAS N. HOGAN | Hartford, Conn. |
| LAWRENCE A. HOWARD, A.B., Yale | New York Law School |
| CLARENCE B. INGRAHAM, JR., Ph.B., Yale | Johns Hopkins Univ. |
| FREDERICK T. JARMAN | Hartford, Conn. |
| ARTHUR D. JOHNSON | Hartford, Conn. |
| JARVIS McA. JOHNSON, A.B., Trinity | Hartford, Conn. |
| FRANK R. LAWRENCE | Hartford, Conn. |
| EDWARD H. LORENZ, B.S., Trinity | Mass. Inst. of Technology |
| FREDERICK W. LYCETT | Trinity College |
| WILLIAM T. LYNCH | Hartford, Conn. |
| ERNEST A. MOORE | Passaic, N. J. |
| FRANK J. MORAN, Ph.B., Yale | Pittsburg, Pa. |
| S. ST. JOHN MORGAN, A.B., Trinity | Wilkinsburg, Pa. |
| TIMOTHY C. O'BRIEN | New York, N. Y. |
| FRANK A. OLDS, Ph.B., Yale | Hartford, Conn. |
| DANIEL L. O'NEILL, A.B., Yale | Yale University |
| CHARLES F. PRATT, A.B., Yale | Hartford, Conn. |
| GEORGE ROBERTS, JR., A.B., Yale | Union Theological Seminary, New York, N. Y. |
| WILBUR C. SEARLE | Worcester Polytechnic Institute |
| GEORGE B. SEYMS, B.S., Mass. Inst. of Technology | Racine, Wis. |
| GEORGE A. SMITH, A.B., Yale | Johns Hopkins Univ. |
| EDWARD A. STILLMAN | New York, N. Y. |
| LOUIE P. STRONG | Hartford, Conn. |
| CLARENCE H. TAYLOR | Hartford, Conn. |
| WILLIAM T. TAYLOR | Hartford, Conn. |
| JOHN F. TRUMBULL, Ph.B., Yale | New Haven, Conn. |
| ABRAHAM TULIN, A.B., Yale | Harvard University |
| G. CLARENCE WOOLLEY | Hartford, Conn. |

## 1900

**AD OMNIA PARATUS**

### HELEN C. LINCOLN, Corresponding Secretary

| | |
|---|---|
| IVA L. ABBEY | Hartford, Conn. |
| AGNESE M. M. AHERN | Smith College |
| ALICE P. AHERN | Hartford, Conn. |
| ELLEN R. M. AHERN | Hartford, Conn. |
| LUCY A. ALLEN | Hartford, Conn. |
| ANNA C. BENNETT | Montclair, N. J. |
| HARRIET R. BLUMENTHAL | Hartford, Conn. |
| HELEN B. BOYCE............Mrs. Joseph T. Tilden, | West Hartford, Conn. |
| EDITH H. BRAINARD | Hartford, Conn. |
| AME M. BROSMITH | Hartford, Conn. |
| L. CORNELLA BULL | New Haven, Conn. |
| MARGUERITE COLTON | Hartford, Conn. |
| LAURA D. CONE | Hartford, Conn. |
| HELEN L. COUCH........Mrs. G. Clarence Woolley, | Hartford, Conn. |
| MARY A. CROSS | Hartford, Conn. |
| HELENA F. CURTIN | Hartford, Conn. |
| MARY B. CURTIS | Hartford, Conn. |
| CHARLOTTE E. CUTLER | Hartford, Conn. |
| CORA E. DAIGNEAU | New York, N. Y. |
| CLARA M. DICKINSON | Hartford, Conn. |
| FLORENCE M. DICKINSON | Hartford, Conn. |
| ELLEN J. DONOVAN | New York, N. Y. |
| NORMA F. EATON............Mrs. Alfred B. Pimm, | Newington, Conn. |
| HELENA H. ELLIOTT | Hartford, Conn. |
| BELLE ELSNER | Hartford, Conn. |
| AMY B. ENO............Died, 1903 | |
| ANNA J. FAGAN | Hartford, Conn. |
| MARY M. FARRELL........Mrs. Frederick W. Barrett, | Hartford, Conn. |
| ANNIE FISHER, B.S., Wesleyan | Hartford, Conn. |
| KATHARINE J. FLYNN | Hartford, Conn. |
| MARGARET L. FLYNN | Hartford, Conn. |
| MARION S. FOWLER | Hartford, Conn. |
| ELLEN G. GILMORE | Hartford, Conn. |
| LAURA E. GLAZIER, A.B., Smith | Hartford, Conn. |
| JESSIE S. GOODWIN | East Hartford, Conn. |
| CAMILLA D. GRISWOLD | Bloomfield, Conn. |
| HAZEL F. HALLAUER | Hartford, Conn. |
| GENEVIEVE L. HERTZLER | Washington, D. C. |
| ALEXINA E. HILLS | Hartford, Conn. |
| MARY E. HOVEY | New York, N. Y. |
| ISABEL M. HUNTINGTON | Hartford, Conn. |
| JULIA L. ISHAM | Hartford, Conn. |
| ETHEL R. JOHNSON | Hartford, Conn. |
| HELEN D. KIRKPATRICK | Hartford, Conn. |
| ADDIE L. KNOX, B.L., Smith | Hartford, Conn. |
| EDITH M. LATHAM | Lutherville, Md. |
| HELEN C. LINCOLN | Hartford, Conn. |
| CLARA E. MAHL | Englewood, N. J. |
| FLORENCE L. T. MIX | Pratt Institute, Brooklyn, N. Y. |
| MARY J. MORIARTY | Hartford, Conn. |

| NAMES | RESIDENCES |
|---|---|
| MARION J. MOULTON, A.B., Mt. Holyoke............ | University of Michigan |
| MARY H. MURRAY................................ | Hartford, Conn. |
| MAY G. NOONAN................................. | Hartford, Conn. |
| MARGUERITA M. O'BRIEN......................... | Hartford, Conn. |
| EDNA A. OLDS, A.B., Smith...................... | Hartford, Conn. |
| EFFIE S. OSTRANDER............................ | Hartford, Conn. |
| EDITH M. PALMER.............................. | Hartford, Conn. |
| MAY C. PARKER................................ | Hartford, Conn. |
| MINNIE P. PIERCE............................. | Hartford, Conn. |
| GRACE E. PURINTON............................. | Mt. Holyoke College |
| FRANCES J. RANSOM, Instructor in Virginia Normal and Industrial Institute........................ | Petersburg, Va. |
| BERTHA C. REED............................... | Hartford, Conn. |
| ETHEL P. RIST................................ | East Hartford, Conn. |
| MABEL G. ROSS................................ | Hartford, Conn. |
| OLIVE K. SAGE................................ | Hartford, Conn. |
| DEETTE SAMSON................................ | Hartford, Conn. |
| HANNAH SAMUELS...........Mrs. William P. Haas, | West Hartford, Conn. |
| FLORA T. SMITH............................... | Weatogue, Conn. |
| JESSIE S. STEANE............................. | Wellesley College |
| LUCY H. SWEET................................ | Hartford, Conn. |
| CATHERINE A. TUITE........................... | Bridgeport, Conn. |
| MAUDE B. UTLEY..........Mrs. John R. McElwain, | Hartford, Conn. |
| BLANCHE E. WELCH............................. | Sheffield, Mass. |
| MARION C. WILLIAMS.....Mrs. William C. Tolhurst, | Hartford, Conn. |
| MARGUERITE F. WOODS.......................... | Hartford, Conn. |
| | |
| ARTHUR W. ALLEN, A.B., Yale................... | Hartford, Conn. |
| GEORGE E. H. BACON........................... | Hartford, Conn. |
| HAROLD J. BARBOUR, A.B., Yale................. | Hartford, Conn. |
| MELVILLE H. BARNARD.......................... | Bloomfield, Conn. |
| JULIUS BONDY, M.D., Columbia.................. | New York, N. Y. |
| FRANK E. BOSSON.............................. | Hartford, Conn. |
| JAMES H. BREWSTER, JR., A.B., Yale............ | Hartford, Conn. |
| GARRET D. BROWER............................. | Hartford, Conn. |
| CHARLES H. BUCK, A.B., Yale................... | Wethersfield, Conn. |
| THOMAS F. J. BURKE........................... | Hartford, Conn. |
| SIDNEY C. CARPENTER.......................... | West Hartford, Conn. |
| S. LEWIS CHURCH, Ph.B., Yale.................. | Olean, N. Y. |
| JAMES H. COBURN, A.B., Yale................... | Hartford, Conn. |
| LEWIS B. COMSTOCK, Ph.B., Yale................ | New Rochelle, N. Y. |
| VAHRAM E. DAVOUD, Ph.B., Yale................. | Niagara Falls, N. Y. |
| SALVATOR D'ESOPO, LL.B., Yale................. | Hartford, Conn. |
| RALPH DEWITT ................................ | Milford, Utah |
| ARTHUR DWYER, Ph.B., Yale..................... | Buffalo, N. Y. |
| WALTER O. EITEL.............................. | Hartford, Conn. |
| FRANK H. ENSIGN, JR.......................... | New Orleans, La. |
| G. BURGESS FISHER, JR........................ | Hartford, Conn. |
| HERBERT F. FISHER............................ | Hartford, Conn. |
| HOWARD R. HASTINGS........................... | New York, N. Y. |
| GEORGE F. KANE............................... | Hartford, Conn. |
| JAMES W. KNOX, A.B., Yale..................... | Yale University |
| WILLIAM J. MCEVOY............................ | Hartford, Conn. |
| BAYARD Q. MORGAN, A.B., Trinity............... | University of Leipzig |
| HAROLD C. MOULTON............................ | Hartford, Conn. |

| NAMES | RESIDENCES |
|---|---|
| CHARLES H. NORTHAM, JR. | Hartford, Conn. |
| KARL E. PEILER, B.S., Mass. Inst. of Technology | Hartford, Conn. |
| FREDERICK A. ROBBINS, JR. | Hartford, Conn. |
| JOHN W. ROBERTS, A.B., Amherst | New York, N. Y. |
| CLIFFORD A. ROBINSON | Hartford, Conn. |
| FRANCIS P. ROHRMAYER | Hartford, Conn. |
| WALTER B. SHERWOOD | Trinity College |
| CHARLES L. SLOCUM | Hartford, Conn. |
| CLARENCE M. THOMPSON, A.B., Brown, Principal of Chilhowee Academy | Trundle's Cross Roads, Tenn. |
| CLAYTON W. WELLES, A.B., Yale | Wethersfield, Conn. |
| HARLAN H. WHITE, Ph.B., Yale | Springfield, Mass. |
| JOSEPH H. WOODWARD, Ph.B., Yale | Hartford, Conn. |

## 1901

### NIL DESPERANDUM

### W. ARTHUR COUNTRYMAN, JR., Corresponding Secretary

| | |
|---|---|
| FLORENCE I. ALLEN | Mt. Holyoke College |
| LENA E. ALLING | Hartford, Conn. |
| AIMEE E. ANGUS | Hartford, Conn. |
| EVELYN BALLERSTEIN | Hartford, Conn. |
| ELSE B. BLUEHDORN.........Mrs. Elmer G. Thrall, | Bridgeport, Conn. |
| MARY G. BUCKLEY | Hartford, Conn. |
| FLORENCE L. BURT | Hartford, Conn. |
| CHARLOTTE W. BURTON | Hartford, Conn. |
| MARGUERITE L. CALLERY | Hartford, Conn. |
| NATALIE CHAMBERS | Hartford, Conn. |
| AGNES J. CLANCY | Hartford, Conn. |
| SARAH E. CLARK | Hartford, Conn. |
| EMELINE P. COUNTRYMAN | New Haven, Conn. |
| JANE C. CULLEN | Hartford, Conn. |
| BLANCHE M. DARLING | Wellesley College |
| ETHEL L. DICKINSON | East Hartford, Conn. |
| CHARLOTTE A. DONLEY | Hartford, Conn, |
| ETHEL C. DUNHAM | Hartford, Conn. |
| ROSE M. DWYER | Hartford, Conn. |
| FLORENCE A. FAIRBANKS......Mrs. Elton F. Strong, | East Hartford, Conn. |
| GRACE M. FLYNN | Hartford, Conn. |
| RENA E. GARVIN | Hartford, Conn. |
| EDITH G. GREEN | Hartford, Conn. |
| HARRIET E. GRISWOLD | Hartford, Conn. |
| EMMA P. HIRTH | Smith College |
| ANNA C. KILFOIL | Hartford, Conn. |
| ELLA C. LESTER | Mt. Holyoke College |
| LUCY S. MATTHEWS......Mrs. Ralph W. McCreary, | West Hartford, Conn. |
| MARGARET A. McCANN | Hartford, Conn. |
| MARGARET M. McEVOY | Hartford, Conn. |
| GEORGIA A. McKEOWN | Hartford, Conn. |
| BERTHA W. MESSINGER....Mrs. William B. Bassett, | Hartford, Conn. |
| LUCY P. MITCHELL | Hartford, Conn. |
| GRACE E. MUCKLOW | Hartford, Conn. |
| ANNA E. O'BRIEN | Hartford, Conn. |
| FLORENCE M. PALMER | Hartford, Conn. |

| NAMES | RESIDENCES |
|---|---|
| KATHARINE PERRY.........Mrs. Harold W. Hough, | Hartford, Conn. |
| MARY E. POND..................................... | Mt. Holyoke College |
| MARY A. READETT................................ | Hartford, Conn. |
| SARAH T. REES.................................. | Smith College |
| MABEL I. REILLY................................ | Hartford, Conn. |
| MARY ROBERTS.................................. | Hartford, Conn. |
| FLORENCE R. ROBERTSON......................... | Hartford, Conn. |
| FRIEDA ROLOFF................................. | Hartford, Conn. |
| MAUD L. ROWBOTHAM............................ | Hartford, Conn. |
| GERTRUDE M. SCOFIELD.....4................... | Hartford, Conn. |
| GRACE J. SHIPMAN.............................. | Hartford, Conn. |
| ANNA D. SODERSTROM........................... | Brooklyn, N. Y. |
| ANNIE E. SPORER............................... | Hartford, Conn. |
| ADA A. STEVENS................................ | Hockanum, Conn. |
| JENNIE I. STINSON............................. | Hartford, Conn. |
| HAZEL P. STRANT.............................. | Hartford, Conn. |
| MARY C. SWEET................................. | Vassar College |
| LUCY M. SWIFT................................. | Mt. Holyoke College |
| MAUDE W. TAYLOR.............................. | Tufts College |
| EDITHA B. TERRY............................... | Hartford, Conn. |
| EMMA J. THOMPSON............................. | Hartford, Conn. |
| ALICE E. TOLHURST............................ | Hartford, Conn. |
| MARY C. TOOMEY............................... | Hartford, Conn. |
| ELIZA N. TRUMBULL..........Mrs. Edwin L. King, | Hartford, Conn. |
| MARY V. WAITE................................ | Cornell University |
| GRACE E. WARFIELD............................ | Smith College |
| LUCY C. WHITON............................... | West Hartford, Conn. |
| CHARLOTTE E. WILE............................ | Hartford, Conn. |
|  |  |
| JOHN H. ALLISON.............................. | Yale University |
| JOHN I. ANGUS................................ | Hartford, Conn. |
| JACOB BALGLEY................................ | Hartford, Conn. |
| CHARLES N. BANNING........................... | Hartford, Conn. |
| RAYMOND A. BEARDSLEE......................... | Yale University |
| EDWARD B. BENEDICT........................... | Hartford, Conn. |
| ROGER H. BLAKESLEE........................... | Trinity College |
| JAMES O. BREED............................... | Hartford, Conn. |
| VINCENT C. BREWER............................ | Trinity College |
| ROBERT H. BROWNE............................. | Hartford, Conn. |
| SIDNEY R. BURNAP, JR......................... | Yale University |
| HOWARD E. BUSHNELL........................... | Princeton University |
| W. ARTHUR COUNTRYMAN, JR..................... | Yale University |
| EDWARD A. DEMING, Ph.B., Yale..............Johns | Hopkins University |
| HAROLD E. DIMOCK............................. | Yale University |
| SOLOMON ELSNER............................... | Yale University |
| ALFRED C. FAIRBANKS, LL.B., Yale............... | West Springfield, Mass. |
| WILLIAM E. FIELDING.......................... | Hartford, Conn. |
| WILLIAM H. FLANIGAN.......................... | Hartford, Conn. |
| TERRY V. GATES............................... | Hartford, Conn. |
| GEORGE A. GAUTHIER........................... | Hartford, Conn. |
| RALPH U. GRIFFIN............................. | West Hartland, Conn. |
| GEORGE C. HADLOCK........................... | Hartford, Conn. |
| W. LINDSAY HALL............................. | Hartford, Conn. |
| C. JARVIS HARRIMAN.......................... | Trinity College |
| GEORGE M. HARRIS............................ | Yale University |

| NAMES | RESIDENCES |
|---|---|
| Anson M. Holcomb.....................Worcester | Polytechnic Institute |
| Edmund G. Howe................................ | Yale University |
| Philip T. Kennedy.............................. | Trinity College |
| Frank R. Knox............................... | Hartford, Conn. |
| Raymond C. Lewis.............................. | Staten Island, N. Y. |
| John J. Lyons.................................. | Hartford, Conn. |
| William F. Mahon.............................. | Hartford, Conn. |
| Edward E. Moran, Ph.B., Yale................... | Shanghai, China |
| Alonzo A. Munsell............................. | Hartford, Conn. |
| Herbert V. Olds............................... | Yale University |
| Samuel J. Plimpton............................ | Yale University |
| John T. Roberts............................... | Yale University |
| W. Blair Roberts.............................. | Trinity College |
| Erle Rogers.........................Worcester | Polytechnic Institute |
| Louis A. Samuels.............................. | Hartford, Conn. |
| Robert W. Seyms.........................Mass. | Inst. of Technology |
| William A. Sheehan............................ | Hartford, Conn. |
| John H. Thompson.............................. | Brown University |
| Dwight W. Tracy, Ph.B., Yale..............Johns | Hopkins University |
| Earl E. Wilbur................................ | Hartford, Conn. |

## 1902

### CONSILIO ET ANIMIS

### Carolyn B. Taylor, Corresponding Secretary

| | |
|---|---|
| Mae C. Backes................................. | Hartford, Conn. |
| Anna I. Ball.................................. | Hartford, Conn. |
| Anna M. Barrows.............................. | Hartford, Conn. |
| Lida A. Belden............................... | Hartford, Conn. |
| Louise M. Belden............................. | Hartford, Conn. |
| Myldred L. Buck.....................Died, 1903 | |
| A. Christina Burnham......................... | Albany, Wis. |
| Carolyn H. Burnham........................... | Hartford, Conn. |
| Elizabeth M. Burt............................ | Hartford, Conn. |
| Marian L. Burt............................... | Hartford, Conn. |
| Ethel C. Cady................................ | Hartford, Conn. |
| Emma L. Chaffee, Mrs. Maurice S. Tooker | |
| Died, 1904 | |
| Alice M. Creedon............................. | Hartford, Conn. |
| Isabelle E. Cunliffe.......................... | Elliott, Pa. |
| Mabel DeBarthe............................... | Hartford, Conn. |
| Sadie P. Dodd................................ | Hartford, Conn. |
| Blanche A. Doebler........................... | Hartford, Conn. |
| Hattie M. Doebler............................ | Hartford, Conn. |
| Clarissa E. Donovan.......................... | San Francisco, Cal. |
| Ida M. Dresser...................Pratt Institute, | Brooklyn, N. Y. |
| Florence J. Duffey..............Adelphi College, | Brooklyn, N. Y. |
| Alice G. Eno................................. | Simsbury, Conn. |
| Mabel L. Fehmer.............................. | Westerly, R. I. |
| Martha Gardner.............................. | Vassar College |
| Helen S. Glazier...........Mrs. Arthur G. Root, | Hartford, Conn . |
| M. Louise Glazier............................ | Hartford, Conn. |
| Kathryn E. Golden............................ | Hartford, Conn. |
| Mary E. Grassier............................. | Hartford, Conn. |

| NAMES | RESIDENCES |
|-------|-----------|
| ALICE S. GRISWOLD | Hartford, Conn. |
| ANNIE C. GYDESEN | Austin, Tex. |
| ANNA L. HASTINGS | Smith College |
| ANNA A. HAWKESWORTH | Hartford, Conn. |
| MARY A. HENDRON | Hartford, Conn. |
| ALICE L. HILDEBRAND | Smith College |
| JANE E. HOLLISTER | Glastonbury, Conn. |
| C. ELINOR HULL | Mt. Holyoke College |
| BLANCHE JACKMAN | Hartford, Conn. |
| FLORENCE W. JACKSON | Hartford, Conn. |
| BLANCHE KASHMANN | Hartford, Conn. |
| FLORENCE M. KEMMERER | Hartford, Conn. |
| ETHEL B. KENYON | Smith College |
| MATILDA KRONSBERG | Hartford, Conn. |
| CLARA E. LANG | Wesleyan University |
| C. ESTELLA LAY.........Mrs. Herbert S. Colton, | Hartford, Conn. |
| RACHEL H. LEVENTHAL | Hartford, Conn. |
| SARA L. MARSHALL | Hartford, Conn. |
| ELIZABETH A. McADAMS | Hartford, Conn. |
| KATHARINE A. McKEOUGH | Hartford, Conn. |
| DAISY E. MINER | Hartford, Conn. |
| MARGARET R. MONTAGUE | Hartford, Conn. |
| JENNIE MOODY | Hartford, Conn. |
| BESSIE M. MOORE | Hartford, Conn. |
| GRACE T. MOORE | Hartford, Conn. |
| HELEN C. MORGAN | Hartford, Conn. |
| HELEN P. MOSES | Hartford, Conn. |
| JENNIE E. MULHALL | Hartford, Conn. |
| JANE E. MULLIGAN | Hartford, Conn. |
| MABELLE C. NEWTON | Hartford, Conn. |
| ETHEL M. POMEROY | Wellesley College |
| MADGE L. PRENDERGAST | Hartford, Conn. |
| EDNA A. RICHMOND | Hartford, Conn. |
| NELLIE A. RISLEY | Hartford, Conn. |
| NELLIE L. ROBBINS | Hartford, Conn. |
| BESSIE L. SCRANTON | Hartford, Conn. |
| HELEN A. SEYMOUR | Hartford, Conn. |
| M. LOUISE SEYMOUR | Mt. Holyoke College |
| MABEL R. SMITH | Belfast, Maine |
| MARTHA L. SPELLACY | Hartford, Conn. |
| FLORENCE C. SULLIVAN | Hartford, Conn. |
| MABEL H. TALCOTT | University of Michigan |
| CAROLYN B. TAYLOR | Hartford, Conn. |
| MARY G. TERRETT | Hartford, Conn. |
| ELIZABETH A. WATERS | Glastonbury, Conn. |
| M. ALICE WHEELER | Smith College |
| BABETTE WIEDER | Hartford, Conn. |
| MABEL A. WRIGHT | Died, 1903 |
| | |
| EDWARD W. ATKINS | Hartford, Conn. |
| HENRY G. BARBOUR | Trinity College |
| RAYMOND W. BARROWS | Hartford, Conn. |
| GARRETT D. BOWNE, JR | Trinity College |
| CLIFTON C. BRAINERD | Trinity College |
| ALBERT L. BROWN | Yale University |
| WILLIAM F. BROWN | Hartford, Conn. |

| NAMES | RESIDENCES |
|---|---|
| JOHN A. CAULKINS | Hartford, Conn. |
| FREDERICK A. CHAMPLIN | Hartford, Conn. |
| WILLIAM J. F. COSKER | Hartford, Conn. |
| HENRY N. COSTELLO | Yale University |
| PHILIP E. CURTISS | Trinity College |
| EVERETT M. DELABARRE | Amherst College |
| RICHARD H. DEMING | Yale University |
| LEON E. DIX | Tufts College |
| GEORGE N. FINLAY | Hartford, Conn. |
| JOHN F. GAFFEY | Hartford, Conn. |
| EDWARD T. GARVIN | Wethersfield, Conn. |
| HOWARD GOODWIN | Yale University |
| ARTHUR R. GRISWOLD | Yale University |
| WILLIAM H. HARRIS | Hartford, Conn. |
| DAVID B. HENNEY | Yale University |
| LEON R. JILLSON | Harvard University |
| ROBERT C. KENNEDY | Hartford, Conn. |
| JOSEPH H. LAWLER | Georgetown University |
| CARL E. LUNDIN | Hartford, Conn. |
| BURDETTE C. MAERCKLEIN | Trinity College |
| JOHN C. MAHON | Yale University |
| NICHOLAS J. McKONE | University of Pennsylvania |
| WILLIAM F. McKONE | Yale University |
| H. WYCKOFF MILLS | Harvard University |
| CLIFFORD B. MORCOM | Hartford, Conn. |
| MATTHEW N. NAHIGAN | Yale University |
| HORACE NORTH | Trinity College |
| JOHN F. NUGENT | Hartford, Conn. |
| CLEVELAND PERRY | Washington, D. C. |
| GEORGE B. POTTER | Yale University |
| JAMES W. ROBERTS | Amherst College |
| HAROLD W. ROGERS | Worcester Polytechnic Institute |
| CHARLES H. SAGE | Hartford, Conn. |
| RALPH W. SMILEY | Harvard University |
| CARLTON W. STARBUCK | Hartford, Conn. |
| RICHARD H. STARKWEATHER | Hartford, Conn. |
| HAROLD B. STILLMAN | Hartford, Conn. |
| SHELDON P. THACHER | Mass. Inst. of Technology |
| EDWIN W. TILLOTSON | Yale University |
| MORRIS TUCH | Bellevue Hosp. Med. College |
| JOSEPH H. TWICHELL | Yale University |
| R. LINCOLN TWITCHELL | Yale University |
| ROBERT L. WAITE | Yale University |
| WILLIAM W. WALKER | Stevens Inst. of Technology |
| RAYMOND W. WEBSTER | Hartford, Conn. |
| ALBERT D. WHAPLES | Newington Junction, Ct. |
| LEWIS B. WHITTEMORE | Yale University |
| RICHARD C. WILLIAMS | Worcester Polytechnic Institute |

## 1903

NITAMUR IN ALTUM

Lucy E. McCook, Corresponding Secretary

| | |
|---|---|
| RUTH E. ABBEY | Hartford, Conn. |
| MARJORIE ALLEN | Hartford, Conn. |
| HELEN E. BAKER | Hartford, Conn. |

| NAMES | RESIDENCES |
|---|---|
| KATHERINE R. BALMER | Hartford, Conn. |
| CLARA G. BARTLETT | East Hartford, Conn. |
| EDITH G. BLACK | Hartford, Conn. |
| BERTHA BONDY | Hartford, Conn. |
| LEILA M. BREWER | Hartford, Conn. |
| FLORENCE G. BRYANT | Wellesley College |
| ANNA L. BUCKLEY | Hartford, Conn. |
| ANNA E. BUTHS | Hartford, Conn. |
| ALICE J. CAMERON | Hartford, Conn. |
| JULIET L. CLAGHORN | Hartford, Conn. |
| ANNE ST. L. CLARY | Hartford, Conn. |
| SARA B. COLE | Hartford, Conn. |
| GRACE M. CULVER | Hartford, Conn. |
| DOROTHY W. DAVIS | Smith College |
| K ESTELLE DOYLE | Hartford, Conn. |
| FANNY L. EITEL | Hartford, Conn. |
| JESSIE L. FENN | Hartford, Conn. |
| ELIZABETH A. FORBES | Hartford, Conn. |
| INEZ F. FOX | Hartford, Conn. |
| KATHERINE E. GOLDBERG | Hartford, Conn. |
| MARY R. HALLIGAN | Rocky Hill, Conn. |
| MINNIE K. HASTINGS | Wellesley College |
| BESSIE E. HATCH | Hartford, Conn. |
| LOUISE M. HENNING | Hartford, Conn. |
| MABEL E. HICKMAN | Hampton Normal Institute |
| BEATRICE M. IRIBAS | Hartford, Conn. |
| CHARLOTTE T. ISHAM | Hartford, Conn. |
| CLARA B. JACOBS | Smith College |
| OLIVE B. JOHNSON | Hartford, Conn. |
| SUSIE A. KRAMER | Hartford, Conn. |
| MARY C. LINCKS | Hartford, Conn. |
| MARY J. LINNON | Hartford, Conn. |
| LOUISE A. MAHL | Hartford, Conn. |
| LUCY E. McCOOK | Hartford, Conn. |
| ELIZABETH C. MERRIAM | Hartford, Conn. |
| HELEN L. MERRIAM | Hartford, Conn. |
| PAULINA MERROW | Cornell University |
| RUTH W. MESSINGER | Hartford, Conn. |
| MARGUERITE MORRISON | Hartford, Conn. |
| CATHERINE E. MULCAHY | Hartford, Conn. |
| RACHEL F. MYERS | Hartford, Conn. |
| HELEN F. PARKER | Hartford, Conn. |
| LAURA H. POMEROY | Smith College |
| EDITH G. PURINTON | Died, 1904 |
| AGNES C. REID | Hartford, Conn. |
| RUTH ROBERTS | Hartford, Conn. |
| EVELYN B. ROBERTSON | Hartford, Conn. |
| ELIZA M. SAUNDERS | Hartford, Conn. |
| JULIA F. SMITH | Hartford, Conn. |
| MABEL C. STEEVES | Hartford, Conn. |
| MARJORIE G. STILLMAN | Hartford, Conn. |
| MAZIE I. STRANT | Hartford, Conn. |
| GRACE C. STRONG | Hartford, Conn. |
| ESTHER F. SUISMAN | Hartford, Conn. |
| ANTOINETTE F. TUTTLE | Hartford, Conn. |
| BERTHA M. WALLACE | Hartford, Conn. |

| NAMES | RESIDENCES |
|---|---|
| HELEN C. WAY | Hartford, Conn. |
| CHARLOTTE T. WELLES | Wethersfield, Conn. |
| RUTH M. WELLES | Mt. Holyoke College |
| FLORENCE M. WHITE | Hartford, Conn. |
| MARY E. WOLLERTON | Hartford, Conn. |
| EMMA E. WUNDER | Hartford, Conn. |
| | |
| ROBERT A. ANGUS | Mass. Inst. of Technology |
| HARRY S. BARTLETT | University of Michigan |
| GOODWIN B. BEACH | Harvard University |
| EUGENE L. BESTOR | New York Homeopathic Med. Coll. and Hospital |
| WILLIAM J. BLACK | Hartford, Conn. |
| CHESTER R. BROWN | New York Homeopathic Med. Coll. and Hospital |
| MORGAN G. BULKELEY, JR. | Yale University |
| HAROLD C. BURNHAM | Hartford, Conn. |
| RAYMOND H. CALLAHAN | Hartford, Conn. |
| WALTER D. CAMP | Hartford, Conn. |
| L. TOULMIN CHALKER | U. S. Navy |
| WARREN S. CHAPIN | Amherst College |
| FRANCIS D. CHILDS | Yale University |
| JOHN J. COX | Hartford, Conn. |
| WILLIAM F. CURRY | Hartford, Conn. |
| RALPH D. CUTLER | Yale University |
| CLINTON D. DEMING | Yale University |
| RAYMOND N. DICKINSON | University of Maine |
| EDWARD L. DONAGHUE | U. S. Navy |
| EVERETT S. FALLOW | Trinity College |
| ABRAHAM FISHER | Hartford, Conn. |
| EDWARD T. FITZGERALD | Hartford, Conn. |
| CLARENCE S. FOSTER | Amherst College |
| LOUIS H. GLADWIN | New York, N. Y. |
| RUSSELL GLADWIN | New York, N. Y. |
| GEORGE S. GLAZIER | Hartford, Conn. |
| SAMUEL J. GOLDBERG | Yale University |
| WILLIAM H. GOODWIN | Died, 1904 |
| PAUL H. GUILFOIL | Trinity College |
| WILLIAM F. GUNN, JR. | Yale University |
| JAMES W. GUNSHANAN | Hartford, Conn. |
| JOHN J. GUNSHANAN | Hartford, Conn. |
| KARL D. HOFER | Hartford, Conn. |
| ROBERT W. HUME | Yale University |
| ARTHUR E. JOYNER | Miami, Fla. |
| MICHAEL F. KEATING | Ecclesiastical Seminary, Piacenza, Italy |
| RICHARD B. KELLOGG | West Hartford, Conn. |
| JOSEPH I. KEMLER | Coll. of Physicians and Surgeons, Boston, Mass. |
| HAROLD M. KENYON | Hartford, Conn. |
| HORACE O. KILBOURN | Yale University |
| HAROLD B. KLINE | Yale University |
| GEORGE D. KNOX | Hartford, Conn. |
| LEROY A. LADD | West Hartford, Conn. |
| JAMES I. LATIMER | Yale University |
| FRANK E. LINNON | Hartford, Conn. |
| MITCHELL S. LITTLE | Yale University |
| C. LEROY MACK | Trinity College |
| OLIN F. McCORMICK | Wesleyan University |

| NAMES | RESIDENCES |
|---|---|
| JOHN A. MCKONE | University of Pennsylvania |
| HENRY E. MORRIS | Hartford, Conn. |
| ARTHUR G. NEWTON | Hartford, Conn. |
| RAYMOND T. PAUSCH | Harvard University |
| RAYMOND J. PEARD | Hartford, Conn. |
| DeWITT C. POND | Trinity College |
| HARVEY C. POND | Trinity College |
| JOHN F. PREU | Hartford, Conn. |
| HOWARD B. PURINTON | Died, 1905 |
| HAROLD W. RIGGS | Yale University |
| CLARENCE W. SEYMOUR | Yale University |
| CLARENCE S. SHERWOOD | Hartford, Conn. |
| ADRIAN B. SLOAN | Hartford, Conn. |
| CHARLES M. SMITH | Yale University |
| HERBERT J. STEANE | Yale University |
| CHARLES SUDARSKY | Hartford, Conn. |
| CHARLES F. TAYLOR | Yale University |
| W. LEROY ULRICH | Yale University |
| DONALD B. WELLS | Yale University |
| GILBERT R. WENTWORTH | Trinity College |
| ROBERT G. WHITE | Yale University |
| G. MORTON WOLFE | Buffalo, N. Y. |
| JOHN C. WOODS | Hartford, Conn. |
| FRED F. WOOLLEY | Yale University |
| HAROLD O. WOOLLEY | Stevens Inst. of Technology |
| THOMAS G. WRIGHT, JR. | Yale University |

## 1904

### HODIE, NON CRAS

ALICE K. O'CONNOR, Corresponding Secretary

| | |
|---|---|
| KATHARINE ADAMS | Tufts College |
| MAUDE E. AGARD | Hartford, Conn. |
| MINNIE B. AISHBERG | Hartford, Conn. |
| CHARLOTTE ALTON | Hartford, Conn. |
| LOIS ANGELL | Vassar College |
| ANNA M. BACHMEYER | Hartford, Conn. |
| HELEN C. BACKES | Hartford, Conn. |
| MARJORIE H. BARROWS | Hartford, Conn. |
| MARY C. BLODGETT | Hartford, Conn. |
| FAITH F. BOLLES | Mt. Holyoke College |
| FLORENCE H. BOWERS | Rocky Hill, Conn. |
| FLORENCE CARTER | Hartford, Conn. |
| HELEN H. CHLOPKOWIAK | Hartford, Conn. |
| FANNIE E. COHEN | Hartford, Conn. |
| MARGUERITE W. COTTER | Hartford, Conn. |
| MARY M. COUGHLIN | Hartford, Conn. |
| GERTRUDE A. COWLISHAW | Hartford, Conn. |
| SARA E. DALEY | Hartford, Conn. |
| MAE E. DIBBLE | Hartford, Conn. |
| GRACE V. DIX | Hartford, Conn. |
| JOSEPHINE M. DRAGO | Hartford, Conn. |
| SADIE A. DUGGAN | Hartford, Conn. |
| EVA E. FAIRFIELD | Hartford, Conn. |

| NAMES | RESIDENCES |
|---|---|
| MAUD L. GALER | Hartford, Conn. |
| NELLIE B. GARVIN | Hartford, Conn. |
| MABEL J. GAUTHIER | Hartford, Conn. |
| JESSICA B. GORMAN | Hartford, Conn. |
| HELEN E. GRAVES | Vassar College |
| ETHEL W. HALE | Hartford, Conn. |
| LOTTIE E. HALE | Hartford, Conn. |
| FLORENCE C. HALL | Hartford, Conn. |
| JOHANNE HANSEN | Hartford, Conn. |
| MARION B. HARRIS | Hartford, Conn. |
| LAURA K. HATCH | Hartford, Conn. |
| MARY A. HEFFERNAN | Hartford, Conn. |
| CLARA F. HEINS | Hartford, Conn. |
| JEANNIE HEPPLE | Hartford, Conn. |
| ADA T. HEUBLEIN | Hartford, Conn. |
| ROSE A. HUBBARD | Windsor, Conn. |
| MURIEL A. JILLSON | Hartford, Conn. |
| MARY E. L. JOHNSON | Hartford, Conn. |
| LILLIAN E. JONES | Hartford, Conn. |
| GLADYS A. JUDD | Hartford, Conn. |
| MILDRED A. JUDD | Hartford, Conn. |
| HELEN B. KEYES | Vassar College |
| MARY E. KILFOIL | Hartford, Conn. |
| AVIS KNIGHT | Mt. Holyoke College |
| LILLIAN C. KOCH | Hartford, Conn. |
| PAULINE E. LEVY | Hartford, Conn. |
| GERTRUDE M. MAGUIRE | Hartford, Conn. |
| ALICE E. MAHL | Hartford, Conn. |
| GERTRUDE E. MAHL | Hartford, Conn. |
| JESSIE M. McCREARY | Hartford, Conn. |
| FLORENCE E. MILLER | Bloomfield, Conn. |
| ALICE L. MOSES | Hartford, Conn. |
| ELLEN A. MULLIGAN | Hartford, Conn. |
| EDWINA A. NAEDELE | Hartford, Conn. |
| ALICE M. O'BRIEN | Hartford, Conn. |
| ALICE K. O'CONNOR | Hartford, Conn. |
| BLANCHE M. PEBERDY | Smith College |
| LOUISE PEILER | Hartford, Conn. |
| FLORENCE B. PINNEY | Hartford, Conn. |
| GRACE M. PINNEY | Hartford, Conn. |
| EDITHE PRUTTING | Hartford, Conn. |
| FLORENCE E. RILEY | Hartford, Conn. |
| KATE RIST | East Hartford, Conn. |
| ALICE S. ROBERTS | Hartford, Conn. |
| ADELAIDE H. ROBERTSON | Hartford, Conn. |
| MABEL E. RUSSELL | Hartford, Conn. |
| EDITH V. SANFORD | Hartford, Conn. |
| ALICE E. SCOTT | Hartford, Conn. |
| MARGUERITE B. SMITH | Hartford, Conn. |
| LENA SPORER | Hartford, Conn. |
| ANNA B. STILLMAN | Rocky Hill, Conn. |
| ORA B. STODDARD | Newington, Conn. |
| GERTRUDE H. TAUSSIG | Hartford, Conn. |
| MARGERY B. TAYLOR | Hartford, Conn. |
| ALICE M. THRALL | Windsor, Conn. |
| MARY VAN ZILE | Hartford, Conn. |

| NAMES | RESIDENCES |
|---|---|
| FLORENCE M. WADSWORTH | Hockanum, Conn. |
| MARJORIE A. WALL | Hartford, Conn. |
| MABEL S. WARNER | Wethersfield, Conn. |
| MILLIE F. WASHBURN | Hartford, Conn. |
| TILLIE I. WASHBURN | Hartford, Conn. |
| MARY L. WEAVER | Hartford, Conn. |
| ETHEL M. WEBB | Simmons College, Boston, Mass. |
| CHARLOTTE M. WIGGIN | Smith College |
| DAISY E. WILBUR | Hartford, Conn. |
| MARY C. WILCOX | Hartford, Conn. |
| MILDRED WILLIAMS | Glastonbury, Conn. |
| FLORENCE P. WOOLLEY | Hartford, Conn. |
| ISABEL WYCKOFF | Hartford, Conn. |
| | |
| EDWARD F. AHEARN | Hartford, Conn. |
| CARLETON M. ALLEN | Yale University |
| NATHANIEL K. ALLISON | East Granby, Conn. |
| CHANNING BACALL | Harvard University |
| SAUL BERMAN | Trinity College |
| CHARLES B. BROWN | Hartford, Conn. |
| LOUIS S. BUTHS | Trinity College |
| H. BISSELL CAREY | Yale University |
| MORRIS B. CLARK | Hartford, Conn. |
| FREDERIC J. CORBETT | Trinity College |
| CHARLES M. CRAWFORD, JR | University of Pennsylvania |
| FERDINAND D'ESOPO | Yale University |
| ROBERT B. ENGLISH | Yale University |
| FRANCIS J. FLYNN | Hartford, Conn. |
| CARL G. F. FRANZÉN | University of Pennsylvania |
| WILLIAM H. GILBERT | Trinity College |
| RALPH E. GOODWIN | Yale University |
| CLARENCE L. GOWEN | Hartford, Conn. |
| HAROLD W. GRISWOLD | Mass. Inst. of Technology |
| EDMUND HELLMANN | Hartford, Conn. |
| MAYO D. HERSEY | Mass. Inst. of Technology |
| ELTON B. HILL | Yale University |
| THOMAS HOOKER | Yale University |
| ROGER H. HOVEY | Hartford, Conn. |
| HENRY W. INGLE | Hartford, Conn. |
| CHARLES E. JONES, JR | Cornell Univ. Med. Coll., New York, N. Y. |
| HAROLD B. KEYES | Yale University |
| PAUL P. KIMBALL | Hartford, Conn. |
| GEORGE W. KING | West Hartford, Conn. |
| LESTER H. KING | West Hartford, Conn. |
| ARCHER E. KNOWLTON | Hartford, Conn. |
| CLARENCE M. KNOX | Yale University |
| L. ROLAND LORD | University of Maine |
| CARL A. MAHL | Hartford, Conn. |
| RAYMOND J. MAPLESDEN | Trinity College |
| JOSEPH B. MARTIN | Hartford, Conn. |
| ARTHUR C. MASON | Windsor, Conn. |
| HARRY D. MATHER | Hartford, Conn. |
| CHARLES W. McKONE | Trinity College |
| LEON B. MEAD | Hartford, Conn. |
| WILFORD B. MUCKLOW | Hartford, Conn. |

| NAMES | RESIDENCES |
|---|---|
| MICHAEL S. O'DONOHUE | Hartford, Conn. |
| JAMES J. PAGE | Trinity College |
| EDGAR B. PECK | Hartford, Conn. |
| HOWARD S. PORTER | Trinity College |
| HARRY A. RAPELYE | Mass. Inst. of Technology |
| WILLIAM J. REID | Hartford, Conn. |
| HAROLD K. REMINGTON | Hartford, Conn. |
| HAROLD E. ROBBINS | Trinity College |
| JAMES R. ROBERTSON | Hartford, Conn. |
| CHESTER S. ROHNE | Yale University |
| CHARLES SCHIRM | Hartford, Conn. |
| CLEVELAND C. SOPER | Hartford, Conn. |
| B. HALSEY SPENCER | Hartford, Conn. |
| ROBERT W. STEVENS | Trinity College |
| CHARLES N. ST. JOHN | Harvard University |
| HORACE V. S. TAYLOR | Yale University |
| MYRTON J. TURNBULL | Hartford, Conn. |
| PHILIP S. WAINWRIGHT | Yale University |
| RALPH W. WAITE | Cornell University |
| LESLIE B. WATERHOUSE | Trinity College |
| HAROLD M. WEBSTER | Hartford, Conn. |
| ALDEN WELLS | Yale University |
| STEPHEN F. WILLARD, JR | Wethersfield, Conn. |
| CHARLES G. WILLIAMS | Hartford, Conn. |
| ROBERT M. YERGASON | Trinity College |

# TABULAR STATEMENT OF GRADUATES FROM 1854

(See note, page 65)

---

| CLASS | Entered | Graduated | Per Cent Graduated |
|---|---|---|---|
| 1854 | 166 | 3 | 2 |
| 1855 | 104 | 8 | 7 |
| 1856 | 86 | 14 | 16 |
| 1857 | 88 | 0 | 0 |
| 1858 | 75 | 21 | 28 |
| 1859 | 90 | 3 | 3 |
| 1860 | 151 | 22 | 14 |
| 1861 | 144 | 12 | 8 |
| 1862 | 100 | 33 | 33 |
| 1863 | 138 | 15 | 10 |
| 1864 | 139 | 21 | 15 |
| 1865 | 108 | 22 | 20 |
| 1866 | 110 | 22 | 20 |
| 1867 | 132 | 14 | 10 |
| 1868 | 132 | 33 | 25 |
| 1869 | 120 | 31 | 25 |
| 1870 | 133 | 31 | 23 |
| 1871 | 150 | 26 | 17 |
| 1872 | 151 | 36 | 24 |
| 1873 | 156 | 45 | 28 |
| 1874 | 174 | 46 | 27 |
| 1875 | 193 | 48 | 25 |
| 1876 | 183 | 51 | 27 |
| 1877 | 172 | 53 | 31 |
| 1878 | 165 | 76 | 46 |
| 1879 | 183 | 56 | 30 |
| 1880 | 196 | 63 | 32 |
| 1881 | 184 | 61 | 33 |
| 1882 | 208 | 72 | 34 |
| 1883 | 200 | 62 | 31 |
| 1884 | 202 | 71 | 35 |
| 1885 | 205 | 73 | 36 |
| 1886 | 160 | 68 | 43 |
| 1887 | 202 | 67 | 33 |
| 1888 | 208 | 87 | 42 |
| 1889 | 221 | 89 | 40 |
| 1890 | 194 | 65 | 34 |
| 1891 | 196 | 76 | 39 |
| 1892 | 240 | 104 | 43 |
| 1893 | 261 | 95 | 37 |
| 1894 | 284 | 100 | 36 |
| 1895 | 276 | 108 | 39 |
| 1896 | 267 | 109 | 41 |

| CLASS | Entered | Graduated | Per Cent Graduated |
|---|---|---|---|
| 1897 | 299 | 101 | 34 |
| 1898 | 316 | 96 | 30 |
| 1899 | 308 | 111 | 36 |
| 1900 | 315 | 115 | 37 |
| 1901 | 293 | 110 | 38 |
| 1902 | 301 | 131 | 44 |
| 1903 | 353 | 139 | 39 |
| 1904 | 383 | 158 | 41 |

Per cent of pupils graduated from 1854 to 1864 . . . . 11.5
"      "      "      "    1864 to 1874 . . . . 21.1
"      "      "      "    1874 to 1884 . . . . 31.6
"      "      "      "    1884 to 1894 . . . . 38.1
"      "      "      "    1894 to 1904 inclusive . . 37.6

Number of graduates from 1854 to 1864 . . . . . . 131
"      "      "    1864 to 1874 . . . . . . 281
"      "      "    1874 to 1884 . . . . . . 588
"      "      "    1884 to 1894 . . . . . . 795
"      "      "    1894 to 1904 inclusive . . . . 1,278

Whole number of graduates from 1848 — Men . . . . . 1,338
"      "      "      "    1848 — Women . . . . 1,790

         Total . . . . . . . . . . . 3,128
Deceased . . . . . . . . . . . . 306

# NAMES OF PUPILS

## SENIOR CLASS

Elizabeth F. Ahern
Anna R. Allis
Clara C. Angus
Mabelle A. Bissell
Agnes M. N. Broughel
Gladys Brower
Annie G. Brown
Annie L. Burns
Mary E. Burns
Esther J. Cady
Mary C. Carey
Marguerite B. Church
Edna M. Clark
Annie M. Cleveland
Ethel Clogston
Marion A. Collins
Hannah Cornfield
Catherine A. M. Coughlin
Mildred Covell
Marion C. Cross
Erma L. Culver
K. Leah Danforth
Eva S. Davis
Mary E. Dillon
Sarah R. Dunham
Helen F. Dwyer
Josephine Dwyer
Agnes G. Egan

Alice H. Farmer
Marion Flagg
Mary C. Fox
Nettie M. Gauthier
Bridget A. Glynn
Dulce Green
Elizabeth R. Harris
Marion E. Hosford
Marjorie F. Howe
Louise G. Hyde
Christine M. Johnson
Helen G. Johnson
Ruth Johnson
Florence J. King
Martha E. King
Sarah Koppelman
Agnes E. Kullgren
Olga R. Kullgren
Mable E. Laraway
Emilie E. Leschke
Rachel S. Leventhal
Irene R. Marcy
Margretta Martin
Mary A. McCarthy
Hazel M. McClunie
Elizabeth A. McDonnell
Helena F. Miller
Jean Mitchell

Mabel Moore
Mary Noack
Helen V. Noonan
Florence E. Oatman
Sarah T. Plummer
Florence P. Roper
Sarah E. Sears
Edith M. Seidler
Helen M. Seidler
Minnie E. Selby
Martha C. Smith
Elsie F. Steinheimer
Florence L. Stronach
Mary A. Sullivan
Arline D. Taintor
Grace H. Taylor
Lulu M. Toohey
Anna V. Toomey
Elinor M. Utley
Nellie W. Viets
Mabelle E. Wander
Sarah A. Ward
Elizabeth H. C. Warner
Marion M. Welch
Emily A. Welles
Annie Wiggin
Imogene M. H. Winter

Paul H. Barbour
O. Lamson Beach
Claude G. Beardslee
Harold C. Bird
Henry L. Bunce, Jr.
William L. Burdick
Raymond M. Burnham
Hollis S. Candee
Frank T. Case
Clifford W. Caulkins
Walter E. Claussen
Chauncey F. Cleveland
Michael A. Connor
William F. Costello
William T. Coyle
Alexander W. Creedon
Edward W. Creighton

William Dwyer
Charles P. Eddy
Paul H. Elsdon
Morris Falk
Hart C. Fenn
Oliver D. Filley
Montague Flagg
E. Selden Geer, Jr.
Charles Gildersleeve
James G. Goodell
Robert N. Griswold
Edward W. Gustafson
Francis H. Hafey
William J. Hamersley
Lewis G. Harriman
Benjamin R. Hawley
Victor Hellmann

Joseph K. Hooker
Robert M. Keeney
Joseph B. Kilbourn
Robert B. King
Charles H. Latham, Jr.
William H. Linton
Robert L. Mason
Robert H. Mather
Thomas C. McKone
Thomas J. Molloy
Harry A. Moran
Allan P. Northend
Solomon Poriss
Warren C. Pratt
Philip W. Raymond
Karl A. Reiche
George W. Roberts

Paul Roberts
Vernon H. Salmon
Arthur H. Samuels
Bertram I. Seward
Owen L. Seward

Mark Skinner
Henry D. Smith
Alfred J. Stafford
Arthur R. St. John
Henry W. Swettenham

Nelson C. Taintor
Percy P. Taylor
Douglas H. Thomson
Meade Wildrick

Girls 83     Boys 65     Total 148

## JUNIOR CLASS

Vera G. Allen
Gertrude Anderson
Grace E. Anderson
Barnekah Angell
Anna M. Bentz
Ethel L. Bonner
A. Louise Brainerd
Caroline E. Braun
Clara M. Bull
Hazel H. Burnham
Signa E. Byorkman
Sadie J. Callahan
Ida M. Case
Harriet J. Chaffee
Mary E. Clark
Bessie Climan
Edith J. Clogston
Sarah I. Cohn
Ruth I. Connover
Freida C. Creighton
Lena M. Crowell
Charlotte M. Culver
Agnes B. Cummings
Estelle P. Cushman
Katherine M. Daly
Helen B. Ericson
Myrtle E. Fallow
M. Louise Farnham
Hazel M. Felty
Alma E. Ferguson
Mary Fisher
Anna E. Franzén
Alice R. Gillette
Mary H. Gladding
Ruth F. Glazier

Elma K. Graul
Annetta H. Hansen
Lucy A. Harbison
Eva M. Hartz
Stella E. Hicks
Philena H. Hinckley
Agnes M. Hogan
Rose Hollings
Eleanor M. Horan
Constance H. Hungerford.
Elsie M. Hurlbut
Miriam E. G. Johnson
Grace A. Jones
Mary J. Kerwin
Alice M. Kinney
Bertha J. Libby
Annie C. Lincks
Marie Macbeth
Ethel E. Marsh
Lena H. Marshall
Mary E. McCann
Helen E. McCarthy
Grace S. McKinney
Florence E. McLaughlin
Leah Miller
Irene H. Mix
Hazel A. Moore
Nina W. Morgan
Helen E. Nemiah
Helen M. O'Connor
Margaret M. E. O'Neill
Grace Parkes
Madeline S. Parkhurst
Harriette O. Patterson
Jennie H. Peterson

Rhoda L. Phillips
Elsa B. Pomeroy
Mae E. Price
Marie R. Prutting
Harriet E. Rankin
Lydia E. Reid
Mary S. Robbins
Alfreda M. Schneider
Susie G. Sloan
Clarabel V. Smith
Maud Smith
Irene E. Squires
Clara M. Stedman
Mamie L. Steinmetz
Bertha M. Stengelin
Norma F. Stoughton
Elsa M. Strong
Bertha F. Thompson
Bessie L. Tillotson
Geneva H. Trumbull
Louise Warner
Mary W. Watkinson
Eleanor M. Welles
Margaret D. Welles
Mary W. Welles
Florence A. Westphal
Laura Wheeler
Norma L. White
Katherine A. Williams
Grace E. Willson
Alice C. Wilson
Mary N. Winslow
Prudence M. Wood

John A. Adams
Carlton B. Barnard
George R. Bestor
Lester A. Bosworth
Louis N. Brody
Francis L. C. Buckley
Edmund P. Burke
George C. Capen
F. Donald Carpenter
Robert P. Carter

Harold B. Chapman
Louis G. Charter
Harold L. Clark
*Charles Cohen
Samuel M. Cohen
Robert T. Costello
William W. Cotter
Frank N. Crane
Edward J. Daly
H. Frederick Day

Frederick D. Dean
William Dorenbaum
Francis T. Fenn
Aaron Fien
George S. Francis
Harold D. Fuller
Harold C. Green
Jacob D. Greenberg
Lewis Gross
Thomas Hewes

* Died Nov. 28, 1904.

Arthur S. Hildebrand
John M. Holcombe, Jr.
Harry H. Howard
Herbert W. Huber
Robert A. Hungerford
Frank Johnston
Harold L. Johnstone
John J. Kennedy
Thomas P. Kennedy
Frederick H. Kenyon
Richard R. King
Arthur Kline
Frederick H. Koch
Alexander Lennox
Peter A. LeRoy
August H. Leschke
Raymond G. Lincoln
Henry J. Marks
Jacob Masur
Morton B. Miner

William L. Montague
Richard E. Moore
Allyn R. Munger
William B. G. Naedele
Arthur F. Newton
Peter E. Nielsen
Walter T. O'Donohue
Alfred W. Peard
Harlan D. Pomeroy
Donald B. Prentice
Harry E. Rau
James J. Riordon
Edward C. Roberts
Philip Roberts
Walter Roberts
Rudolph F. Roloff
Harold C. Rood
Samuel Rosenthal
John F. Sagarino
Douglas T. Smith

Irving W. Smith
O. Harrison Smith
Arthur H. Soper
George Squires
Harold H. Storrs
Alec G. Stronach
Raymond H. Sullivan
Harry F. Sweet
John H. T. Sweet, Jr.
Charles C. Tomlinson, Jr.
Jacob Vogel
David Weinerman
Andrew Welch
J. Newell Welch
Raymond P. Wheeler
Fred E. Wiley
Howard C. Wiley
Franklin O. Williams
William J. Witschen
Dayton T. Wyckoff

Girls 103     Boys 90     Total 193

## THIRD CLASS

Jessie L. Abrams
Carolan Alton
Madeline L. Andrews
Florence A. Atkins
Mabel I. Baker
Mercedes E. Balfe
Helen L. Bartlett
Bertha J. Beaudoin
Florence Benedict
Annie C. Berry
Emma C. Berry
Carrie E. Bonner
Anna M. Bowen
Charlotte S. Brainerd
Clara E. Bray
Bertha L. Britten
Gertrude M. Brott
Fannie E. Brown
Florence M. Brown
Helen I. Brown
M. Louise Buckland
Florence E. Burton
Caroline F. Camp
Cora M. Chatfield
Rose Cheesick
Agnes E. Christie
Louise C. Clancy
Ruth H. Colby
Maud A. Coleman
Mary M. Collins
Jane M. Conway
Margaret G. Coughlin

Myra D. Cross
Marjorie L. Cummings
Ellen C. Cunningham
Helen M. Curtiss
Anna V. Daly
Catherine M. Daly
Edith L. Davis
Frances L. Davis
Dora I. Day
Ellen C. Donley
Marion L. Dow
Ethel M. Down
Emily A. Dwyer
Helen F. Egan
Marion T. Fitzgerald
Helen F. Fogerty
Irma Fontaine
Elizabeth J. Gibson
Ethel B. Gilbert
Minnie B. Gilnack
Fanny L. Gladding
Vera A. Green
Helen M. Greer
Jessie Griffing
Grace E. Griffiths
Viola V. Gruninger
Susan G. Halliday
Sarah F. Harrison
Frances M. Hartman
Wilhelmina E. Herman
Mary P. Herzer
Faith G. Holcomb

Grace E. Jackson
Jean A. Jackson
Clara L. Jenkins
Ethel M. Jennings
Emily Joslyn
Eleanor M. Joy
Helen G. Judge
Fannie Kashmann
Hester M. Kibbe
Elizabeth A. Killin
Abbie J. Langrish
Carmeleita T. Latimer
Grace Lombard
Ethel H. Love
Bernice L. Loveland
Mary E. Loydon
Eleanor Macbeth
Alice M. MacLeod
Lillian E. Martin
Susie E. Martin
Marion F. Maxfield
Ethel F. May
Kate H. Mayo
Mae R. McEntee
Clara McFetridge
Mary J. McGinn
Genevieve L. Mead
Ellen E. Merrow
Beatrice R. Metcalfe
Elsie G. Miller
Annie R. Moore
Marjorie P. Moore

Carrie W. Moses
Ruth Moyer
Anna G. Murphy
Mary C. Murphy
Jennie C. Murtaugh
Abbie R. Newberry
Inez V. Newberry
Karen M. Nielsen
Lucy B. O'Connor
Pearl M. O'Keefe
Katarina M. Outerson
Florence M. Ozon
Ida B. Parker
Marion A. Parker
Idah A. Peck
Hortense I. Perry
Cora B. Pierce .
Edyth L. Pindar
Rose E. Pinkham
Bessie Pintus

Kristine Rask
Katherine A. Riley
Marion H. Roberts
Annie I. Robertson
Katherine L. Rowe
Etta F. Ruffkess
Annie B. Sanford
Clara E. Sears
Carolyn B. Segalla
Mary Shaw
Maude S. Simonds
Florence E. Simpson
Adele R. Smith
Emma V. Snider
Ethel M. Spencer
Mabel I. Sponsel
Marjorie A. Stevens
Bessie B. Stoner
Georgia S. Strant
Lucy E. Strant

Elsie V. Taylor
Esther Taylor
Daisy F. Tobey
Grace L. Townsend
Louise R. Tracy
Emma M. Trebbe
Olive E. Ulrich
Mary E. Wade
Susan J. Wade
Katchen M. Wagner
Louise S. Warren
Katharine R. Westphal
Alice L. White
Jennie L. White
Marion H. White
Hazel C. Wiseman
Carolyn M. Woolley
Laura V. Wooster

Willis F. Abbey
Robert C. Allen
Arthur H. Badeau
Charles H. Bardons
Walter E. Batterson
J. Watson Beach
Howard W. Beardsley
Isaac Becker
Erle M. Beebe
William Berman
Frederick H. Bidwell
Charles E. Blake
Charles K. Bragaw
N. Howard Brewer
Francis P. Britt
U. Hayden Brockway, Jr.
St. Clair Bromfield
Clarence H. Browne
Malcolm G. Buckland
Wesley H. Bucklee
Ralph C. Bulkley
De Witt M. Bull
Vere I. Burdick
Ray U. Carpenter
Jesse L. Case
Sherman Cawley
Joseph B. Champlin
Martin J. Cleary
Francis W. Cowles
Dennis J. Coyle, Jr. .
William H. Cronin
Andrew C. Culver
Malcolm W. Davis
Winfred G. Deming
C. Harold Dodge

Edward B. Duffy
Robert W. Dwyer
Philip G. Eaton
Harry L. Edlin
Frederick B. Edwards, Jr.
Frederic Emens
James P. English
Earl E. Ensign
Herman J. Fenselan
Harry J. Foster
Leon R. Foster
Rudolph H. Fox
Philip M. Freeman
Charles W. Gaines     .
Davis Glater
Albert E. Goethner
Henry K. Goldstein
Sidney N. Greenberg
James P. Greer
John F. Griffin
Ray M. Griffin
Charles D. Griswold
Henry S. Griswold
Samuel A. Griswold
James E. Gross
Edward T. Guinan
Thomas C. Gunshanan
William E. Haaser
Frank S. Hart
Frederick H. Hartleben
Raymond H. Hartz
Robert D. Hastings
Rudolph C. Hauert
John M. Hayden
William J. Hickmott, Jr.

Irving W. Hicks
Asa A. Hollings
Lewis Hollings
John T. Horan
Thomas E. Hughes
George H. Humphrey
Harold C. Jaquith
Percy C. Jencks
Ervin D. Johnson
Philip J. Jones
Richard P. Jones
Edward W. Keefe
Austin J. Kilbourn
Jonathan F. Kilbourn
John M. Kingsley
Harold L. Klein
Louis Kofsky
Joseph I. Kopelman
William J. Langdon
John F. Lawler
Thomas H. Lawler
William S. Lines, Jr.
Paul G. Macy
Clarence H. Mahl
Robert H. Martin
Warren S. Mather
Frederick R. McKernan
William B. B. McKone
Donald J. McRonald
Clarence G. Mellen
Arthur B. Mercer
John G. G. Merrow
Robert J. Metzger
William J. Mills
Eugene F. Mitchell

Philip H. Moss
Jasper R. Moulton
Francis J. Murphy
Clifford R. Murray
James P. Murray
Theodore C. Naedele
Ernest M. J. Oakley
Patrick J. O'Connor
Roderick O'Connor
Oliver Parkes
George T. Patterson
Clarence H. Pearl
Everett L. Pease
Grafton M. Peberdy
Arthur R. Peck
Howard L. Peck
Clarence L. Perkins
Harry L. Perkins
Dexter S. Phelps, Jr.
Simon F. Phillips

James Porteus
Wilbur C. Prior
Harry K. Rees
Edwin H. Richards
Leslie H. Richmond
G. Sherman Ripley
Ralph H. Roberts
Walter K. M. Rodgers
Edwin E. Sage
W. Clifford Sage
Charles T. Sanford
William O. Sanford
Louis E. Schoenborn
John H. Scoville
Harold C. Scranton
Raymond H. Segur
Abraham M. Shapiro
Eugene D. J. Shaw
Wilton W. Sherman
Jacob Shulansky

Allan K. Smith
Thomas S. Smith
Karl L. Sommer
Charles S. Spencer
Lawrence E. Stevens
C. Wardell St. John
Arthur N. Story
Robert C. Stoughton
John Strempfer
Paul H. Taylor
Robert E. Vail
Edward B. VanZile
Edwin V. Vedder, Jr.
John C. Warner
Arthur B. Watson
Edward F. Welch
Guy P. Wilcox
Frank E. Wilson
Francis Winslow, Jr.
Clarence S. Zipp

Girls 154        Boys 165        Total 319

## FOURTH CLASS

Margaret M. Ahern
Viola M. Allen
Florence W. Archer
Blanche E. Atwood
Louise E. Atwood
Marion F. Barker
Edith T. Bartlett
Elsie N. Bauer
Ethel M. Beeman
Inza W. Bennett
Anna A. Bergenholtz
Alice G. Bernard
Helen J. Bolf
Elsie M. Bolles
Leah E. Bowdoin
Olive Boynton
Pauline R. Breslav
Mary H. Britt
Nettie E. Brody
Dorothy Brown
Grace D. Browne
Lisla A. Buckland
Edith M. Burdick
Helen Burdick
Florence E. Busch
Mildred A. Butts
Margaret C. Byrne
Mary J. Cairns
Helen D. Calhoun
Margherita T. Carey
Marjorie Case
Florence E. Cederberg

Matilda E. Chesky
Theresa H. Clancy
Mildred E. Clark
Florence L. Claussen
Marion L. Cleveland
Anna T. Code
Katherine C. Coffey
Marguerite G. Coleman
Anna F. Cosgrove
Flora E. Crane
Mary E. Crombie
Sophia Crost
Helen D. Crowley
Marion S. Cummings
Frances J. Curtin
M. Louise Curtin
Claribel S. Curtis
Helen T. Daly
Marie K. Daly
Emma W. Daniels
Lillie A. Day
Etta M. Dimon
Madalene F. Dow
Alice I. Downing
Frances C. Dunham
Mary J. Dunne
Augusta E. Elkin
Mary E. Elwood
Marion Feinberg
Sarah G. Finley
Catherine M. Foley
Helene Z. Fossum

M. Florence Franzén
M. Florence Gaffey
Mary E. Gaffey
Leslie A. Garvin
Jennie E. Gleszer
Margery Goddard
Smeralda A. I. Godin
Celia T. Goldberg
Grace Goldberg
Cornelia W. Goldenblum
Margaret T. Grady
Annie E. Greenberg
C. Estelle Greene
Florence W. Griswold
Sarah M. Guilfoil
Enola M. Hale
Anne B. Hansling
Ruth Harrison
Alma S. Hastings
Carrie L. Hastings
Helen Hatch
Helen E. Haviland
Effie N. Hazard
Mabel E. Henry
Annie Herron
Mary F. Hewins
Helen J. Higgins
Helen M. Hodge
May E. Hoey
Katherine L. Hogan
Marjorie M. Howe
Ellen C. Hughes

Pauline G. Hughes
Anna A. Hynes
Luisita Iribas
Grace L. Jacks
May E. Jackson
Alma A. Jaeger
Elizabeth E. Jewett
Esther A. Johnson
Gertrude M. Johnson
Marion A. Johnson
Marguerite L. Jones
Wilhelmina J. Kalausch
Martha J. Kane
Sadie C. Kane
Helen M. Kearney
Nellie M. Keating
Christina R. Keleher
Hilda M. Keller
Lucy A. Kelly
May A. Kennedy
Alice M. Kenyon
Dorothy Kenyon
Edith King
Matilda N. Kirkpatrick
Edith Knight
Esther A. Kullgren
Lillian H. Lang
Mary C. Langdon
Edith Lasher
Gwendolynne P. Laub
Anna M. Leahy
May L. Leggett
Annie C. Lennox
Josephine A. Lincks
E. Gladys Lincoln
Frieda A. Litz
Rena L. Lohmes
Florence G. Long
Marion C. Maercklein
Anna J. Magee
Catherine T. Maher
Lottie M. Mahl
Elizabeth A. D. Mahon
Sadie Malley
Florence E. Mather
Madeleine H. Matzen
Reise A. Maxfield
Mary Mayo
K. May McBeth
Nellie E. McCarthy
Winifred J. McCarthy
Winifred J. McCarty
Mary T. McDonald
Blanche R. McEvoy

M. Estelle McGill
Annie C. McNally
Maude Meacham
Elsa C. Mellgren
Caroline W. Merriam
Ruth S. Miller
Florence Mills
Blanche Mitchell
Esther T. Molin
Gertrude E. Morrill
Elisabeth R. Morrison
Helen R. Morrison
Rachel Morton
Ella L. Mulcahy
Esther B. Murray
Johanna B. A. Neumann
Florence M. O'Brien
Mary A. O'Connor
Loraine A. Osborn
Susie E. Packard
Lucy Parker
Mabel Parkes
Helen J. Peck
Jeannette A. Perrault
Alice C. Phillips
Gertrude L. Pond
Lena E. Popp
Elizabeth B. Post
Hazel F. Prentiss
Violet H. Ray
Helen G. Raymond
Mary E. Redigan
Mary A. Rees
Mary E. Reilly
Frances A. Rieckel
Fay L. Robbins
Helen H. Roberts
Marguerite Rockwell
Grace I. Rogers
Helen S. Rose
Sarah F. Rosen
Helena S. Rosenthal
Elsie L. Rothschild
Loretta E. Ryan
Florence M. Salzer
Leila D. Samson
Helen A. Saunders
R. Helen Schmelz
Louise E. Schoepflin
Fayoline Sedgwick
Edith D. Seymour
Agnes C. Shaughnessy
Agnes F. Sheridan
Mary Silverman

Edith A. Simmons
Tirzah J. Sisson
Bessie B. Smith
Elsie L. Smith
Mary H. Smith
Grace E. Sponsel
Marie B. Sproat
Edith L. Stengelin
Rhoda F. Stillman
Annette M. St. John
Josephine F. St. John
Janet T. Stone
Louise H. Stratton
Grace I. Strickland
Fannie W. Strong
Netta M. Strohg
Helen I. Sullivan
Mae G. Sullivan
Mary J. Sullivan
Elizabeth A. Swettenham
Ida F. Swift
Sarah H. Swift
Florence E. Taylor
Edith R. Thompson
Sadie J. Thompson
Sarah I. Thompson
Dora M. Tobias
Helen A. Tracy
Grace M. Treadwell
Mary E. Treat
G. Inez Tuttle
Florence M. VanGompf
Sally VanZile
Clara E. Viets
Gertrude M. Wade
Edith Wallace
Evelyn L. Wander
Josephine E. Ward
Olive H. Watkinson
Minnie J. Weisner
Anna D. Welch
Marion Welles
Sadie E. Wenick
Elizabeth G. White
Miriam Whitney
Anna Wiener
Helen W. Wilbur
Lela M. Wiley
Margaret H. Williams
Rebecca Wineck
Lois W. Woodford
Harriet B. Woodruff
Dorothy Woolley
Helen E. Young

Moses Abuza
Chun Wing Sen Afong
Philip A. Ahern
Raymond S. Alvord
Carl J. Anderson
Leonard A. Ashby
William J. Audet
E. Raymond Barlow
J. Welles Baxter
Hart J. Beach
John C. Beck
Charles R. Bedford
Hyman Beizer
Frederick A. Bennett
Jacob Berenson
Louis S. Berman
Reuben Berman
Charles N. Best
George F. Bill
Clarence S. Birden
David W. Blanchfield
Joseph L. Boyce
William A. Boyle
F. Nelson Breed
Edward C. Brinley
Leo Britton
Kingsley L. Brown
William F. Burns, Jr.
James R. Butler
Charles C. Byrne
Henry M. Callahan
Daniel J. Carroll
Everett E. Case
Howard T. Case
Leonard T. Clark
Edward S. Cleveland
George H. Cohen
Richard J. Connelly
Chauncey A. Crawford
Tracy E. Crouse
John L. Cully
James A. Curry
Thomas B. Curry
Michael J. Davern
Archibald R. Davie
Roger W. Davis
Stanley H. Davis
Warner B. Day
Walter H. Deacon
Bertrand K. Dean
Michael A. D'Esopo
James H. Dillon
James N. Doolittle
Jacob Eckstein
Howard R. Eddy
Carl A. Edmond
Robert W. Elliott, Jr.

Carl Emerson
Edward J. Emmett
John P. English
Edward H. Fahy
John L. Farrell
John F. Fenton
Joseph F. Finnegan
Simon Fish
Robert T. Frisbie
John A. Fritze
Samuel S. Garfinkel
Warren A. Gentner
Edward F. Gibbs
Harry A. Ginsburg
David D. Glanz
Samuel Glater
Charles R. Goddard
Louis Greenberg
Thomas J. Griffin
Abraham B. Gross
Ralph L. Hadaway
Robert D. Hadlock
Clarence L. Hamilton
Arthur H. Harris
Harold C. Hart
Henry P. Hastings
Carl I. Hellstrom
Edwin G. Hellyar
John M. Henry
Lewis B. Herrick, Jr.
Thomas W. B. Hogan
Harold D. Holden
William T. Holleran
Leonard W. Hollis
Raymond R. Hurd
H. Max Hurvitz
Roy E. Hutchins
Charles W. Jackson
Howard K. Jackson
Hugo W. Jaeger
Harold H. Jameson
William C. Jensen
Crompton T. Johnson
Frederick H. Johnson
George W. Johnson
Benjamin Katz
Morris Kessler
George T. Keyes
Thomas C. Kilfoil
Benjamin W. Kitchen
Arthur C. Koch
Charles D. Koenig
Samuel Kramer
George A. Kronsberg
Evan F. Kullgren
Edward T. Lally
Francis P. Langzettel

James E. Lehan
Clarence T. LePard
George D. Loomis
Richard S. Lyman
D. Stanley MacCallum
Robert G. MacDermid
Louis P. Mack
Howard P. Mahl
William E. J. Mahl
Merle B. Mann
Harry W. Manning
Robert W. Marchant
Louis H. Marte
Irving R. Martin
Timothy A. McCarthy
Laurence H. McClure
Charles A. McLaughlin
Edmund J. McLaughlin
Thomas F. Meagher
Meyer Michelson
Maxwell V. Miller
Edwin V. Mitchell
Ray W. Moody
Robert C. Moran
John J. Moriarty
Miles Mosher
John B. Motto
William A. Neilson
Royal C. Nemiah
Frederick B. Newell
William W. Nielsen
Francis J. Nolan
Henry J. O'Farrell
Cornelius F. O'Leary
Francis R. Olmsted
Henry M. O'Loughlin
Carl H. Olson
Stuart R. Osborn
George A. Ott
Harold L. Parker
Richard H. Phillips
John W. Phoenix
Joseph H. Pierce
L. Bertrand Pillion
Victor E. Preissner
Thomas B. Preston
Robert E. Price
A. Erwin Rankin, Jr.
Howard O. Ray
Robert S. Ray
Dudley W. Redfield
Harvard J. Reilly
Earl U. Richmond
Ralph G. Risley
John W. Robbins
Raymond W. Robbins
Robert W. Rollins, Jr.

10

| | | |
|---|---|---|
| Allan B. Rood | William C. Skinner, Jr. | Edward J. Wadsworth |
| Howard F. Root . | Clarence C. Smith | Alan W. Waite |
| Harold Rowe | Philip A. Sparrow | Herbert D. Waldron |
| John G. Sadoian | George M. Spidell, Jr. | Merritt S. Ward |
| Robert T. Scott | Maximilian Sporer | Charles E. Watkins |
| Michael Segal | Russell D. Steane | Ratcliffe C. Welles |
| Ralph J. Sexton | W. Ernest Steven | Irving M. Wickham |
| John J. Sheedy | Jacob Suchawolsky | Russell A. Wilcox |
| Ronald E. Sherman | John E. Sullivan | George L. Witham |
| Charles P. Shirrell | Reuben Taylor | George S. Wood |
| Solomon A. Shlimbum | Chester C. Trieschmann | John A. Worthington |
| Clarence H. Skaats | Horace N. Trumbull | Harry Yudowitch |
| Andrew H. Skau | Daniel F. Wadsworth | Henry Zimmerman |

Girls 258     Boys 210     Total 468

## SUMMARY

| | | |
|---|---|---|
| Senior Class . . . . . . . | Boys 65, | Girls 83 — 148 |
| Junior Class . . . . . . . | " 90, | " 103 — 193 |
| Third Class . . . . . . . | " 165, | " 154 — 319 |
| Fourth Class . . . . . . . | " 210, | " 258 — 468 |
| Graduate Students . . . . . . | | 10 |
| Total . . . . . . . . . | | 1,138 |

The foregoing list includes the whole number of different pupils registered since the beginning of the present school year, September, 1904.

# INDEX OF GRADUATES

**Barber**
1895 Gerald S.
1898 Laura M.

**Barbour**
1863 Joseph L.
1864 Lucius A.
1880 Lucy A.
1884 Clarence A.
1887 Amy L.
1890 Daisy F.
1896 Lucius B.
1897 Florence A.
1897 Robert W.
1900 Harold J.
1902 Henry G.

**Barchfeld**
1884 Josephine
1895 Helen M.

**Barker**
1871 Mary G.
1878 Mary E.
1898 Clarence L.

**Barnard**
1868 Henry D.
1877 Emily V.
1892 Mabell A.
1900 Melville H.

**Barnes**
1882 Julia R.

**Barnett**
1884 Grace C.

**Barney**
1877 D. Newton

**Barrett**
1896 Marion L.

**Barrows**
1869 Harriet F.
1880 Benjamin S.
1895 Rosa L.
1902 Anna M.
1902 Raymond W.
1904 Marjorie H.

**Bartholomew**
1894 William C.
1897 Jeannette B.

**Bartlett**
1868 Charles G.
1871 Charles L.
1876 Charles H.
1877 Philip G.
1878 Louise L.
1890 Alexis P.
1892 Warren T.
1893 Edith E.
1895 Alice M.
1896 S. Russell
1903 Clara G.
1903 Harry S.

**Barton**
1876 Minnie

**Baskerville**
1898 Albert A.

**Bassett**
1868 Mary S.

**Batterson**
1887 Emily L.

**Bauer**
1889 Caroline M.
1891 Pauline M.

**Bayliss**
1892 Grace L.

**Beach**
1852 Francis
1865 Mary C.
1871 T. Belknap
1886 Louis L.
1893 Carroll C.
1903 Goodwin B.

**Beadle**
1858 Heber H.
1890 H. Leonard
1890 Harry A.

**Beardslee**
1901 Raymond A.

**Beardsley**
1893 Mary A.
1895 Grace R.

**Beaumont**
1876 Minnie L.
1877 Fannie E.

**Beckwith**
1872 Eliza A.
1896 Grace E.

**Beebe**
1871 Anna R.
1893 Robert L.

**Beers**
1864 Henry A.

**Begg**
1889 William R.

**Belden**
1868 Joshua
1873 Augusta I.
1874 Ida G.
1874 William P.
1890 Herbert E.
1892 Addie S.
1892 Caroline S.
1893 Alice D.
1895 Clifford H.
1902 Lida A.
1902 Louise M.

**Bell**
1889 George N.

**Benedict**
1895 Elmer C.
1901 Edward B.

**Bennett**
1887 Maud I.
1889 Edith M.
1889 Frederick F.
1892 Mary M.
1892 Arthur P.
1893 M. Toscan
1897 Norma B.
1900 Anna C.

**Benton**
1891 Collins W.

**Bergen**
1894 Francis P.
1898 M. Henry

**Berman**
1904 Saul

**Berry**
1878 Charles P.
1882 Nellie E.
1885 Jennie E.

**Bestor**
1903 Eugene L.

**Bevin**
1875 Anna M.

**Bidwell**
1869 Kate M.
1871 Jane A.
1876 Lawson B.
1877 Walter D.
1878 Kate L.
1880 Grace C.
1881 Daniel D.
1883 Howard E.
1884 Jonathan C.
1885 Annie M.
1888 Frederic C.
1889 Mary A.

**Bigelow**
1856 Sophia W.
1867 Georgiana
1885 Julia E.

**Bill**
1889 Eliza A.
1889 Rosa L.
1896 Elizabeth R.
1897 Francis W. H.

**Billings**
1896 Mary E.

**Bingham**
1880 Emma L.
1880 Edwin H.

**Birch**
1877 Fanny J.

**Birkenmayer**
1886 Helen J.

**Birkery**
1895 Edward L.

**Birmingham**
1896 Mary E.
1899 Katherine G.

**Birney**
1886 Reginald

**Bissell**
1872 Hattie
1878 Caroline D.
1879 Lillian L.
1890 Clinton S.
1893 M. Eleanor
1894 Herbert G.

**Black**
1903 Edith G.
1903 William J.

**Blake**
1869 Henry A.
1886 Gertrude V.
1891 Mary J.

**Blakeslee**
1891 Leila H.
1895 Henry J.
1901 Roger H.

**Blanchard**
1858 Joseph L.

**Bliss**
1848 Charles M.
1849 Henry I.
1875 Charles H. J.
1878 Walter
1881 Mary F.
1882 Grace E.
1882 Mary L.
1893 Myra E.

**Blodget**
1871 Henry

**Blodgett**
1856 Anna E.
1858 Jane F.
1860 Roswell F.
1904 Mary C.

**Bluehdorn**
1901 Else B.

**Blumenthal**
1900 Harriet R.

**Boardman**
1880 Howard F.
1883 Emma J.

**Bogert**
1879 Lillian M.

**Bolles**
1851 Caroline A.
1852 Edwin C.
1904 Faith F.

**Boltwood**
1878 George S.
1879 Lucius

**Bond**
1885 Marion W.

**Bondy**
1900 Julius
1903 Bertha

**Bone**
1881 Robert D.

**Booth**
1870 Mary E.
1874 Lillian M.
1895 James W.

**Bosson**
1900 Frank E.

**Boswell**
1879 Charles M.

**Bosworth**
1895 Mabel L.

**Boutelle**
1896 L. Gertrude

**Bowers**
1865 Emily E.
1873 Alice A.
1874 Arthur E.
1887 Herbert O.
1904 Florence H.

**Bowles**
1887 Helen A.

**Bowman**
1879 George E.
1898 Maud F.

**Bowne**
1902 Garrett D.

**Boyce**
1900 Helen B.

**Boyd**
1897 Frederic R. C.

**Boyle**
1879 Charles P.
1882 Sara A.

**Brace**
1865 Ella J.
1883 Lucy M.

**Brackett**
1893 Edward S.
1897 Ella N.

**Bradley**
1895 Grace A.

**Bragaw**
1899 Allen C.

**Bragg**
1889 Hattie A.

**Brainard**
1883 Homer W.
1887 Charles E.
1893 Howard DeW.
1896 Morgan B.
1897 Daniel E.
1898 Newton C.
1900 Edith H.

**Brainerd**
1902 Clifton C.

**Brandt**
1877 Edward P.

**Bray**
1898 Henry T.

**Breed**
1897 Charles A.
1901 James O.

**Brewer**
1878 Carrie E.
1887 Everett P.
1901 Vincent C.
1903 Leila M.

**Brewster**
1866 Julia R.
1900 James H.

**Bridgman**
1878 Myron H.

**Briggs**
1870 Emma A.
1891 S. Lillian

**Brigham**
1863 Mary A.
1891 Clement H.
1895 Alice
1896 Clara
1896 H. Eleanor

**Brinley**
1895 John H. W.

**Briscoe**
1873 Willis A.

**Britton**
1899 Agnes G.

**Brockett**
1882 Calista V.

**Brocklesby**
1862 John H.
1865 Arthur K.
1865 William C.

**Brockway**
1899 Bessie N.

**Brodie**
1889 Alice L.

**Brokaw**
1895 Lottie E.
1897 Neva A.

**Bronson**
1862 Edward B.

**Brooks**
1853 James S.
1865 Ezra
1884 Grace C.
1885 Charles M.

**Brosmith**
1900 Ame M.

**Broughton**
1896 Lyman D.

**Brower**
1900 Garret D.

**Brown**
1873 Jennie M.
1884 George M.
1886 Fannie F.
1887 M. Grace
1893 Helen
1894 Cardella D.
1895 Robert D.
1896 Loraine S.
1897 Helen E.
1902 Albert L.
1902 William F.
1903 Chester N.
1904 Charles B.

**Browne**
1883 Pauline
1891 Marion B.
1901 Robert H.

**Brownell**
1880 Jane L.
1881 Grace
1881 Harriet M.
1883 Henry B.

**Bryant**
1866 Percy S.
1872 James S.
1896 Henry G.
1903 Florence G.

**Bryden**
1892 Florence B.

**Buck**
1862 Ellen M.
1874 Horace H.
1878 Lucy F.
1879 Mary E.
1880 George D.
1885 Florence K.
1887 John H.
1894 Clara B.
1896 Winthrop
1900 Charles H.
1902 Myldred L.

**Buckingham**
1892 Susie A.

**Buckley**
1901 Mary G.
1903 Anna L.

**Budde**
1892 Minnie L.

**Budge**
1896 Benjamin

**Buffington**
1896 Eva M.

**Bugbey**
1878 Carrie E.

**Bulkeley**
1852 Charles E.
1882 Mary M.
1887 Alice T.
1894 Sally T.
1903 Morgan G.

**Bulkley**
1880 Stephen
1892 George E.
1896 Daisy M.

**Bull**
1876 Arthur E.
1889 C. Sanford
1900 L. Cornella

**Bullard**
1877 Alice
1884 Herbert S.

**Bullock**
1878 N. Florence
1888 Lillie M.

**Bunce**
1848 Jonathan B.
1856 Charles H.
1879 James M.
1884 Philip D.
1887 John L.
1888 Anne K.
1897 Grace W.

**Bundy**
1879 Harriet M.

**Burbank**
1856 Julia B. ·
1858 Katherine ·

**Burch**
1877 George W.

**Burdett**
1899 Ralph H.

**Burdick**
1884 Grace C.
1890 Howard H.
1891 Gertrude A.
1895 Elizabeth L.
1895 Edwin P.
1897 Elsie

**Burke**
1900 Thomas F. J.

**Burkett**
1869 William H.

**Burnap**
1892 Clara A.
1901 Sidney R.

**Burnell**
1886 Bessie R.
1896 Harriette J.

**Burnham**
1869 Norman H.
1873 Ida J.
1878 Louise D.
1882 Mary A.
1885 Charles R.
1894 Mabelle
1902 A. Christina
1902 Carolyn H.
1903 Harold C.

**Burr**
1874 Mary C.
1893 Alice E.

**Burt**
1869 John F.
1882 Ada E.
1896 Alice M.
1901 Florence L.
1902 Elizabeth M.
1902 Marian L.

**Burton**
1901 Charlotte W.

**Burwell**
1895 Lena A.

**Bushnell**
1901 Howard E.

**Buths**
1903 Anna E.
1904 Louis S.

**Butler**
1889 Louis F.

**Butler**
1892 Clara M.
1892 Marshall A.

**Butterfield**
1879 Josie M.

**Cadwell**
1883 Harriet C.

**Cady**
1885 Jennie S.
1892 Ernest H.
1897 Florence G.
1897 Mary E.
1902 Ethel C.

**Cairns**
1880 Elizabeth J.

**Calder**
1892 Matilda S.
1894 Helen B.
1897 William P.

**Caldwell**
1862 Frances A.
1882 Ernest L.

**Calhoun**
1874 J. Gilbert
1876 Mary R.
1881 Fannie R.

**Callahan**
1894 John F.
1903 Raymond H.

**Callender**
1861 Harriet E.

**Callery**
1901 Marguerite L.

**Calnen**
1898 Genevieve M.

**Cambridge**
1879 Bertha A.

**Cameron**
1903 Alice J.

**Camp**
1855 Henry W.
1869 Charles H.
1873 Elizabeth
1878 Walter G.
1894 Josephine L.
1897 Burton H.
1903 Walter D.

**Campbell**
1899 James N. H.

**Canfield**
1875 Charles W.

**Capron**
1882 Clara D.
1886 Bertha C.
1888 William C.

**Carleton**
1885 Arthur S.
1887 Herbert
1890 Mabel L.
1895 Guy M.
1897 Bessie G.

**Carpenter**
1877 Harriet B.
1878 Martha L.
1887 Lillie B.
1893 Marcia S.
1900 Sidney C.

**Carr**
1879 Albert
1892 Bernard J.

**Carrier**
1852 Martha E.

**Carey**
1879 E. Louise
1891 Nellie S.
1904 H. Bissell

**Carroll**
1893 M. May
1894 Margaret A.
1899 Mary C.

**Carter**
1889 Charles P.
1892 Elizabeth S.
1899 Ethel
1899 William L.
1904 Florence

**Case**
1878 Minnie J.
1880 Charles G.
1881 Miron J.
1884 Jennie S.
1884 Burton O.
1895 Herbert M.
1896 Eliza N.
1896 Helen E.

**Casey**
1899 Viola M.

**Castle**
1880 Mary E.
1882 Louise

**Caswell**
1887 Jean G.
1891 Frederick K.

**Catlin**
1849 Julius
1855 Benjamin S.
1875 Mary L.

**Caulkins**
1902 John A.

**Chaffee**
1886 Amasa D.
1902 Emma L.

**Chalker**
1903 L. Toulmin

**Chamberlin**
1894 Mary E.

**Chambers**
1901 Natalie

**Champlin**
1896 Lottie M.
1899 Frank C.
1902 Frederick A.

**Chandler**
1868 Flora J.
1889 Charles B.

**Chapin**
1865 Mary J.
1869 Josephine M.
1875 Elizabeth N.
1881 Martha B.
1899 Alice V.
1903 Warren S.

**Chapman**
1872 Alice M.
1874 Alice W.
1886 Leila B.
1888 Emeline S.
1892 Frederick S.
1893 John W.
1896 Louis B.
1898 Henry E.

**Charter**
1881 Hattie L.
1887 Susie R.

**Chase**
1876 Charles E.
1882 E. Helena

**Cheney**
1879 Louis R.
1821 G. Herbert
1883 Walter B.
1884 Thomas S.
1884 William C.
1887 Henry R.
1888 Howell
1888 Knight D.
1888 Mark
1891 Sherwood A.
1892 Ward
1893 Richard O.
1894 Clifford D.
1890 Russell

**Chickering**
1881 Frances E.

**Chieng**
1881 Wan Kwei

## Childs
1865 Frank R.
1874 William H.
1879 Samuel B.
1903 Francis D.

## Chlopkowiak
1904 Helen H.

## Christiansen
1897 Katrina

## Chung
1879 Mun Yew

## Church
1868 Louise A.
1900 S. Lewis

## Claghorn
1903 Juliet L.

## Clancy
1901 Agnes J.

## Clapp
1894 Louise C.

## Clark
1860 James W.
1867 Charles H.
1869 Susan T.
1869 George N.
1870 Charles W.
1870 John F.
1873 Sidney W.
1875 George H.
1880 Elizabeth B.
1880 Eunice A.
1882 Fanny M.
1884 Harriet A.
1885 Charles M.
1888 Robert
1800 Anna W.
1890 Caroline C.
1890 Lena H.
1892 Walter H.
1894 Lucy M.
1894 Horace B.
1896 Mary H.
1898 William D. B.
1899 Eliot R.
1901 Sarah E.
1904 Morris B.

## Clarke
1894 Mary W.

## Clary
1903 Anne St.L.

## Cleary
1885 Lizzie A.

## Cleasby
1894 Harold L.
1898 Bessie M.

## Clemons
1857 William H.

## Cleveland
1898 Edmund J.
1899 Elsie H.

## Clifford
1884 Kate F.

## Coburn
1900 James H.

## Cody
1891 M. Isabel
1895 Nellie T.

## Coe
1892 George H.
1896 Grace A.

## Cohen
1904 Fannie E.

## Coit
1876 Hattie J.

## Cole
1808 Richard H.
1899 Francis W.
1903 Sara B.

## Coleman
1881 Mary E.
1896 Gertrude V.

## Collins
1863 Charles T.
1869 Atwood
1880 William E.
1899 Viola I.

## Colton
1897 Harold B.
1900 Marguerite

## Colver
1883 Lizzie L.

## Comings
1870 Emma S.

## Comstock
1900 Lewis B.

## Condit
1852 Stephen

## Cone
1873 Ella B.
1882 Leah J.
1884 Robert B.
1887 Clara M.
1890 Harry F.
1892 Florence M.
1893 Lillian C.
1900 Laura D.

## Conklin
1882 May H.
1885 William P.
1889 Charles W.

## Conklin
1889 William E.
1891 Edna D.
1896 Clara L.

## Conrads
1898 Clara S.

## Conroy
1884 Mary F.

## Cook
1876 Mary E.
1883 Albert S.
1892 Agnes A.
1897 Mary J.

## Cooke
1862 Oliver D.
1868 Mary A.
1876 Hattie E.

## Cooley
1869 Emma E.
1875 Grace E.
1882 Francis R.
1898 Joseph F.

## Coombs
1889 Kittie E.

## Corbett
1904 Frederic J.

## Corbin
1884 Frank W.
1884 William H.
1886 Annie L.
1891 Harvey W.

## Cornish
1873 Kate A.

## Cornwell
1873 Hattie E.

## Corson
1887 William R. C.

## Cosker
1902 William J. F.

## Costello
1883 Minnie G.
1894 Elizabeth M.
1902 Henry N.

## Cotter
1904 Marguerite W.

## Couch
1900 Helen L.

## Coughlin
1891 Matthew E.
1904 Mary M.

## Countryman
1901 Emeline P.
1901 W. Arthur

## Courtice
1893 Mary J.

## Cowles
1875 John S.
1875 Thomas
1877 Arthur W.
1893 Luzerne S.

## Cowlishaw
1898 James E.
1904 Gertrude A.

## Cowperthwaite
1881 Ellanora

## Cox
1903 John J.

## Crane
1862 Elizabeth M.
1873 Georgia A.
1878 Alice R.

## Craver
1890 D. Howard

## Crawford
1904 Charles M.

## Creedon
1902 Alice M.

## Cressy
1893 Louis A.
1896 Morton S.

## Crocker
1891 Alice M.

## Cross
1896 Harry I.
1899 Charles M.
1900 Mary A.

## Crowe
1895 Helen C.

## Crowell
1880 Albert D.

## Cullen
1891 Charles H.
1899 Charles A.
1901 Jane C.

## Culver
1903 Grace M.

## Cummings
1878 Nellie M.
1886 Alice T.
1892 Carrie E.
1896 Frances W.

## Cunliffe
1902 Isabelle E.

**Curry**
1868 Albert M.
1903 William F.

**Curtin**
1900 Helena F.

**Curtis**
1888 Robert W.
1889 Carrie B.
1896 Edith C.
1896 Elizabeth A.
1898 Alice L.
1900 Mary B.

**Curtiss**
1885 Elsie A.
1899 Elizabeth W.
1902 Philip E.

**Cutler**
1900 Charlotte E.
1903 Ralph D.

**Daigneau**
1900 Cora E.

**Daley**
1904 Sara E.

**Danforth**
1881 Mary

**Daniels**
1869 Lillie E.
1879 Phebe A.
1880 Lorenzo

**D'Arche**
1889 Valsorine F.

**Darling**
1901 Blanche M.

**Darrow**
1875 Fanny G.

**Davenport**
1893 Elizabeth L.

**Davidson**
1882 William B.

**Davis**
1862 G. Pierrepont
1873 Frederick W.
1876 Marion L.
1878 Belle C.
1889 James W.
1891 Gertrude E.
1893 Gustavus F.
1897 Carl W.
1898 George E.
1903 Dorothy W.

**Davison**
1885 Suvia

**Davoud**
1900 Vahram E.

**Dawson**
1869 Ida V.

**Day**
1866 Arthur H.
1882 Harriet G.
1882 Thomas Mills
1884 Sarah C.
1886 Arthur P.
1888 Clive

**DeBarthe**
1902 Mabel

**Decker**
1894 Kathryn E.
1897 John A.

**Delabarre**
1902 Everett M.

**DeLeeuw**
1881 Esther

**Deming**
1868 Charles C.
1868 Henry C.
1873 Edward
1879 L. Clerc
1880 William C.
1882 Adelaide
1894 Florence
1899 Clara B.
1901 Edward A.
1902 Richard H.
1903 Clinton D.

**Denison**
1881 Clara M.
1896 May L.

**Dennis**
1879 Charlotte W.
1886 Rodney S.

**Denslow**
1877 Lizzie W.

**Derby**
1892 Nellie E.

**D'Esopo**
1900 Salvator
1904 Ferdinand

**Deutsch**
1878 Eva

**Dewey**
1861 Daniel P.

**DeWitt**
1900 Ralph

**Dibble**
1892 Mary E.
1895 Ida B.
1904 Mae E.

**Dickenson**
1889 Gertrude E.
1895 Elizabeth C.
1898 Edwin C.

**Dickerson**
1888 Julia A.

**Dickinson**
1861 Emma C.
1881 Mary L.
1900 Clara M.
1900 Florence M.
1901 Ethel L.
1903 Raymond N.

**Dillingham**
1888 Mabel B.

**Dimock**
1881 Edwin F.
1901 Harold E.

**Dix**
1902 Leon E.
1904 Grace V.

**Dobie**
1860 Samuel W.

**Dodd**
1862 Caroline B.
1902 Sadie P.

**Doebler**
1902 Blanche A.
1902 Hattie M.

**Donaghue**
1903 Edward L.

**Donley**
1897 Georgett E.
1901 Charlotte A.

**Donovan**
1899 Annie Z.
1900 Ellen J.
1902 Clarissa E.

**Dooley**
1882 Sarah A.

**Dorsey**
1886 Mary

**Dougherty**
1883 Mary J.

**Dow**
1876 Etta M.

**Dowling**
1897 Mary J.

**Doyle**
1903 K. Estelle

**Drago**
1904 Josephine M.

**Dresser**
1890 Elsie J.
1897 Gertrude M.
1902 Ida M.

**Driscoll**
1897 Isabelle G.
1897 Raymond F.

**Dudley**
1896 Clara L.

**Duffey**
1893 Francis J.
1899 Lillian R.
1902 Florence J.

**Duffy**
1892 Gertrude F.
1897 Elizabeth P.

**Duggan**
1895 Mary E.
1897 Ellen H.
1899 Anna M.
1904 Sadie A.

**Dunham**
1850 Austin C.
1883 Adele A.
1899 Donald A.
1901 Ethel C.

**Dunning**
1898 Anna M.

**Dustan**
1893 Grace N.

**Dwight**
1884 William B.

**Dwyer**
1899 Ellen C.
1900 Arthur
1901 Rose M.

**Easton**
1859 Morton W.

**Eaton**
1888 Myrah
1890 Edward B.
1900 Norma F.

**Eaves**
1885 Minnie F.

**Eckhardt**
1894 Winifred M.
1897 Malcolm M.

**Edwards**
1867 Frederick B.
1889 Florence G.
1894 Gaston H.
1895 Nellie F. V.
1896 Stanley W.

### Fox

1849 Charles E.
1872 Charles J.
1874 Inez J.
1878 William S.
1887 Mary C.
1903 Inez F.

### Francis

1868 Mary C.
1874 George Bell
1875 Minnie
1877 Anna L.
1877 Arlan P.
1881 Frederick W.
1891 Everett M.
1893 Bernice E.
1895 Arthur D.

### Franklin

1895 Bessie L.

### Franzen

1904 Carl G. F.

### Frasick

1878 Seymour F.

### Frayer

1888 Cordelia M.

### Freeman

1887 Harrison B.
1888 Elizabeth B.
1888 Frances H.
1894 Louise R.

### French

1862 Georgiana L.
1880 Alice L.
1881 Alfred W.

### Frisbie

1895 Florence S.
1898 Edward W.

### Fuller

1869 Ella A.

### Futter

1897 Leon N.

### Gaffey

1902 John F.

### Galacar

1891 Frederic R.
1893 Laura J.
1895 Mabel F.

### Galer

1904 Maud L.

### Gallagher

1862 William D.

### Gallaudet

1851 Alice C.
1851 Edward M.
1881 Grace W.

### Gallaudet

1889 Denison
1889 Edson F.

### Galpin

1866 Samuel L.

### Galvin

1892 Mary F.

### Gardner

1902 Martha

### Garvan

1883 Mary E.
1890 Edward J.
1891 Elizabeth F.
1893 Francis P.
1897 Genevieve F.

### Garvie

1894 John S.

### Garvin

1896 Ethel M.
1901 Rena E.
1902 Edward T.
1904 Nellie B.

### Gates

1877 Harry T.
1877 William E.
1901 Terry V.

### Gauthier

1899 Carrie A.
1899 Flora E.
1901 George A.
1904 Mabel J.

### Gaylord

1875 Edward B.
1877 Andrew S.
1886 William A.

### Geer

1889 Anna B.
1894 Frederick P.
1899 Elene E.

### Giddings

1889 Bertha S.
1893 Edith M.

### Gilbert

1873 Mary E.
1873 George E.
1874 Charles M.
1876 Mary E.
1881 Hattie E.
1884 Alma L.
1886 Zulette K.
1888 Edna S.
1888 Edwin R.
1904 William H.

### Gill

1891 Frank C.

### Gillette

1858 Elisabeth H.
1864 Ellen F.
1873 William H.
1875 Flora J.
1887 Hattie
1889 Mary P.
1890 Edwin C.
1899 Emma T.

### Gilman

1885 George H.
1886 Martin L.
1892 Julia E.

### Gilmore

1900 Ellen G.

### Gladwin

1885 Carrie L.
1889 Samuel F. P.
1903 Louis H.
1903 Russell

### Glazier

1856 Theodore C.
1863 Sarah M.
1865 Luther C.
1875 Mary A.
1880 Charles M.
1887 Robert C.
1892 Alice B.
1895 Clara M.
1900 Laura E.
1902 Helen S.
1902 M. Louise
1903 George S.

### Gleason

1882 Mary A.

### Glen

1891 Christine F.

### Goldberg

1903 Katherine E.
1903 Samuel J.

### Golden

1902 Kathryn E.

### Goldsmith

1886 Lillie

### Goldthwaite

1851 Jane
1853 Mary

### Goodell

1896 Louis A.

### Goodenough

1896 Gertrude L.

### Goodman

1866 George F.
1877 Emilie
1880 Annie
1891 Mary E.
1892 Richard J.

### Goodrich

1860 Frederick E.
1868 Martha S.
1875 Nellie S.
1878 Isabella E.
1884 Grace
1886 Mabel E.
1888 F. Zulette
1888 Harold B.
1890 Lillys M.

### Goodridge

1855 Edward

### Goodwin

1851 James J.
1854 Sheldon
1860 Henry S.
1875 Carolyn A.
1888 Ralph C.
1896 Harriet L.
1897 James L.
1900 Jessie S.
1902 Howard
1903 William H.
1904 Ralph E.

### Gorman

1876 Charles F.
1904 Jessica B.

### Gorton

1882 L. Belle

### Gott

1896 Marion E.

### Gould

1889 Willard J.

### Gowdy

1883 Kate R.

### Gowen

1904 Clarence L.

### Grant

1887 Ralph M.
1896 Horace R.
1897 L. Mabel
1899 Louis L.

### Grassier

1902 Mary E.

### Graves

1886 Frank W.
1892 F. May
1894 Martha W.
1895 Gertrude I.
1896 Arthur H.
1898 Effie S.
1904 Helen E.

### Green

1892 Eleanor T.
1899 Ethel E.
1899 M. Helene
1901 Edith G.

**Hellmann**
1904 Edmund

**Hendee**
1872 Abner

**Hendrick**
1886 Jessie V.

**Hendron**
1902 Mary A.

**Henke**
1883 Franceska A.

**Henney**
1870 William F.
1874 David
1879 Mary C.
1897 James B.
1902 David B.

**Henning**
1903 Louise M.

**Henry**
1866 Martha F.

**Hepple**
1904 Jeannie

**Herrick**
1882 John W.

**Hersey**
1904 Mayo D.

**Hertzler**
1900 Genevieve L.

**Heublein**
1904 Ada T.

**Hibbard**
1879 Philena

**Hickman**
1903 Mabel E.

**Hickmott**
1875 Martha E.

**Higgins**
1885 John W.
1888 Joseph J.
1896 Grace A.

**Hildebrand**
1902 Alice L.

**Hill**
1904 Elton B.

**Hillhouse**
1880 Sadie B.

**Hilliard**
1896 C. Cordelia
1899 Elisha E.

**Hills**
1860 Charles D.
1874 Anna G.
1877 Hattie
1880 George C.
1886 Carrie E.
1888 Sara W.
1888 John H.
1889 Grace M.
1890 Katherine L.
1893 Alice M.
1894 Effie M.
1894 Jane R.
1894 Laura K.
1896 Rowland B.
1899 Annette M.
1900 Alexina E.

**Hinckley**
1899 Clara B.

**Hirth**
1897 Augustus C.
1899 Joseph E.
1901 Emma P.

**Hitchcock**
1882 Alice W.

**Hoadley**
1899 Eva M.

**Hobson**
1898 Bertha P.

**Hodge**
1870 Ida E.

**Hodgman**
1878 Walter E.

**Hofer**
1903 Karl D.

**Hogan**
1894 Margaretta B.
1899 Thomas N.

**Hoisington**
1887 Frederick R.
1891 Nancy L.

**Holaday**
1899 Grace L.

**Holbrook**
1883 Grace H.
1883 Nellie G.
1885 Mary A.

**Holcomb**
1852 Daniel E.
1873 Jessie F.
1884 Annie L.
1885 Harriet E.
1888 Eliza J.
1901 Anson M.

**Holcombe**
1864 James W.
1865 John M.

**Holcombe**
1883 Annie E.
1892 Harold G.
1896 Emily M.

**Holland**
1888 Olga C.

**Hollister**
1854 Arthur N.
1870 Emma G.
1880 Carrie E.
1897 J. Robinson
1902 Jane E.

**Holman**
1852 Lavinia M.

**Holmes**
1865 Elizabeth K.
1868 Harriet T.

**Holt**
1898 Lucius H.

**Hood**
1898 Nellie E.

**Hooker**
1856 Elma J.
1860 Thomas
1874 Edward B.
1885 Edward W.
1898 W. Brian
1899 Isabel K.
1904 Thomas

**Horey**
1887 Margaret A.

**Horton**
1860 Ann E.
1879 Harry I.

**Hotchkiss**
1851 Ellen M.
1893 Laura A.
1894 Philip L.

**House**
1852 Juliette
1858 William W.
1871 Henry S.

**Houston**
1872 Ella M.

**Hovey**
1896 Alice L.
1900 Mary E.
1904 Roger H.

**How**
1882 James
1884 Charles A.

**Howard**
1861 Maria
1869 Charles P.
1885 Leland

**Howard**
1887 Arthur W.
1887 Harry
1893 Frank E.
1895 James L.
1899 Helen E.
1899 Lawrence A.

**Howe**
1870 Daniel R.
1895 Fannie B.
1901 Edmund G.

**Hoxie**
1897 Grace M.

**Hubbard**
1869 William D.
1882 Mary A.
1884 Annie L.
1888 Charlotte L.
1898 Mary E.
1904 Rose A.

**Hudson**
1849 William M.
1878 Regina M.
1880 Frances B.

**Hull**
1902 C. Elinor

**Hume**
1903 Robert W.

**Humphrey**
1884 Alice F.

**Hunn**
1894 William W.

**Hunt**
1856 Emma M.
1858 Albert L.
1877 Ada W.
1880 Hattie O.
1893 Lucy O.
1894 Grace S.

**Hunter**
1872 Dwight W.
1878 Frederick E.
1880 Isabella D.
1890 Jeannette B.

**Huntington**
1860 Samuel
1862 Henry K.
1875 Charles G.
1878 Mary L.
1879 John W.
1883 Bert D.
1885 Joseph S.
1885 Robert W.
1892 Mary G.
1895 Caroline T.
1897 Ellen A.
1900 Isabel M.

**Knowlton**
1904 Archer E.

**Knox**
1890 Lena I.
1892 Robert C.
1900 Addie L.
1900 James W.
1901 Frank R.
1903 George D.
1904 Clarence M.

**Koch**
1904 Lillian C.

**Kramer**
1903 Susie A.

**Kreuzer**
1877 George C.

**Kronsberg**
1902 Matilda

**Lacy**
1898 Joseph·R.

**Ladd**
1886 Herbert I.
1903 Le Roy A.

**Lally**
1891 Mary J.

**Lamb**
1886 Charles T.
1888 Annie W.
1892 Chauncey B.
1897 Ora F.

**Landon**
1894 Grace W.

**Landrigan**
1899 Mary A.

**Lane**
1888 Bertha G.
1893 Sarah E.

**Lang**
1902 Clara E.

**Langdon**
1899 Anna L.

**Lanman**
1893 Laura T.

**Larkum**
1898 Newton W.

**Latham**
1892 Maud E.
1900 Edith M.

**Latimer**
1862 Hannah P.
1887 Edward H.
1903 James I.

**Law**
1894 Sally P.

**Lawler**
1886 Annie M.
1902 Joseph H.

**Lawrence**
1893 James W.
1895 Thomas F.
1899 Frank R.

**Lawson**
1899 Anna E.

**Lay**
1902 C. Estella

**Leavenworth**
1873 Frederick A.

**Leavitt**
1887 Blanche

**Lee**
1882 Edward T.
1883 Mary S.
1888 Henry N.

**Leete**
1886 William H.

**Leonard**
1874 Fannie I.

**Lester**
1901 Ella C.

**Leventhal**
1902 Rachel H.

**Levy**
1904 Pauline E.

**Lewis**
1877 Mary B.
1881 Gertrude O.
1888 Mary L.
1889 T. Jarvis
1901 Raymond C.

**Liang**
1878 Tun Yen

**Lincks**
1903 Mary C.

**Lincoln**
1874 Charles G.
1881 Fannie M.
1898 Richard C.
1900 Helen C.

**Linnon**
1903 Mary J.
1903 Frank E.

**Litchfield**
1865 Julia G.

**Little**
1876 George H.
1903 Mitchell S.

**Loomis**
1862 Caroline H.
1864 James S.
1866 Martha E.
1868 Annie D.
1871 Sarah H.
1872 Sarah E.
1879 Allyn C.
1881 Hiram B.
1889 Archie H.

**Lord**
1884 Archibald E.
1887 Isabel E.
1904 L. Roland

**Lorenz**
1897 Annie
1899 Edward H.

**Lorenzen**
1899 Ida M. E.

**Losty**
1884 Kate J.

**Lounsbury**
1889 Ralph R.

**Lucas**
1879 Fannie C.

**Luce**
1896 Cortlandt F.

**Lundin**
1902 Carl E.

**Lux**
1886 William K.
1888 George L.
1889 Alice G.
1893 Henry E.
1895 Edith M.

**Lycett**
1899 Frederick W.

**Lyman**
1851 Theodore
1869 Helen L.
1870 Frederick S.
1877 Arthur H.
1882 Edward E.
1896 L. William
1897 Annie B.
1897 Pauline A.

**Lynch**
1891 William J.
1899 William T.

**Lyon**
1888 Mary
1889 Irving P.

**Lyons**
1898 Bertha J.
1901 John J.

**Mac Bride**
1898 Herbert S.

**Mack**
1898 F. Elizabeth
1903 C. Le Roy

**Maercklein**
1902 Burdette C.

**Maguire**
1848 Dominick
1895 Kittie L.
1904 Gertrude M.

**Mahl**
1898 Grace E.
1900 Clara E.
1903 Louise A.
1904 Alice E.
1904 Gertrude E.
1904 Carl A.

**Mahon**
1899 Mary E.
1901 William F.
1902 John C.

**Mallory**
1895 Clara F.

**Mairson**
1897 Rosaline

**Malone**
1880 Emma J.

**Maloy**
1892 Mary A.

**Maltbie**
1894 Anne L.
1897 William M.

**Mandlebaum**
1878 Flora
1885 Frederick S.

**Mangan**
1881 Lizzie V.

**Manley**
1881 Mary H.

**Maplesden**
1904 Raymond J.

**Marchant**
1887 Mary

**Marsh**
1886 Mabelle S.
1888 Katharine H.
1896 Edena L.
1898 Charles W.

**Morrow**
1876 Thomas R.

**Morse**
1858 Augustus
1864 Ella G.
1888 Madaline K.
1898 Everett H.

**Moseley**
1870 Gilbert G.
1872 Belle S.
1883 Edward E.
1889 Georgia M.

**Moses**
1902 Helen P.
1904 Alice L.

**Moulton**
1900 Marion J.
1900 Harold C.

**Mowry**
1874 Leverett N.

**Mucklow**
1901 Grace E.
1904 Wilford B.

**Mulcahy**
1894 Bridget T.
1894 Thomas P.
1903 Catherine E.

**Mulhall**
1881 Nellie T.
1902 Jennie E.

**Mullen**
1895 Margaret A.

**Muller**
1874 Christine E.
1887 Mary St. L.

**Mulligan**
1848 John
1850 Thomas P.
1902 Jane E.
1904 Ellen A.

**Munroe**
1887 Nettie L.

**Munsell**
1901 Alonzo A.

**Murphy**
1893 Daniel F.

**Murray**
1900 Mary H.

**Myers**
1899 Ella L.
1903 Rachel F.

**Mylecraine**
1875 Nettie

**Naedele**
1904 Edwina A.

**Nahlgan**
1902 Matthew N.

**Naramore**
1883 Martha J.

**Nason**
1886 Charles R.
1896 Grace A.

**Nevers**
1885 Jessie I.
1889 Hattie H.

**Newberry**
1886 E. Florence
1890 Herbert C.

**Newcomb**
1877 Warren P.

**Newell**
1886 Roger S.
1894 Eleanor
1898 Robert B.

**Newton**
1862 Anna C.
1878 Charles W.
1881 Lillian L.
1897 Elizabeth
1902 Mabelle C.
1903 Arthur G.

**Ney**
1882 Edward M.
1896 Elsie L.

**Nichols**
1888 Helen C.
1889 Elma A.
1890 Edwin B.

**Noble**
1880 William B.
1891 Harriet E.
1899 Mary E.

**Noonan**
1900 May G.

**Norris**
1891 Charles F.
1894 T. May

**North**
1890 Eva M.
1902 Horace

**Northam**
1899 Katherine T.
1900 Charles H.

**Northrop**
1874 Lena S.

**Norton**
1870 Elizabeth
1889 Arthur W.
1899 Ada I.

**Nugent**
1902 John F.

**O'Brien**
1894 Edward D.
1897 Mary I.
1898 Thomas J.
1899 Timothy C.
1900 Marguerita M.
1901 Anna E.
1904 Alice M.

**O'Callahan**
1898 J. Frank

**O'Connor**
1904 Alice K.

**O'Donohue**
1904 Michael S.

**O'Flaherty**
1889 Mary P.
1894 Hannah P.
1896 Ellen P.

**Olds**
1899 Frank A.
1900 Edna A.
1901 Herbert V.

**O'Leary**
1892 James F.

**Olin**
1885 Hattie I.

**Olmsted**
1852 Bertha
1870 Frank H.
1881 Harry D.
1888 Robert E. S.
1891 Frederick E.
1895 Amy E.
1897 John
1898 George F.

**Olsen**
1899 Alice M.

**O'Nell**
1894 Mary A. Z.
1897 Kathryn C. G.

**O'Neill**
1899 Daniel L.

**Osborn**
1897 Mary G.

**Ostrander**
1900 Effie S.

**Oviatt**
1868 George A.

**Owen**
1855 Charles H.
1860 Henry E.
1862 Jane A.
1867 Edward T.
1889 Flora B.
1895 Katherine B.

**Packard**
1858 Sarah C.
1863 Irene H.

**Page**
1904 James J.

**Pagram**
1885 Annie M.

**Palmer**
1889 Mary A.
1892 Warren P.
1898 Isabel L. F.
1900 Edith M.
1901 Florence M.

**Pardee**
1876 Cora A.

**Parent**
1877 Arthur M.

**Parish**
1859 Roswell

**Parker**
1871 Frances A.
1900 May C.
1903 Helen F.

**Parkhurst**
1895 Harleigh

**Parrish**
1869 Nellie A.

**Parsons**
1848 John G.
1849 John C.
1858 Elizabeth W.
1868 William B.
1876 Annie L.
1886 Belle M.
1889 Francis
1890 Louis M.

**Pasco**
1858 Henry L.

**Patterson**
1871 Martha A.

**Pattison**
1895 Alice V.

**Patton**
1872 Robert W.

**Patz**
1884 Bertha E.
1897 Ida E. L.

**Rice**
1878 James Q.
1879 Anna B.

**Rich**
1887 Elisha R.

**Richards**
1891 Edith K.
1893 Edith S.
1894 Alfred E.
1898 Kathryn R.

**Richardson**
1887 Lillian A.

**Richmond**
1902 Edna A.

**Ricker**
1892 Edith E.

**Riddle**
1887 Mary M.

**Riggs**
1903 Harold W.

**Riley**
1868 Alice M.
1890 Mary A.
1904 Florence E.

**Ripley**
1881 Lewis W.

**Risley**
1894 Edith L.
1897 Edith E.
1898 Anne W.
1902 Nellie A.

**Rist**
1869 Owen D.
1898 Helen B.
1900 Ethel P.
1904 Kate

**Robbins**
1870 Edward D.
1875 Charles W.
1877 Ellie B.
1877 Jane E.
1879 Mark T.
1881 Caroline T.
1883 Mary E.
1883 Mary S.
1883 Samuel B.
1888 Harriet
1889 Anna C.
1896 Bertha T.
1900 Frederick A.
1902 Nellie L.
1904 Harold E.

**Roberts**
1852 Emily G.
1861 William H.
1869 James H.
1873 Henry

**Roberts**
1888 Helen M.
1888 Homer C.
1890 Mary C.
1891 H. Louise
1893 Sarah R.
1895 Alfred E.
1897 Helen
1898 Elise A.
1898 Charles A.
1899 George
1900 John W.
1901 Mary
1901 John T.
1901 W. Blair
1902 James W.
1903 Ruth
1904 Alice S.

**Robertson**
1901 Florence R.
1903 Evelyn B.
1904 Adelaide H.
1904 James R.

**Robinson**
1849 Henry C.
1852 Alfred S.
1858 Caroline E.
1868 Harriet L.
1875 Mary A.
1881 Lucius F.
1883 Lucy T.
1884 Ella A.
1885 Henry S.
1889 John T.
1891 Mary S.
1892 Henry H.
1900 Clifford A.

**Rockwell**
1880 Anna G.
1899 Jessamine

**Rodgers**
1875 Wellington J.
1889 Clarence M.
1891 Ashmead G.

**Rogers**
1865 Georgiana C.
1884 Gertrude H.
1888 Knight E.
1901 Erle
1902 Harold W.

**Rohne**
1904 Chester S.

**Rohrmayer**
1900 Francis P.

**Roloff**
1901 Frieda

**Ronald**
1890 Charlotte K.

**Rood**
1879 Frank W.

**Root**
1866 Charles H.
1876 Rachel W.

**Rosenthal**
1896 Sadie F.
1897 Edith H.

**Ross**
1900 Mabel G.

**Rossiter**
1892 Irmagarde

**Roulstone**
1876 Eliza J.
1882 Jennie M.

**Rowbotham**
1901 Maud L.

**Rowell**
1853 Harriet
1856 Mary

**Rowles**
1872 M. Louise

**Rowley**
1885 Jennie P.
1888 Arthur M.
1898 Robert L.

**Royce**
1888 William R.

**Russ**
1897 Charles C.
1897 Henry C.

**Russell**
1885 Angie J.
1897 Thomas W.
1904 Mabel E.

**Ryan**
1879 Dennis F.
1885 Edmund J.
1889 Nellie S.
1893 Winifred A.
1895 Mary C.
1898 Louise G.

**Ryder**
1890 Pauline L.
1891 George H.

**Sadd**
1881 Walter A.

**Sage**
1895 William P.
1900 Olive K.
1902 Charles H.

**Sames**
1883 William J.

**Samson**
1900 De Ette

**Samuels**
1900 Hannah
1901 Louis A.

**Sanford**
1904 Edith V.

**Saunders**
1875 Herbert H.
1880 Mary E.
1884 Jessie E.
1903 Eliza M.

**Savage**
1891 Wilfred W.

**Sawtelle**
1892 Albert G.

**Sawyer**
1891 Edith P.

**Schaefer**
1881 Augusta S.

**Schirm**
1904 Charles

**Schulze**
1861 Eliza W.

**Schwab**
1880 Alice
1884 Emma N.
1890 Josephine H.

**Scofield**
1901 Gertrude M.

**Scollon**
1864 Terrence

**Scott**
1883 Julia A.
1885 Frederick A.
1889 John J.
1904 Alice E.

**Scranton**
1902 Bessie L.

**Scudder**
1868 Henry T.

**Searle**
1889 Franklin H.
1899 Wilbur C.

**Sears**
1849 Martha A.
1872 Alida A.
1875 Agnes M.
1895 David L.

**Seaver**
1882 Cora J.

**Seavey**
1870 Alice L.

**Sprague**
1875 Effie P.
1884 Ada J.
1892 Harriett B.
1894 Sarah T.

**Spring**
1874 Mary C.

**Squire**
1876 Wilbur H.

**Squires**
1894 Lillian M.

**Stamm**
1871 Anna M.
1875 Louise R.

**Standish**
1895 Emma L.

**Stanley**
1865 Elisha
1871 Grace G.
1873 Ellen C.
1882 Sarah E.
1898 Mary B.

**Starbuck**
1902 Carlton W.

**Starkweather**
1858 Mary A.
1860 Sarah W.
1902 Richard H.

**Starr**
1885 Martha K.
1889 Mary S.

**Steane**
1900 Jessie S.
1903 Herbert J.

**Stearns**
1868 Charles C.
1870 George M.
1873 Alice M.

**Stebbins**
1883 Josephine M.

**Stedman**
1863 Ernest G.

**Steele**
1864 Elizabeth J.
1878 Ada E.
1885 Charlotte B.
1888 James E.
1890 Edward L.
1894 M. Adella
1895 Elizabeth S.
1896 Andrew G.

**Steeves**
1903 Mabel C.

**Sterling**
1882 Alice U.

**Stern**
1876 Max
1882 Clotilde M.
1889 Minnie
1890 Julia

**Stevens**
1877 Margarette M.
1878 Annie L.
1885 Nellie H.
1885 Nellie K.
1901 Ada A.
1904 Robert W.

**Stickney**
1872 Jeannie R.

**Stiles**
1882 Josephine
1882 Edgar C.
1885 Charles W.

**Stillman**
1850 Albert E.
1875 Mary F.
1878 Kate S.
1894 H. Robbins
1899 Edward A.
1902 Harold B.
1903 Marjorie G.
1904 Anna B.

**Stinson**
1901 Jennie I.

**St. John**
1898 George C.
1904 Charles N.

**Stockbridge**
1866 Lucy W.

**Stocker**
1893 Frank H.

**Stoddard**
1880 Frank R.
1886 Martha A.
1904 Ora B.

**Stokes**
1893 Martin C.
1895 Maria F.

**Stone**
1878 Charles G.
1882 Sarah E.
1883 Lillian A.
1884 Frank E
1885 Fannie G.
1889 Clara L.
1889 Jane W.
1892 Elisabeth W.
1893 Henrietta E.
1896 Edward C.

**Storrs**
1885 J. Gertrude
1885 Lewis A.
1887 Rose W.
1898 Charles H.

**Strant**
1901 Hazel P.
1903 Mazie I.

**Strong**
1868 William H.
1887 Frederic C.
1897 Edwin A.
1899 Louie P.
1903 Grace C.

**Studley**
1884 Carrie L.

**Sturmdorf**
1896 Leonice C. M.

**Sturtevant**
1890 Harry C.
1892 Florence M.
1894 Albert M.
1897 F. Raymond

**Sudarsky**
1903 Charles

**Suisman**
1903 Esther F.

**Sullivan**
1865 Cornelius
1895 Margaret M.
1897 Robert J. F.
1902 Florence C.

**Sumner**
1860 William G.
1878 Alice

**Surridge**
1893 Alice V.

**Sweet**
1878 Clara M.
1890 F. Benoni
1900 Lucy H.
1901 Mary C.

**Swift**
1877 Mary B.
1881 Harriet L.
1889 William E.
1893 Loretta G.
1895 Charles R.
1901 Lucy M.

**Sykes**
1883 Helen F.
1893 Abbie M.
1898 Florence P.

**Taintor**
1870 Mary E.
1888 Harlan H.
1897 James S.

**Talcott**
1879 Elizabeth H.
1891 Lillian G.
1902 Mabel H.

**Tallman**
1899 Marion G.

**Tarbox**
1872 Emma I.

**Taussig**
1904 Gertrude H.

**Taylor**
1881 Mary C.
1882 Bertha E.
1891 May F.
1891 Harry K.
1893 Ellsworth M.
1894 Lillian M.
1894 Charles L.
1896 Alice R.
1897 Howard F.
1899 Clarence H.
1899 William T.
1901 Maude W.
1902 Carolyn B.
1903 Charles F.
1904 Margery B.
1904 Horace V. S.

**Teel**
1896 Winifred R.

**Ten Eyck**
1891 Nellie E.

**Terrett**
1902 Mary G.

**Terry**
1850 Alice E.
1865 Henry T.
1866 Susie E.
1868 Edward C.
1875 Harriette C.
1892 James
1901 Editha B.

**Thacher**
1865 Charles H.
1874 Elizabeth
1902 Sheldon P.

**Thompson**
1870 Sarah J.
1879 Herbert W.
1882 Belle
1889 Arthur R.
1892 Susie C.
1893 Harriet M.
1900 Clarence M.
1901 Emma J.
1901 John H.

**Thomson**
1895 Leontine M.

**Thorpe**
1878 Walter E.

**Weed**
1887 Nathan A.
1893 Clara E.
1897 Helen A.

**Weeks**
1892 Jessie W.
1892 Mabel C.
1895 May L.

**Weiser**
1872 William F.

**Weltzel**
1865 Charles T.

**Welch**
1873 George K.
1874 Olive C.
1878 Alice L.
1878 Archibald A.
1878 Edward G.
1879 Mary
1879 Edward M.
1882 Frances G.
1882 Henry K. W.
1883 Sarah
1884 Lewis S.
1887 Julia A.
1899 Alice C.
1900 Blanche E.

**Weld**
1850 Lewis L.

**Weldon**
1880 John
1887 Charles H.

**Welles**
1855 George P.
1860 Edgar T.
1868 Mary N.
1876 Ida E.
1878 Martin
1879 Mary C.
1886 Edwin S.
1889 Lemuel A.
1893 Florence C.
1893 Katharine
1893 Harry L.
1894 Franklin G.
1894 John T.
1896 Georgiana
1900 Clayton W.
1903 Charlotte T.
1903 Ruth M.

**Wells**
1878 Anne M.
1883 Mary A.
1885 Elizabeth M.
1886 Hannah C.
1889 Clara E.
1891 Maud E.
1893 Ernest A.
1893 James D.
1897 Ida J.
1897 Ralph O.
1903 Donald B.
1904 Alden

**Wenk**
1872 Emma E.

**Wentworth**
1903 Gilbert R.

**Wesley**
1882 Cora M.

**Wesson**
1859 Charles H.

**West**
1880 Agnes D.

**Westcott**
1896 Anna G.

**Whaples**
1897 Heywood H.
1902 Albert D.

**Wheeler**
1884 Stella J.
1889 Mary P.
1889 Arthur L.
1892 Lillian E.
1902 M. Alice

**Wheelock**
1876 Adelaide S.
1891 Kate P.

**White**
1874 Frank C.
1876 Isabelle G.
1877 Richard A.
1878 Hattie H.
1880 Charlotte E.
1882 Henry C.
1888 Annie I.
1890 Mabel F.
1893 Charlotte F.
1894 Clara A.
1894 Ruth D.
1896 Margaret M.
1897 Alonzo P.
1900 Harlan H.
1903 Florence M.
1903 Robert G.

**Whitehouse**
1886 Fannie M.

**Whiting**
1850 Samuel
1890 Roberta E.

**Whitmore**
1850 Matthew N.
1874 Charles O.
1881 William R.
1887 William F.
1892 Hattie G.
1896 Harold B.

**Whitney**
1874 Elizabeth A.
1881 Josephine A.
1882 Nettie L.

**Whiton**
1894 Clara A.
1898 Mary F.
1901 Lucy C.

**Whittelsey**
1896 Esther I.

**Whittemore**
1902 Lewis B.

**Whittlesey**
1873 Una C.
1876 Heman C.

**Wickham**
1879 Clarence H.
1882 Almeron W.

**Wieder**
1902 Babette

**Wiggin**
1904 Charlotte M.

**Wightman**
1891 Alanson H.
1895 Susan W.

**Wilbur**
1901 Earl E.
1904 Daisy E.

**Wilcox**
1882 Addie I.
1887 Kate S.
1893 Mary E.
1894 Alice L.
1904 Mary C.

**Wile**
1901 Charlotte E.

**Wiley**
1873 Annie A.

**Wilkinson**
1892 Clara B.

**Willard**
1858 Dwight D.
1863 DeForest
1876 Nellie B.
1879 Lizzie H.
1904 Stephen F.

**Willes**
1884 Flora N.

**Williams**
1862 Jane E.
1865 Francke S.
1872 Lucy S.
1872 Horace B.
1873 Arthur
1874 Abby M.
1875 Mary R.
1876 Laura C.
1878 Emma L.
1878 Emmet S.

**Williams**
1881 William E.
1883 C. Louise
1884 Mary
1886 David N.
1887 Julia S.
1887 Mary A.
1887 Henry L.
1888 Abram C.
1889 Philip K.
1890 Alice S.
1892 Ella M.
1894 Arthur C.
1895 Ethel L.
1895 Rena B.
1898 Edith C.
1900 Marion C.
1902 Richard C.
1904 Mildred
1904 Charles G.

**Willis**
1891 Harriett E.

**Wilson**
1880 Laura C.
1881 Charles F.
1884 J. Willis
1892 Florella W.
1899 Daisy A.

**Winter**
1886 Carrie P.

**Witham**
1894 Aurilla R.

**Witherell**
1893 Georgia M.

**Wolcott**
1877 Alice E.
1877 Emma
1878 Mary W.
1881 Cora
1887 Helen L.
1892 Charles B.
1894 Mary L.
1896 Grace

**Wolfe**
1903 G. Morton

**Wollerton**
1903 Mary E.

**Wong**
1879 Kai Kah

**Wood**
1881 Annie C.

**Woods**
1896 Jessamine B.
1900 Marguerite F.
1903 John C.

**Woodford**
1877 Addie J.
1882 Carrie B.

FIRST HIGH SCHOOL BUILDING, 1847-1870

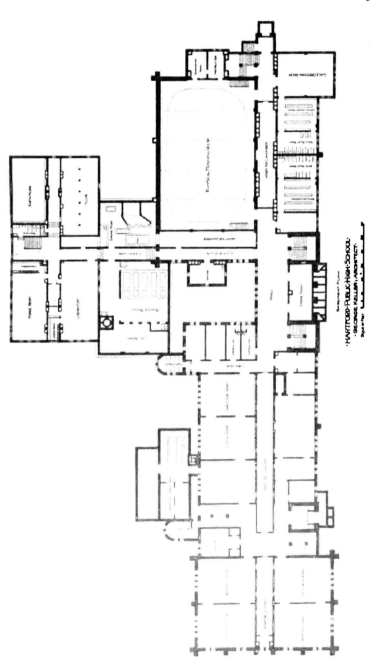

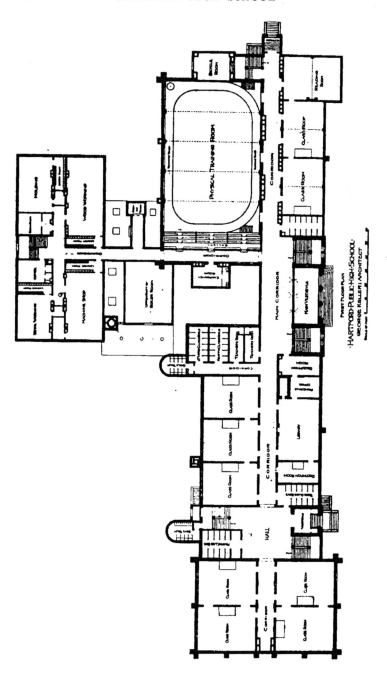

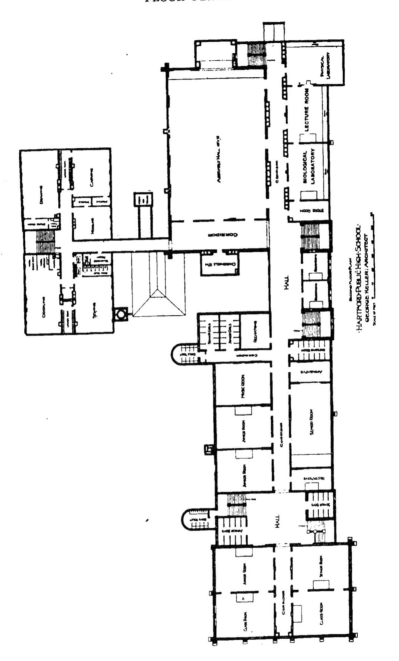

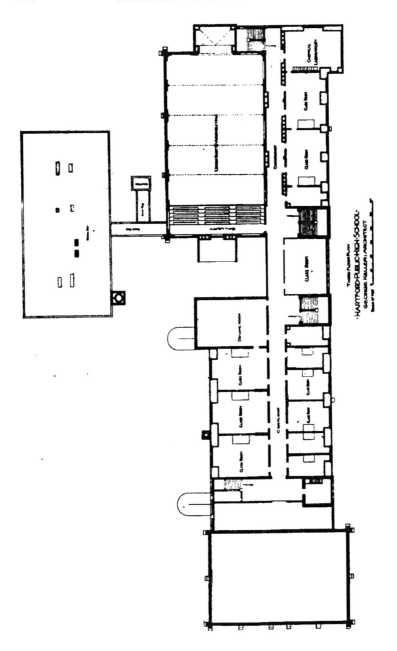

9 781146 256940